KING KONG – OUR K

King Kong – Our Knot of Time and Music

A personal memoir of South Africa's legendary musical

PAT WILLIAMS

Portobello
BOOKS

Published by Portobello Books in 2017

Portobello Books
12 Addison Avenue
London
W11 4QR

Copyright © Pat Williams

A CIP catalogue record for this book is available from the British Library

9 8 7 6 5 4 3 2 1

ISBN 978 1 84627 653 8
eISBN 978 1 84627 654 5

Typeset in Bembo by Avon DataSet Ltd, Bidford on Avon, B50 4JH

Printed and bound by CPI Group (UK) Ltd, Croydon, CR0 4YY

www.portobellobooks.com

for all those
who shared in the miracle
of *King Kong*

for Dan,
With love and gratitude
beyond measure

and
for Daūd Jān,
beloved man to sail the seas with,
who brings me laughter, courage and heart's ease

Ubuhle balomhlaba Bulana Wentxa
Tyambu Aboyiswa Lukhltla
Kwa Nobudenge.

The beauty of this world
Is like a blossom.
It cannot be hidden by weeds,
Nor destroyed by ignorance.

Todd Matshikiza, from 'Sad Times, Bad Times',
the overture to *King Kong*

Introduction

This book is a memoir of my part in *King Kong*, South Africa's first and most famous musical, snapshots from a story that began nearly sixty years ago, with a first production which became an exceptional and unexpected triumph, and a second which was an unmitigated disaster. At the time of writing, a very promising third one is due to open in August 2017.

Given the depredations of time and memory, what follows can't be a documentary account. I have never kept a diary, so what I write is comprised of shards and splinters of some of the events lying about in my mind from those days, bolstered by research and reading and conferring with others who were there, and strung on a very substantial thread of autobiography. And the context of my account is the social and political atmosphere of apartheid South Africa, now fading, I think, from most people's awareness, and perhaps never known, except in an over-simplified way, to younger readers. These are the three threads plaited together throughout this book.

A great deal has been written about what happened in those brave days during which *King Kong* was conceived, and what it 'meant' – articles, books, one PhD thesis, and a monograph by people who weren't there. So although from this distance what I write is largely impressionistic (except at electric moments when events burned themselves into my memory in vivid detail), it is both a partial history and a chance to tell the story as I remember experiencing it – and in doing so, also an opportunity to set the record straight in a tale from which some people were in danger of being airbrushed out.

As far as has been possible for me, I have checked facts with surviving others who were there, or reminded myself by reading contemporary records – in particular the invaluable book, *King Kong: A Venture in the Theatre*, by Mona Glasser, wife of the show's musical director, Stanley Glasser, written very soon after the show opened in Johannesburg and published in 1960 – and for the existence of which I am very grateful. From time to time I have quoted her directly, though more usually I have paraphrased the information I have drawn from her book. However, because we never met during this period, she knew very little about my part in the story.

Other people involved in the tale, in particular Arnold Dover, the choreographer, and to an extent even the stage director Leon Gluckman, as well as many people in the cast, are either absent or figure very little in my account, simply because both at the time and in the subsequent years, our paths seldom or never crossed.

The week I started thinking about perhaps writing a memoir, two old friends died within days of each other: Joe Mogotsi, beloved friend, charismatic singer and actor, and beacon of the Manhattan Brothers vocal group, who played Lucky the gangster, one of the lead roles in *King Kong*; and Arthur Goldreich, artist and architect, the set designer and exuberant live wire of the 'creative team'.

The three of us, together with all the others who made and played in the show, were and remain inextricably linked by the strength and depth and durability of the extraordinary *King Kong* experience. Now, after numerous efforts over decades had failed to bring about a revival, the show, which we thought might have died, is coming back to life – in a new production by another exceptional South African, Eric Abraham, producer and impresario of extraordinary determination, generosity and patience. He has a genius for enabling films and theatrical productions of distinction to come into being. I am deeply indebted to him for this, and for many other reasons.

Finally, I need to emphasise that this memoir has been written many decades after most of the events took place. So it is likely that – in ignorance of facts which might have amplified, corrected or changed my point of view – certain of my recollections and attendant assumptions have become distorted into a personal legend of my own making. If I have offended anyone in the process, I offer my whole-hearted apologies, and ask their forgiveness.

1

'This thing is bigger than both of us!' The banal words are a parody, of course, a hangover from melodrama and the movies, but they signal an experience not at all banal and beyond all words. Couples say or think it, for instance, when they find themselves suddenly tumbled about more or less helplessly within a huge wave of love. And in essence, this is what happened over several months in 1958 and '59, when a group of us worked together to create South Africa's first musical, based on the life of a boxer who had very recently died. His fighting name was King Kong.

We couldn't have known that in the process of making the show we would be tumbled about in a powerful wave of . . . well it was, it really *was*, love. Those who conceived of the show, others who got it onto a stage, the people who performed it or played the music, and later, all the audiences too — between us we broke through insane and cruel restrictions, both of law and convention, which in South Africa up till that point had kept people of different races apart, and which had seemed as rigid as iron, as unbreachable as, say, the prison on Robben Island. Inconceivable, unthinkable — but somehow it happened. Remembering how we were, and how events unfolded, I think the word 'love' is the right one.

Perhaps, also, the whole event could be seen as rather

like what some African tribes, so I've heard, call a 'knot of time', when people, place, the moment itself, and other ingredients and forces one isn't even aware of, come together as if in chemical eruption, and produce a Phenomenon, of a dimension and consequence far beyond what was originally conceived. In our case, the Phenomenon profoundly affected our lives, propelling all of us to another country, and a handful to world fame. But in a real sense the success wasn't personal. Such a Phenomenon seeks out its human constituents. If not us, it would have been others.

I was twenty-three at the time it all began, a successful journalist married to a respected consultant cardiologist, living comfortably in a spacious Dutch-gabled house standing on two acres of land. I had an eighteen-month-old son, and a good job on the *Rand Daily Mail*, Johannesburg's influential morning newspaper. Four servants eased my sun-filled days. My life looked like utter paradise.

I doubt if anyone at the time could see how lonely and unhappy I was. Even before *King Kong* was on the horizon, I had suggested several times to Joe, my husband, that ours was not a marriage in any sense, really, and that we should separate or divorce.

Then one Tuesday in August there was an early-evening phone call from my friend Irene Menell. The conversation remains lit in my memory. We'd known each other since our teens. 'Pat, we're thinking of doing a musical,' she said in her warm and spirited voice, coming straight to the point. 'And we thought you could write the lyrics for it. Can you come over?'

I was as energetic and immediate as she was. 'When?' Behind the matter-of-fact question, however, surged excitement and the sheer pleasure of new life stirring, the whiff of a chance to be part of . . . whatever this turned out to be. There had never been a home-grown musical in South Africa before, this would be 'a first', and I was ripe for the challenge.

'Well, *now*,' she said. 'If you can, that is.' I sensed that she was in a room with others who, so I imagined, had just agreed on me joining them, and were waiting.

Speculation, exuberance, curiosity and relief raced around my head so fast they could barely be differentiated. They generated a spurt of energy, a gush of fuel from the deeps. When Irene phoned I had been lying apparently exhausted in bed with what I had called flu – while at the same time being well aware that it was not. Irene's call cut through all of that. Life, which seemed to have been folding its arms waiting for me to do something, *anything*, I suppose, to break out of my misery, now rushed towards me at full force.

'I'm coming. I'll be there as soon as I can,' I told her, throwing on my clothes and running down the corridor, explaining the flurry to Joe as I went, and hearing his baffled words trailing after me: 'I thought you had flu?'

'Well yes, but that doesn't matter now . . .'

As I sped towards the garage I heard him from a distance saying, bemused: 'I'll never understand you . . .'

The Menells lived fifteen minutes away, in a brick house, outside which they had built a patio, from which an external staircase led up to Clive Menell's studio. The house, set in a luxuriant garden, a small one by wealthy South African standards, was worlds away from our empty acres of unremarkable neat lawn and the occasional flower bed. This garden was a living entity, a flourishing harmony of shrubs, established trees and bright flowers. Each time I was in it, however briefly, it lit me with pleasure, as true gardens always do. I remember the fragrance of roses, freesias and eucalyptus, and though indigenous flowers weren't yet the fashion in South African gardens, here, in places, were proteas and aloes as well.

Twenty minutes after the phone call I had run through that garden, smitten once again by its beauty, charged up the stairs to the studio, and was sitting happily with the two others Clive and Irene Menell had brought together – the composer Todd Matshikiza, and Arthur Goldreich, who was to design the sets. They had already been meeting for two or three weeks, and thought of me to write the lyrics because they knew the weekly satirical verses I wrote in the *Rand Daily Mail*, for which I was also reporter and deputy film and drama critic. We would be working in the comfortably cluttered studio room at the top of the house. I remember red, white and brown striped Spanish curtains, an upright piano, a number of small, stylised stone sculptures, mostly of animals, a few African wood carvings, rich textiles and artefacts which spoke of European travel, a pottery wheel in one corner, and paintings on the walls, mostly portraits, very accomplished, done by Clive.

Soon we were all absorbed in visualising the first of the set pieces for the show, which was to be about the rise and fall of the boxer Ezekiel Dhlamini, known as 'King Kong' – a true and ultimately tragic story, so familiar to us that

4

no further explanation was needed. The function of the scene, and the song in it, was to establish King Kong as star of the boxing ring, and his popularity among the people of the township.

The song, which came to be called 'Oh Those Marvellous Muscles', was to be a swaggering celebration, prelude to a boxing match between King Kong and an inferior and less charismatic challenger – as all fighters were, at that point in the story, when matched against him. And as in any traditional story, the King Kong of our show was to be a hero, a giant, and a loner.

This had been just as true in real life. King Kong was South Africa's black heavyweight boxing champion, who strode through the adulation of the fans without appearing to notice it. And rather like Muhammad Ali, who, it was later rumoured, might play him in an American production of our musical, he was also a magnet for women, whether they were interested in boxing or not. He liked them well enough, but didn't attach himself to anyone in particular, or welcome their adulation, so legend had it – that is, until he became entangled with the woman who would prove to be his downfall. In 'Oh Those Marvellous Muscles', King Kong sings disdainfully as all the girls crowd round:

> Women are the same
> all the same,
> flapping round like moths round flame.

'Muscles' was to come right after the overture, and was the show's first big number, in which an admiring crowd celebrates him at the height of his powers and popularity. And the music for it was exciting, exuberant and unforgettable – just like Todd Matshikiza, the man who wrote it.

From the first moments of that meeting I was committed, utterly in love with Todd's music and indeed with the whole enterprise, and the harmony I felt with the small group of people I would be working with – and then, as time went by, with the growing *King Kong* community of musicians, performers, organisers, costume makers and supporters. Most of us were in our early twenties, young and inexperienced, with Todd perhaps slightly older. He was determinedly secretive about his age – I assumed because he felt robbed of opportunities by the circumstances of his life; that without the obstacles he inevitably faced as a black man in those days, he could have done so much more, and done it sooner. Though as I learned later, he had in fact written an enormous amount of music of all types, and was also a virtuoso piano player. But whatever our ages, we came from disparate segments of our segregated and unhappy country, and for the most part had no pretensions or even ambitions to be in show business. We really didn't know what we were doing, other than just following our noses.

We knew, and at the same time could hardly be bothered to know, that as the weeks went by we would be flying in the face of precedent, ignoring social and conventional rules, and breaking the actual laws of the land as well. We couldn't avoid it. This was probably the first time black people and white had ever worked so openly together on a project which was not in any way political or 'subversive' – though of course many people saw what we were doing as both those things, and they didn't take kindly to it.

My mother, for instance, walked into my house one day as I sat at the dining-room table working on the script and did her best to pull me away, physically pull me, from the typewriter. She was upset and hysterical.

'You have to stop this right now!' she screamed at me. 'Stop this terrible thing you're doing. You'll harm your family. Stop it *immediately*. All this unspeakable nonsense with these *Kaffirs!*' She spat out the word with distaste, just as many white people did.

'Mum, don't worry about it. It'll be OK. You'll see. It's important to me that I do this. It's a wonderful chance. I'm loving it.'

'I tell you, my girl,' she said, 'if you don't stop right now this minute, I'm going into town straight away to speak to your editor, and tell him he must forbid you to carry on. Maybe he can talk some sense into you. And if he can't, I'll tell him to fire you.'

Even though the *Mail*'s editor, Laurie Gandar, was an enlightened man with regard to our race laws, I dreaded an embarrassing scene in the office, a scene my mother was quite capable of making.

I found myself howling with fury, 'Don't you dare! Don't you dare!'

'It's for your own good!' she shouted.

'Mum, if you do that, it's the end. You hear? The *end*. I'll put down the phone when you ring, I'll leave the house if you come near it. Anyway, I'm sick of you turning up here five times a day unasked. And don't think I don't know who it was who got rid of my kittens when I was at work! Well, it's enough now.'

It was all coming out, after years of subterranean strife, diplomacy and restraint.

She got the message and backed off, fearing quite rightly that if she did not, she might lose me altogether.

My poor mother. She was struggling. But I was struggling myself at this point, so couldn't see her at all clearly. She was uneducated, in the sense that, like many South African white women of her day, after she left school her potential and imagination were never nourished or engaged. Instead she lived within a trance of unhappiness and frustration, and soon after I was born, became addicted to barbiturate drugs. I imagine they cushioned her from the emptiness she felt. For much of her life thereafter, I was told later, she took dozens of pills a day, faking doctors' prescriptions by putting 100 or even 1,000 where ten had been prescribed, and if not lying seemingly comatose in bed, would be bumping into furniture when she walked, slurring her words when she spoke, and either ignoring me or telling me in no uncertain terms how much I was not the daughter she wanted. Not unusual, I think, in that generation. She liked to tell how, having given birth to me at home prematurely, she had left me on the verandah to cry all night when I was just three days old because she intended to train me from the start. I know now it could have resulted in infanticide. But at four a.m. the neighbours called the police, and I was brought back in. Over the years, my mother would relate this story with pride to all and sundry as if it merited some sort of accolade.

So inevitably we had no attachment, no meaningful communication, only what, in her frustration, she harshly commanded from me. Depressed herself, she felt terribly out of control, and so tried to control absolutely everything and everyone around her, including her 'unworthy' daughter. No wonder she physically pulled me from the typewriter. She didn't begin to see me for who I was. If she had, I used to think and hope, she might actually have liked me. But instead, to mask her frustration and unhappiness, she retreated into the daydreams to be found in romantic novels from the library.

My mother wasn't the only one who thought my involvement with *King Kong* was foolhardy. I grew up, and still often moved in, an almost tribal social circle – a network of apparently like-minded young people who seemed always to have known, or known of, each other, and whose parents all knew each other too. Gossip, not always accurate, about what a few of us were doing, making a musical by 'working with blacks', spread easily in such a network, and as it did, the criticism and finger-pointing began.

Prejudices I hadn't suspected surfaced not only from friends of my parents, but from friends of my own whom I had always thought of as 'liberal' and tolerant. Much of the criticism circulated behind my back, I later realised, but sometimes also to my face. My clever friend Natalie, for example, left wing herself and also a professional psychologist, which on both counts I thought would have made her sympathetic, told me how irresponsible and neurotic I was, involving myself in dangerous and lunatic nonsense, and that I should not under any circumstances go on with it. I'd rue the day. This was an obstacle I hadn't expected.

Another friend, Judy, whom I saw a lot of socially even though we were not particularly close, invited me for tea one afternoon. Once the white-jacketed-and-gloved black servant had set down the silver pots, the cups, the plates of sandwiches and the cakes and left the room, she came to the point. She also, like Natalie, had studied psychology at university, and clearly thought this gave her license. How could I be wasting my time with 'these' people? It was irresponsible and immature, even neurotic. She implied that working for black people was fine if it was just 'charity work' – but *this*, working *with* these people, side by side, equally, hurling myself into this stupid and unrealistic project – this was breaking all the rules. For a start, what about my husband, and my social position?

'Joe doesn't mind,' I said. 'Why should he? After all, one of his close friends, and a colleague, is Yusuf Dadoo.'

Yusuf Dadoo was the leader of the Indian National Congress, and deeply involved in the protest movement.

'That's not the same thing,' said Judy. 'They're both doctors. And from what I hear, Dadoo is an educated, cultured man. Some Indians are. So it's quite different.'

'Oh, you mean not like mixing with black scum from the townships?' I said sourly.

Over the years more than one friend had challenged me for 'breaking the rules' by paying my servants a decent wage. I was spoiling the market for the rest of them by paying well over the odds, they said, even though the ones who objected loudest were for the most part richer than me.

And now, with *King Kong*, they were once again calling me immature and irresponsible, charging me with putting my family at risk by consorting with people from whom we whites should be keeping our distance, because, as well as being black, they were so alien from us, by which they meant inferior and probably dangerous. I should listen to wiser heads than my own.

Fast forward: the following year, during what became a necessary headlong dash out of South Africa, I was lucky enough to spend a memorable week with Julius Nyerere, then Prime Minister and later President of Tanzania. I had approached him as a journalist wanting an interview, and we ended up talking almost non-stop for most of the day we met and for much of the week that followed. I think I must have been the first South African white 'specimen' Nyerere had a close encounter with. He was immensely curious about my own attitudes, and whatever else he could learn from me about other white people in my country, and how they thought. At one point we were talking about colour, and as far as I'm concerned, he said the last word on it. Pinching a bit of the skin on the back of my hand, he said, 'Ah yes, this,' shaking the skinfold gently, 'is a terrible problem for those for whom it is a problem.' That's it, in a nutshell.

Decades later, on a visit to South Africa, I was interviewed about the *King Kong* days for an 'academic video' by an intense young white drama student. Time had switched opinions around now, and the student's interest was very different from that of my psychologist girlfriends.

'What did you see as the issues, the socio-political meaning and relevance of what you were doing?' she asked.

I could only stare at her, unable to get my head around the question. 'We didn't think like that. We were just trying to create a musical and get it on a stage.'

★

Before I pick up the story again, I want to signal the atmosphere of the times, which these days is mostly forgotten, indeed perhaps never even known by most of the young. We were very isolated: the outside world had not even begun to notice the distortions within which we lived. South Africa was slugged almost senseless by the infection which was apartheid. It was like trying to live well without quite enough air. If you were white, life was cut and styled for comfort and convenience. We must have had the highest standard of living in the world, perhaps in the history of the world. Even low-grade jobs earned good houses, good cars and one or more servants. Most of us whites were spoiled, in the exact sense of that word – conditioned by upbringing, to a greater or lesser degree, to think that the separateness was a law of nature, not merely restrictions brought about by unjust political laws.

But if you were black, then you were legally oppressed; no stranger to injustice, violence and brutality. You had no vote, no material advantages, few chances. Virtually your every move was controlled by the State. Skilled jobs were reserved for whites. Yet for many black South Africans, perhaps most, the pressure of these difficulties acted rather like a furnace which strengthened and tempered. I was a young journalist, perhaps twenty, when a colleague burst gleefully into the reporters' room: 'D'you know what Nelson Mandela and Walter Sisulu are doing? I've just seen them. They've qualified as lawyers, but they're not being allowed inside law court chambers, so for the moment they're setting up their practice on the pavement outside!' I marvelled at their purpose and courage.

My parents' superior attitude to the black people was typical of most white people in the country then, and certainly those in the social group in which I was raised. Few of them had spent even five minutes of social time with someone black. They were just servants in our homes – but any of them could be summoned on the street with a 'Hey, John' – it was always 'John' – to carry parcels, help with a heavy load, deliver a message. Nelson Mandela described how one day, very near the court where he'd been defending a client, he saw an elderly white woman whose car was sandwiched between two others. So he immediately went over and pushed the car to help free it. 'The English-speaking woman turned to me and said, "Thank you, John,"' he wrote in his autobiography.[1] 'She then handed me a sixpence coin which I politely refused. She pushed it towards me and again I said no, thank you. She then exclaimed: "You refuse a sixpence. You must want a shilling, but you shall not have it!" and then threw the coin at me, and drove off.' A typical encounter, played out many times.

Mandela, typically, offered his help voluntarily, rather than being summoned. However, when I was growing up I would be excruciatingly embarrassed and ashamed on each of the many occasions when my mother imperiously curled her finger and beckoned a passing 'John', requiring some menial task to be done on the instant, depositing afterwards threepence, or sometimes sixpence, into a stooping 'John's' cupped hands, with never a please or a thank you; if any word at all, it would be just a curt 'Here!' as the money dropped into his palm.

To the majority of people like my parents, non-white people were probably only real when they surfaced in front of them. They seemed unable to see them as flesh and blood, or imagine them as people with their own families, as well as their own culture, traditions, talents, resources; participators in life's joys and sorrows. And it would have been a truly unthinkable thought to them that the very oppression and disenfranchisement non-white people lived under very often made for lives richer in what *really* matters than were our own. My parents, for instance, thought that it would be only communists and dangerous radicals who would have anything to do with 'the blacks', and that such people should be in prison anyway. Indeed, the State thought so too, for to be a communist had by that time become illegal.[2]

It was exactly the same the other way round, of course. Only a very small minority of black people had the experience of any social contact with whites. But they knew more about us than we did about them because, being on the underside, and working for us, they had the opportunity more easily to study us and come to know us, seeing in intimate detail not only our strengths and limitations, but also our dishonour.

So it really was something of a miracle that the show came about at all.

★

I'd been thrown in at the deep end. Todd Matshikiza, the composer, Clive and Irene Menell, and Arthur Goldreich, the set designer, had been working on the shape and structure of the show for a few weeks before I arrived, and had already conceived some of the set pieces. It had all begun, Irene told me, with a lunchtime conversation between Clive and Todd who, in spite of all social restrictions, had somehow met and become friendly. Todd told him that he and white lawyer and novelist Harry Bloom had decided to collaborate on a musical 'revue', loosely structured around the life of the heavyweight boxer Ezekiel Dhlamini, known as King Kong, who two years earlier, in 1957, had drowned himself in a dam on a prison farm. Harry once mentioned to me that the idea had been triggered by the British writer Wolf Mankowitz, who had recently been visiting Johannesburg and suggested to him that the King Kong story cried out to be put on stage or film.

A few years before Wolf Mankowitz's visit, the talent of black musicians and singers in Johannesburg had begun to be presented in concerts and revues – events most white people would never have seen, though they may well have noticed and dismissed the tattered posters here and there on lampposts announcing the latest township jazz concert. So it probably needed an outsider like Mankowitz to see the potential in that pool of extraordinary talent, and in the almost mythic possibilities in the story of King Kong.

Mankowitz was tuned in to the drama, humour and resilience of the disadvantaged from his own background in London's East End, where he set most of his work. He had written a string of successful books, stage shows and films, perhaps the best known of which was *A Kid for Two Farthings*, a whimsical tale about a boy who buys what he thinks is a unicorn, in order to grant the wishes of the adults around him. The 1955 film version, directed by Carol Reed, at the time a name to conjure with, had starred Celia Johnson, David Kossoff and Diana Dors.

Clearly Mankowitz, the outside eye, the outside ear, saw and heard and was inspired. I imagine him homing in on the vivid presence of black people on the city's streets, many down at heel or in shabby work-drab clothing, many others energetic and colourful, dressed in sharp style; handsome people on the whole, but all of whom would normally have to step off the pavement to make way if a white person came towards them. He would have picked up on the hoarse, haunting tunes of jiving little boys, as they played their penny whistles at every street corner . . . a breathy *obligato* to the sounds of the city's traffic. And he would have noticed that as darkness fell black people disappeared, banished by curfew back to the townships.

And he would have somehow come across Harry and Todd, and visited the townships with them or others, seeing what only a very few open-minded and fortunate tourists would have had a chance to see — if they fell in with the right people. It's very likely, for instance, that Mankowitz would have visited the popular 'Back of the Moon' *shebeen* (the very *shebeen* in our musical) and that he was also taken to the Bantu Men's Social Centre, always bursting with music and song and the arts. And I am sure he would have recognised the instinctive kinship the township musicians felt with the America of the prohibition era of the 1930s. As Chicago had its speakeasies, so Johannesburg's townships had their *shebeens*, which in both cases provided the added thrill of the illicit. After an hour or two of illegal drinking in a *shebeen* and chatting and listening to the musicians and entertainers there, Mankowitz would have become aware that the township people shared Chicago's experiences and idioms for their own world of gangsters, speakeasies, gospel singers, dapper dudes, honkytonk musicians, jazz, and violent death. Within disadvantage, talent and creative energy express themselves in whatever ways are available.

And music was in the air! There were superb musicians and singers everywhere, there were bands and groups, there were concerts galore, the whole place was saturated with talent. This was the very matrix out of which a musical could emerge, and Mankowitz would have known it instantly. All it needed was the right story – and King Kong's story had already been in the newspapers. To my knowledge, it was the first 'human interest' story about a black man ever to reach the pages of the white South African press. His life, his court appearance and the manner of his death were simply too unusual to be ignored, and so his story had actually earned a few lines in the *Rand Daily Mail*, the newspaper on which I worked. What had caught the public imagination was that when King Kong had been brought to court accused of murder, this muscle-man of few words suddenly waxed eloquent, and demanded that the judge should sentence him to death. What is more, Todd had actually known him, and had been in court that very day, covering his trial for the immensely popular *Drum* magazine, which reflected to its black readership, with style and journalistic flair, many aspects of their lives

17

and their culture. I wish I'd asked Todd more about that court appearance when I had the chance.

Once the *King Kong* revue had been mooted, Todd had enthusiastically set to work on the music. However, as he told Clive over their lunch, out of the blue Harry phoned him from Cape Town to say he had decided to live there, which meant the King Kong idea would have to be dropped. A bitterly disappointed Todd, who up till that point had been fizzing with musical ideas for the project, told Clive how extremely upset he was.

Although their stations in life were poles apart, an important segment of the two men's emotional lives were surprisingly similar. Clive, born into massive privilege, was a tall, good-looking, gentle man, responsive, thoughtful, careful and principled. Sensitivity, amusement and tolerance were written into his face, which seemed to have a layer of defensive skin too few, so you could instantly see his spirits lift or pain leave its mark. He was a gifted painter, far more suited, I was convinced, to the life of an artist or history professor than to what he was – a principal in Anglo-Vaal, one of South Africa's more junior mining houses, and the first to diversify from mining into industry.

But when I mentioned that idea to Irene years later, I found out I was wrong. Irene told me that to Clive, the work was not only family duty to be shouldered, but also intrinsically interesting. And of equal importance to him was the fact that it also provided an influential platform from which to work for change in South Africa. Anglo-Vaal controlled gold, platinum, diamonds and base metals, and much of the heavy industry, even though it was not quite in the same league as Anglo-American, the organisation headed by that other powerful magnate, Harry Oppenheimer, South Africa's foremost industrialist and last of the latter-day 'rand lords'.

Todd, on the other hand, a qualified teacher and superb musician, born into an intensely musical family, and himself possessor of an unparalleled musical genius and a sparkling, poetic and jazz-like literary talent too, was slogging away at a job he would rather not have done, as a Gillette razor-blade salesman in the townships. And he was doing it for precisely the same reason as Clive – out of a sense of responsibility, in his case to his family. But whereas doors opened for Clive wherever he went in the world, Todd's movements were tightly controlled by South Africa's rigid 'pass' laws. If his papers were in some way, no matter how trivial, not quite in order, he could be picked up and sent to prison. Indeed, as he told me, this had happened – he had been arrested and locked up just because he was walking through the city with something as inconsequential, perhaps, as a misspelled date, in his 'passbook'.

And right here is one of the many paradoxes of our country in those days. The separation of individuals by skin colour was written into law and statute. But there were very few of those laws, if any at all, which the majority of white people, comfortable within their privilege, would even have *wanted* to break.

And yet, in spite of this harsh separation of the races, Clive and Todd were good friends, with an unmistakable rapport. They were part of a small but growing 'grey area' in which people who refused to accept apartheid's insane restrictions mixed as freely as they could. Those of us who were white but who at a personal level ignored the colour line, deciding we would not live by the government's ignorant and brutal imperatives, found something we couldn't have predicted – that, by walking over the lines that officially barred us, we had given up something not worth having, and in its place had gained a richness in terms of human friendship, a greater capacity to see and understand, and a wider reach. So many gifts conferred, so much given back, more than we could have dreamed of, simply by ignoring the country's endemic prejudice. Ignoring it to the best of our ability, that is, given how conditioned from birth we all were – there were certainly pockets hidden deeply in both my mind and body, finally scoured away only as I came to know myself better. Father Trevor Huddleston, the inspirational Anglican bishop living and working in South Africa at the time, wrote, in 1956: 'I have never understood, or been able to understand, how White South Africa can so lightly forfeit a richness of life; can, on the contrary, build around itself such mighty and impenetrable barriers of pride and prejudice and fear.'[3] And that is precisely what I had come to see for myself.

When Todd, still very depressed and seemingly hopeless about the dropped King Kong project, phoned Clive not long after they had lunched together, Clive instantly set his mind completely at rest. The project must not die, he said. There were other people he could work with; other ways of going ahead. How about a *proper* musical, for example, not just a revue? Revues were familiar and plentiful, but there had never been a musical in all South Africa's theatrical history. How about *that*? He and Irene would make it happen, he promised. Todd told me later what a relief it had been to hear those words. He knew Clive to be an honourable man.

That night, Clive told Irene what he had undertaken. 'I took a deep breath,' she later told me, smiling at the memory, 'and I thought, "*What has he got us into?*" Neither of us knew a thing about musicals. Clive was a businessman. I was a lawyer, and a busy mother. What would be demanded of us? It took a few moments. Then I saw that Clive was determined and serious and had given his word, so I mentally rolled up my sleeves, and said, "OK. I'll be in there for whatever it takes."'

Irene is like that and always has been, since I first knew her in our teens: strong, reliable, clear-headed, brave, responsible, humorous and far-seeing.

I see I'm slowly assembling the cast of characters here. Others among them were those who dropped in to our 'creative meetings' from time to time and stayed while we worked, listening, sharing the fun, and occasionally making a suggestion. If it were a Sunday, Todd would often come with his wife Esmé and their adorable small children, Marian and John. Esmé was a social worker, calm and beautiful, impressively intelligent and formidably 'together'. She had a lovely voice, gentle and measured, which at the same time communicated a will of steel. Sometimes our friend Robert Loder would drop in. He had been living in South Africa for several years, working first at Father Trevor Huddleston's school and mission, and now within Oppenheimer's Anglo-American organisation. He was endlessly generous with his time and advice – and his contacts, negotiation skills and experience would play a large part both in raising money and getting *King Kong* into theatres both in South Africa and London.

Much later on it might be Joe Mogotsi and Nathan Mdledle of the vocal group Manhattan Brothers who came by, or the singer Miriam Makeba, all of them experienced professionals, and already informally in our sights for central roles in the show.

The flamboyant and romantic John Rudd, scion of an illustrious family, was another drop-in visitor. The son of an Olympic champion and grandson of Charles Dunell Rudd, Cecil Rhodes' friend and partner in the formation of De Beers and Consolidated Goldfields, John himself had been awarded the Sword of Honour at Sandhurst, and was commissioned into the Coldstream Guards. Now back in South Africa, his birthplace, he was working as a journalist and businessman, and his imagination was utterly caught when he heard Todd's music and watched *King Kong* grow. About eighteen months after our show opened, police raided his flat and found him in bed with the black dancer Dorothy Tiyo, a member of the *King Kong* cast. This was illegal. The Immorality Act[4] forbade white and non-white individuals to make love to each other. Unsurprisingly, their arrest and twenty-one-day trial hit the headlines around the world, the courtroom was packed each day, and in the end John and Dorothy were each jailed for six months. In separate prisons, of course, with very different privileges, or lack of them.

We were already a community, and growing all the time. But the 'creative team' itself was just the five of us, four of whom were white. Clive and Irene, the fulcrum and enablers, and though in the end invisible, actually at the heart of it all; Todd and myself; and Arthur Goldreich, nominally designer of the sets and costumes, but actually, along with Todd, a wellspring of fun, brimming with manic energy, savouring life's absurdities and its tender moments too. He was a talented and successful architect, well respected in South African circles, a fine artist, draughtsman and designer – and at our meetings also our engine, providing the steam and fizz that gave us lift-off. In years to come he was to write his name into South African history (of this, more later), and even at this point he must have been deeply involved in the political underground. Irene and I subsequently came to the same conclusion: that the party-like atmosphere he generated when we met at the studio, his role in creating the show, his flamboyance and playfulness, may have been, for him, a way of decompressing any hidden tension, and also a means of deflecting attention away from himself, if perhaps the Special Branch were watching him.

But it was also consistent with Arthur's personality. He was a man of deep seriousness, but also a natural storyteller; a clown and a mimic; an effortless entertainer – lanky, seemingly rubber-limbed, good-looking, and irresistible to just about every woman. It must have been hard for Hazel, his wife. In the song 'Oh Those Marvellous Muscles', King Kong complained that 'women are the same, all the same, flapping round like moths round flame' – but whereas King Kong could sometimes be irritated by the attention of too many women, Arthur loved them all.

Whenever we met to take the show to its next step, it was Arthur who created the magic that brought it to life. He literally 'entranced' us as he played out how a scene would 'feel' on the stage. One memorable evening as we sat building up the first of the show's set pieces – the township waking up in the morning, which would be acted out more or less silently to the music of the overture – Arthur began to describe how the scene would unfold and what it would look like. 'Can't you just see it!' he suddenly shouted, and then the power of his vision could keep him in his seat no longer. Leaping from his chair he became, really *did* seem to become, a washerwoman, a child, the dogs, a bus, a bicycle . . . He bounded about the room, peopling it with the men, women, children and animals who were part of the township opening its eyes to the new day, acting out exuberant and wonderful exaggerations, describing with wildly flailing arms, and uninhibited sound effects, in his strong but clearly enunciated South African accent, the motion of people, the sweep and size of houses, the life that moved in the early morning, even the clucking of the chickens. And we saw it all, as if hypnotised. Todd's elegiac overture, heart-stirring and melancholy, mirrored in its rhythms and melodies what Arthur conjured up for us – the waking before dawn of the men getting ready for work and queuing for the bus, the fires lit, the women setting about the chores of the day, the children, the dogs, the chickens, the rickety bicycles . . .

Arthur's stage-sets, where all this would take place,

were just as remarkable: stylised emblems, coloured rhomboids, squares and rectangles piled one on another, leaning against and supporting each other, and in front of them, high, perpendicular telegraph poles. His angular, abstract designs, mainly in oranges, reds and blacks, stood perfectly for, and were instantly recognisable as, the tin houses and corrugated iron shacks of the townships, yet at the same time spoke of something else, a spirit and jauntiness beyond the visible reality.

I'm amazed at how little detail I remember about the course of these meetings, when we were building the show's set pieces. They have mostly all coalesced into one, yet the essence remains – the camaraderie and high spirits and joy in what we were doing. It sounds crazy, but that particular evening when Arthur became a bicycle (he really somehow *did*) will never die in my memory, nor has it faded for the others there that night. Sometimes we still remind each other about it when we reminisce. I also remember Clive's quiet amusement and Irene's serene smile, and also her warmth, humour and steadiness as she made sure that food and drink were available, and that notepaper and props were there as we needed them.

Another meeting: Todd in teasing mode. He turned up looking absolutely shattered – a bad day in the township, he explained. It was a bad night before too, man, he added, miming a glass to his lips. At the Back of the Moon *shebeen*, I rather think. No way would it have been the government's licensed beer hall.

Then he brightened up, and flashed one of his widest, happiest smiles. 'But I also wrote this tune for the *shebeen* scene.' Anticipation rustled through the room. We needed a song for that, and it would be an important one. 'But,' he went on, 'I was so drunk, man, I can't remember any of it.'

Covertly, he waited for our groans.

'Oh no, man, that's *terrible!*' 'Todd, no *way!* You *must* remember it!'

And when we had registered sufficient alarm he unfolded a two-inch square piece of paper, written in tiny tonic solfa, solemnly put it on the piano's music rest, and peered at it closely, shaking his head, trying vainly, it seemed, to remember. His timing was masterly. Then after a few heart-stopping, blatantly theatrical false starts and dramatic moments of blocked memory, he began to play, he and we glorying in the melody, as he went on and on, frolicking with his latest theme. Our *shebeen* in the show, like the popular one in the real world, was called 'Back of the Moon', and that became the name of the song he played that night:

> Back of the Moon boys,
> Back of the Moon boys,
> Right behind the shanties
> Is the Back of the Moon!
> Behind all the shacks, boys,
> Built for the blacks, boys,
> Right behind is the Back of the Moon![5]

In time I came to see that Todd needed his tiny squares of paper to hastily jot down a melody in tonic solfa before the tunes disappeared of out of his head, as good creative ideas tend to do if not very quickly recorded. The paper came from a Croxley 'jotter', little two-inch square offcuts bound into a pad, which were given away by the Croxley stationery company as free samples. They were as useful and popular as Post-it notes today. We all had them. We got used to Todd carefully propping one of the tiny squares on the piano's paper rest, peering at the *doh*s and *reh*s and *me*s in a histrionic, and no doubt also partly genuine, effort to remember how the music went.

He was so convincing that I thought for a long time that he must have had very little musical education – though I now think this was an impression he was encouraging and sending up at the same time. My assumption was born out of the inescapable brainwashing in which I and those like me had been saturated, combined with the presence of all those scraps of paper written in tonic solfa, *plus* the fact that Spike Glasser, a music graduate recently returned from London, was later brought in specifically to orchestrate Todd's music. But as I later came to see, I had assumed that he, like me, had grown up in a house barren of books or ideas, with parents who had no interest in learning, taking it for granted that this was a default for him just as it was for me, because I also knew how little opportunity there was for black people to study painting, music or any of the arts. So without enquiring further, I decided that Todd was an instinctive genius, but without technical grounding. How stupid and patronising!

I could have learned the truth at the time, had I asked him. In fact it was only years later when Esmé, by then Todd's widow, took issue with a description I had written which spoke of Todd's brilliant musicianship, saying that he was 'made of music' but innocent of training or musical education. In fact, she told me, he had graduated from St Peter's College in Johannesburg with a diploma in music and a teaching diploma as well, and he also taught English and maths. He came from a family of ten, all saturated in music and learning. Everything I had longed for while I was growing up, in fact.

Working with Todd was magical. I have only to think of him to find myself smiling, the world brighter, my heart warm. If he was not smiling himself he was laughing, his face cracking with humour, his whole being bursting with amusement in life. He was about five foot four in height, I'd guess, with eyes as dark and shining as new olives, seemingly always rubbing his hands together and chuckling with glee, alert and alive to whatever was happening around him. His very presence seemed to say that life, each moment of it, was there to be relished. He warmed our spirits just by walking through the door. But this is no caricature. He was unusual and extraordinary, possessed enormous intelligence and generosity of spirit, and inspired affection and admiration, I imagine, in everyone who knew him. There were also great depths of darkness and sadness and profound human understanding in him too, a deeply layered subtext to all the humour and creative joy. You could see it in him if you caught him off guard. And you can hear it in all the music that poured from him, tumbling out of him like water, as from a seemingly endless spring. Indeed, since the first production, more than half a century ago, the *King Kong* music, first on vinyl, then on cassette and now on CD, has never once gone out of print. What is more, no one who has heard Todd's melodies for *King Kong* can ever forget them. You can play them over and over again, and they never wear out.

I can't count how many times down the years people who heard those melodies would, unbidden, sing lines of their lyrics to me, if we happened to meet. When I attended the opening of Cape Town's Fugard Theatre in 2010, many people who had been in the audience that night were coming up to me and doing just that. Another occasion that sticks strongly in my mind was when, in 2011, I was in Johannesburg visiting Dr Joe Teeger, who had been doctor for the *King Kong* cast. A phone call came in from one of his patients. It happened to be someone I had known since childhood and he was phoning from his bed, weakened by terminal cancer. Joe finished his conversation with him and handed me the receiver. To my amazement, ill as he was, he immediately began to sing:

> Back of the moon, boys,
> Back of the moon boys,
> Top *shebeen* in Joburg is the back of the moon!
> By day you are boys, boys,
> Now make a noise boys,
> Be a man at the back of the moon!

He knew it perfectly.

We were concocting the show set piece by set piece, and having so much fun it never felt like work. Somehow it had evolved that whenever Todd played what was to become the Back of the Moon song, we would all sing to its tune in a ridiculously boisterous way: 'Hi good-looking what's cooking good looking!', grinning at each other, feeling high and happy, visualising people coming into the *shebeen* singing those words, giving each other wide smiles and high fives. Those lines were never actually in the lyrics, but they became and remained our privately sung greeting.

Fast forward: I am sitting in London with a few South African friends, ten or so years later, watching the TV news of the Apollo 8 spacecraft going into orbit and thereby giving most viewers their first sight of the other side of the moon. 'Back of the Moon' is the song the BBC selects to accompany the TV newsreel of the event. We all cheer loudly.

People often ask songwriters which comes first, the music or the words. In our case, there was no choice, because it was so hard for Todd and me to meet, given the limitations apartheid imposed on where we could meet, plus the fact that we both also had jobs, which made the 'when' difficult too. So Irene and Clive decided it was necessary for me somehow to have the music available even when Todd was not. In these digital days, the solution would be child's play, but at the time it was remarkable that the Menells could organise a home recording at all. The technology was extraordinarily cumbersome: ten-inch reel-to-reel spools and bulky recording equipment the size of a small fridge. As the tapes slowly turned, Todd sat at the piano in the Menells' studio, playing one song after another, and also playing *with* them, lifting and submerging the melodies, rolling and bouncing them in a sparkle of notes, with an exuberance and inventiveness reminiscent of those great jazz originals, Art Tatum and Fats Waller. Had Todd's path taken him to America, I know with complete certainty that he would have been one of their number, joyfully and justifiably celebrated.

The tape recordings were transferred to vinyl 78s, which I would play at home, doing my best − no easy task − to lift out a simple line of melody from all the variations, as Todd frolicked and swung with his compositions. The music he recorded that day has such beauty it breaks my heart, because for all its ease and lightness and expressive melody, there is a deep undertow of sadness and, yes, here it is again, love. I think this is the element that catches the heart, rendering the music unforgettable. But it was a puzzle to pick out a clear line of melody from all Todd's variants and embellishments, as he played on and on, and I was never sure I had it right.

'Did I get it?' I'd ask Todd anxiously. 'Is that it?' as I showed him how a lyric ran over what I had picked out. 'Yes, yes, that's it absolutely,' he would say airily, quickly dismissing my doubts. But I was always uneasy, worrying that I had perhaps elided bits, or introduced extra notes where he may not have wanted them.

Those discs had turned out to be a brilliant solution to the difficulties of meeting. But on rare occasions, when we could free ourselves at the same time, Todd and I did manage to get together. There was a café in Fordsburg, a suburb at the western edge of Johannesburg, where no one cared about colour. It was in all respects basic, as well as low-key and friendly, and no eyebrows were raised at my presence, though often I was the only white person there. Well before our time, Fordsburg had been developed to house white gold miners and artisans, but as apartheid began to be enforced it ended up as a mostly Indian neighbourhood. It was also a kind of no man's land for those who enjoyed its non-racial atmosphere and were prepared to ignore apartheid's restrictions. Back in the 1930s, the Afrikaner writer Herman Charles Bosman was one such, and had cranked out protest pamphlets there on a dilapidated old press. In the 1950s playwright Athol Fugard worked there as a clerk in the Native Commissioner's Court. He says his time in Fordsburg was traumatic: 'I saw more suffering than I could cope with. I began to understand how my country functioned.'[6] My husband Joe's friend and colleague Yusuf Dadoo also spent time there during the years of 'struggle'. So, I'm told, did Nelson Mandela. It was that sort of place, and to me it felt wonderfully non-judgemental and comfortable.

Todd and I worked well together. Right from the start we had found a relaxed rapport, a place of shared understanding and fun, connecting almost as if we were children playing together. We were on the same side, in a place of ease and straightforwardness. Friendship had somehow been established with few questions asked or words spoken, as it often is when people work together towards a shared goal. We had our eyes on that, rather than on ourselves or each other, or what was in it for us. Except for one time, that is, in the Fordsburg café, when work had reached a natural break, and . . . 'Do you think this show could make any money?', Todd wondered.

'I don't know, Toddy. If it's a great success, all the seats sold out for the three weeks . . .'

'. . . and if the profit on each seat is [whatever it was we thought], then probably we could make . . .'

'. . . say, £60 each?'

We lowered our voices, ashamed at even saying it out loud, this talking about money, and how much of it, if any, would be for us, even though the sum we'd come up with was so modest, really. Then feeling quite uncomfortable about thinking so basely, we dropped the subject abruptly.

In the event, before it went to London in 1961, so utterly inconceivable at the time of our conversation, *King Kong* broke all records, and was seen by an estimated 65,000 people in just over 100 performances in South Africa's four main cities – though I have also seen that number put at 200,000 – two-thirds of whom were white. The music of *King Kong* was played in Johannesburg *shebeens* and on black radio stations all over the country, and for the first time in living memory, black stars had white fans and groupies. The show was to have a powerful effect on social attitudes in our country – and the £60 became an irrelevant, amusing memory.

If we couldn't make it to the café, Todd would come to my house in Houghton, near Killarney, one of Johannesburg's older and most exclusive suburbs. The house had been built by a judge for himself and his family, and today, to my astonishment, it has become a conference centre. Todd and I would work in the study, a cosy room with deep sofas and a view of the ivy-covered colonnade outside and the circular marigold and freesia bed in the centre of the driveway beyond. Then, at the end of the session, it was always necessary for me to write a 'Special' – that is, a 'pass' to protect Todd from summary arrest: 'Please let my boy Todd pass late tonight. He has been working late for me.' My 'boy' was a man, and older than I was, but that was irrelevant. Such indignities borne by Todd and all the other men with such dignity. I remember alto sax player Kippie Moeketsi, acknowledged by all the township musicians as 'the father of South African jazz', saying that so many were the dangers an African man might have to face after he left home in the morning, that each day his mother would say goodbye to him as if it might be for the very last time.

*

The car was a marvellous place to try out lyrics. To, and particularly from, work, when I had time to take a longer and prettier way home, a winding route over a high hill, with views of the city below, I would sing words and lines into the music, trying them out, seeing if they made sense, or could rhyme, or express anything close to what I hoped for – and whether I could get my tongue around the words when sung in the rhythms dictated by the music. I found out that words had to flow, in most circumstances without consonants too close together. 'King Kong, killer gorilla' I would sing out exuberantly, in a voice unselfconsciously awful – but of course here nobody had to listen. 'That's me! I'm him! King Kong!' I'd sing, full of beans, trying out whether the words would be easy on the tongue, with the rhythms and note lengths. At other times I wanted sharp consonants, lots of them: 'I say that Lucky's King, King Kong keep out!' yells Lucky the gangster, when his girlfriend deserts him for King Kong. The explosive consonants carried right through that song, which I called 'Damn Him!' It had the rhythms of a Sotho war dance, I later learned, and the explosive consonants carried right through it worked well, when sung with furious intensity by Joe Mogotsi.

Sometimes thoughts I'd wanted to express didn't quite yield their meaning if they were to fit. 'Oh we'll walk down the future's long shore,' I chanted, in one of the romantic numbers, 'and it's ours, ours, no one's ever been there before.' It just wouldn't do, and after stubbornly trying to make it fit I had to compromise: the line as sung became 'and it's ours, ours, none before', which was better than the discarded: 'Oh we'll walk in the future's bare land, and it's ours, ours, no footprints on the sand!'

It was probably about October 1958. I was utterly happy singing away in the car, feeling the warmth of the sun through the open window. As a child, I had never been sung to by anyone, nor even consciously been aware of singing. Indeed at my first singing lesson in secondary school the teacher sent me out because my voice was so hopelessly awful, and told me I need never come back. Ever since, shamed, I had avoided trying to sing in public. But alone in the car I was the happiest of singers. I'd sway as I sang, exaggerating vowels until they sounded like something out of America's deep south, but always trying to find the best solutions I could to what I took to be the melody lines I had found so hard to unravel from Todd's wonderful improvisations.

One of the most difficult to find a clear melody line for was the 'Death Song', which King Kong sings from his prison cell while awaiting trial for murdering his girlfriend. The 'tune', as Todd played it, seemed to weave up and down, and in and out of, a sea of sound, as if the melody line surfaced first in the one place, then in the other. So it had to be written in fragments and phrases. Looking back, though, I realise that it was the most heartfelt of all the lyrics:

> I see clouds floating by . . .
> A face . . . a name . . . a place . . .
> Drift on.
> The thing that mattered so . . .
> My girl . . . long ago . . .
> Has gone.
> The whole world fades away,
> Melts away.
> Sun is dull . . . grass is grey . . .
> Nothing real.
> My world has shrunk away,
> Colour gone . . . people gone.
> I'm alone . . . I'm alone.
>
> I'd do it once again, I know,
> Knowing so,
> I'm strong.
> I'd kill that girl again
> And show . . . other men
> I'm Kong.
> Oh hear me Judge,
> I say:
> 'I choose to die, and this is why:
> You cannot change your road

Nor load . . .
When your name's
King Kong.'

Fast forward: the following year Evelyn Waugh wrote an account, in the London weekly *Spectator*, of an evening spent dining with the governor general of what was then Rhodesia. At about 10 p.m. his host put on the 'Death Song' from *King Kong*, and after the thoughtful silence that followed, Waugh felt it was time to go. He subsequently learned that when the governor general wanted his guests to leave, he always played the 'Death Song' from *King Kong*. I read Waugh's article and smiled to myself with understanding. That song *is* a conversation stopper.

At a certain point, as we worked out the story we were telling, we wondered whether we could actually get black characters and white onstage together. Yes, it was against the law. But could we risk it? Work out how to do it somehow? If not, what would we do about the white characters? Voices off, perhaps? I suggested black actors wearing white masks, as in Genet's play 'The Blacks'. I still think it was a great idea, – a powerful, and traditional, metaphor. But none of the others were comfortable with that. In the end, we stuck with black characters only. Even the policemen were black – as indeed in the townships many were. The decision was taken, in the end, not for political reasons, but for what we called 'coherence'.

As I've said, we had all known from the start that what we were doing was at some point going to involve breaking the law. In fact, we broke it for the first time very early on, because it was illegal for people of different colour to drink together. But how on earth can you work with jazz musicians without any booze around? It's unimaginable. Yet in those days black people could only drink legally in licensed 'beer halls', government run and supervised, serving weak, tepid beer. And never, never, officially, could blacks and whites drink together. For blacks the penalty could be prison; for whites, usually a fine. Sanctioned social drinking, of course, would also have made for friendship between the races, which in turn would have led to a weakening of the tension between them, so essential for the regime.

Nevertheless, drink flowed at all our meetings. Come to think of it, you could say Clive and Irene were running a free *shebeen*. Irene would put a large bowl of innocuous alcohol-free fruit punch on top of the cupboard in the studio, and the booze on the table. Any knock at the door meant we would freeze for a moment while Irene shoved all the bottles back into the cupboard as fast as possible, and locked it.

One day, when some of the musicians and all the Manhattan Brothers were present, and Todd and I had most of the songs completed, the knock came. There was a split second of shock. Anxious glances exchanged. Irene moved like lightning to hide all the evidence of drinking, sweeping bottles into the cupboard and filling the quickly drained glasses (no point in wasting good liquor!) with orange juice and ginger ale. But sighs of relief all round – it was Clive's father, Slip Menell, who told us he had brought with him a couple of visitors, steel millionaires from Detroit and their wives, to hear some of our music. Just for a bit, he said. After some moments of commotion and shifting around to make space, they came in. Two gussied-up ladies in designer Halsten sack dresses, accompanied by one tough, shortish husband built like a small tank, and another tall, lanky and laconic. All four were utterly charming. Except as film stereotypes, I had never met their like before. They were flying back to Pittsburgh next day – via Paris, one of them said, because that was the best place to buy shirts. My young colonial eyes widened.

The drinks reappeared, and whiskies, brandies and beers (proper beer, not the government muck) were poured for all. When the guests were settled, the musicians grouped themselves in a corner and the concert began: 'This is the music from the *shebeen* scene' . . . 'This comes after the boxing match' . . . 'Here's the first love song.' The Manhattans and Miriam Makeba were in fine voice and style, and the few other musicians present played discreetly underneath and around their sound. The Detroit four were wonderfully enthusiastic. At that point South African music had hardly reached the ears of those outside our own townships, let alone America. Miriam, a slender and seemingly shy young woman then, would within a year be taking the sound – and our songs – to America. But this was in the unthinkable future.

When the musicians stopped, and had been sincerely applauded, three of the Detroit visitors urged the fourth, whose name was Doris Gershenson, to 'play some of your songs, Doris'. 'Oh no,' I thought. 'After all this great music, some rich woman is going to sing to us, and then expect us to be polite about it.' To her credit, she said, 'No no, they don't want to hear *me*' – too right, sister – but the Americans wouldn't let up, then out of politeness we feebly joined in, and in the end Doris was persuaded. With an unnecessary degree of fuss, I thought uncharitably, she moved the piano until she decided it was exactly where she wanted it, took off her many rings with ostentation, carefully set them down to the side of the piano, and began to play.

And oh, how she played!

As stylish and accomplished as any night club entertainer. I'd never heard anything as assured. She was sensational.

And then the thunderbolt!

'Here are some of the songs I've written,' she said. And proceeded to perform some of the great hit songs of the 1940s. There was special material written for Nat King Cole, special material for Danny Kaye, songs for the Ink Spots, Billie Holiday and Ella Fitzgerald, as well as for Bing Crosby and the Andrews sisters, names to conjure with in those days, and song after song from the hit parade of the decade before, including 'Into Each Life Some Rain Must Fall', and many more from movies we'd all seen – all the songs, for instance, from the Rita Hayworth film *Gilda*, including 'Put the Blame on Mame', which I often used to sing burlesque style in my bedroom when no one was home, bumping and grinding, and feeling just great. There was 'Whispering Grass', one of my all-time favourites, along with 'Tampico', which I had a cherished, much-played record of, but which Doris said was her orphan child, and hadn't done as well as the rest of them. As I write I am vividly reliving the mounting disbelief and excitement. We wouldn't let her stop. A magic was happening in the room. We were suddenly in touch with a world we had thought was far beyond our reach: unattainable not only geographically but mentally, because it was a world beyond apartheid, a world beyond the colonies – and a world which contained the giants. Now that world appeared within touching distance. A Representative had come.

Doris said: 'I'll play you some of my father's music now.' And told us how, when Fred Fischer, her father, first came to America from Germany, he played piano for a while in a black brothel. (Clive's father, I distinctly remember, looked decidedly nervous at this, and tried uncomfortably to nudge her away from such inflammatory talk which breached all our country's taboos – hard to believe now, but sex and skin colour in the same sentence panicked white minds and snapped them shut.) 'He wrote many great songs,' said Doris. 'How about this one?' And she played that great driving glory of a song . . . 'Chicago'.

There are tears in my eyes as I write, all these years later. It was as if, in the hologram that was King Kong whole and undivided, here in a small fragment of that hologram, the entirety of our 'Phenomenon' was represented. A small Knot of Time. There was a roar, yes, really, a roar, from the musicians, all the black people in the room. Some were actually shouting for joy! Their song! *Their* song! Theirs! They had played it and sung it and loved it and lived it! 'Chicago'! Can you believe? *'Chicago!'*

The room was turbulent with emotion. I remember she also played 'Ma, He's Making Eyes at Me', 'Peg o' my Heart', and much else her dad had written, but even though we all knew and loved those other songs too, by then they were almost an anti-climax.

I had been amazed, lifted up by meeting this formidable woman, so human and so wonderfully ordinary, who had written some of the songs that were in my bloodstream; someone, in fact, from a world I longed for while being marooned in my island of social narrow-mindedness. And she must have been able to read something about my situation from my face and demeanour. Possibly she'd been through it herself, and saw the confusions of my life, family, marriage, motherhood, career, all of that, in the days before the impending wave of feminism had got going. She took my hand when we said goodbye, held my eyes steadily, wished me luck in what I was doing, and said, with directness and concern: 'Always remember, nothing, absolutely nothing, is as important as home and family.'

How I pondered those words. Coming from someone as successful as she, someone who seemed to see through my own boiling troubles, and sense that what had started as a fugitive germ of an unthinkable thought, had grown into the knowledge that I was planning to make a run for it. For that is what was happening. I'm not proud of what I did in my desperation, and was heartsore for many, many years at the consequences, the harm and hurt of my actions. But that's how it was, and Doris Fisher, who wrote, among so much else, 'You Always Hurt the One You Love', clearly had the eyes and the experience to detect it.

*

It had never occurred to me until the experience of meeting the cast and musicians of *King Kong* that people who were 'disadvantaged' or 'underprivileged' could be having a rewarding life – and in real terms, often a much better one than many of those 'on top'. I was only just beginning to learn, from living life rather than theorising about it, that the truth of things existed beyond and in spite of any words or labels. And I was beginning to see, too, that well-established, comfortable lives tend to make for widespread homogeneity in a community. It's a trade-off. By reducing the danger, disadvantage and brutality and making life safer throughout society (as happily has been largely achieved in Britain), the potential for excellence is actually reduced, because people have a much narrower range of experience, and are actually less tempered and tested.

Indeed this thought sometimes arises when I remember the many times of such joy and harmony among us all, as we sat in the Menells' studio, sometimes with the exceptional musicians playing the songs and all of us singing them (me, with my weak voice, almost under my breath, but singing even so). These were times of such pure happiness that it felt as if our hearts would burst, as our emotions – and something deeper too, and more valid than emotion – soared on the wings of joy and friendship and work sincerely done. It would have been impossible for anybody in the whole world to be happier than we at such moments. We were radiant with it. This was the surfacing of the reality of our Phenomenon. Here it was. Sheer love, transcending any of its stereotypes in the 'mundane' world.

2

Memory is a shifting mist. Writing this account, I was puzzled that although Harry Bloom had been, with Todd, the first to initiate the idea of a *King Kong* revue following a nudge from Wolf Mankowitz, I couldn't remember him ever being present when we were working together to create the show. Yet he is on public record as the sole begetter and author of *King Kong*. How had he come to play such a big role, claiming the lion's share of the publicity, if he wasn't even around while we created and shaped it? I knew he had moved to Cape Town, but surely he must have come to Johannesburg and worked with us at least *sometimes*? He must at least have played *some* part in building the scenes? Where was he?

The fact that I just couldn't remember Harry's presence, however often I tried, was finally explained, to my relief, when I referred to Mona Glasser's book about *King Kong*, which was published in December 1960, not quite two years after the show had opened. Her husband Stanley Glasser, known as Spike, was the musical director of the show, and much of his work with the musicians took place in their house. So hers is as close to a contemporaneous version of events as one is likely to get. She knew the timeline. And according to what she wrote, it seems that Harry actually *wasn't* part of our delightful creative team working on *King Kong*.

Clive Menell had reassured Todd that the music he had already written for a *King Kong* revue would not be lost after Harry's departure, and that he would get something going, somehow – but as a musical rather than a revue. That was what had brought us all together as a team in the first place, and it was how, between us, we had shaped the show. A recent conversation with Irene Menell confirmed this, and reminded me that it was Clive himself who had actually written the show's outline – the scaffolding, so to speak, from which we worked. He had created a sequence of events – episodes which built the story from where it starts, with King Kong at the height of his powers, and followed it through to his tragic end.

Clive set it all within the frame of a single township day, starting with people waking up and getting ready for the day ahead, and ending with the tired men slowly returning home from work, after which the whole township settled down for the night. It was Clive's outline which was the basis for the big set pieces on which we were working, planning what happened in them and where the songs would fall. And that outline actually remained the spine and structure of the finished show. Clive and Irene's aspiration was to make *King Kong* South Africa's contribution to jazz opera – and at the same time to showcase the musical genius of Todd Matshikiza. Their models were *Porgy and Bess*, and *West Side Story*. Indeed, the latter had opened in New York just weeks before we began to work together on *King Kong*, and Clive and Irene had seen it there.

Mona's book relates that some months later, when Harry was passing through Johannesburg, he visited the

Menells and discovered how far we had progressed with *King Kong*. When he became aware of how much we'd already achieved, he rushed away, very excited, and in the two nights he was in Johannesburg, according to Mona, wrote forty pages of script ideas, notes and suggestions, gave them to the Menells – and then left again for Cape Town. One or two friends commented at the time on what had already occurred to me – that when Harry saw how the show was shaping up, he wanted to be part of it after all. A very human reaction. It was, as he reminded us, his idea in the first place. Well, yes . . . and, er, Wolf Mankowitz's too. However, when we looked at Harry's document carefully, we saw that it made full use of the work we had done so far, and though enthusiastic and promising, with vivid scraps of dialogue here and there, it did not, in fact, take us a great deal further. As much as a contribution, it felt, in a sense, also like him staking a claim.

And given Harry's absence, we were still without a script or scriptwriter. So what happened next was predictable. As the only other writer in the group, Clive asked me if I would take on the complete 'book' – script as well as lyrics. I felt utterly terrified. Then, just like Irene had done earlier, I rolled up my mental sleeves, took a deep breath, and said yes.

*

It seemed to all of us that my task would not be too hard. We were clear how the story unfolded, so it would just be a question of stringing together all the set pieces we'd built, and hanging them on the agreed storyline. Up till this point the script's conception had been a cooperative effort, and our understanding was that the team would continue to offer me ideas and suggestions where necessary.

In any case, the thrust of the scenes was already set: the washerwomen, acting as chorus during the overture as the township wakes up, would establish the mood and look of the show. Next came the moment we would meet the adoring, excited crowd and a swaggering King Kong, just before a boxing match. Then we had King Kong boasting about himself in song; then there would be love songs between the two couples who were the leading and supporting characters; then King Kong gets involved with Lucky the gangster's girl; after that, Lucky vows vengeance on King Kong; then there would be the wedding of King Kong's trainer and girlfriend, a celebration which turns dark and doom-laden, as King Kong kills the girl he has stolen from Lucky when he sees her flirting with Lucky again; and finally the climax, the murder trial, where King Kong, the silent loner, finds his voice and speaks to the court from his heart.

And after the whole story is told, we return to the township where we started: the men coming home from work, the washerwomen taking down the dry laundry, and all of them mourning the loss of their hero. At the very end, as dark descends and night falls, all that is left is the solitary, plaintive sound and sight of a small boy playing the penny whistle. That last scene was so inevitable that we had all, independently, already thought of it for ourselves. And, indeed, it worked beautifully.

But then, when I first sat down to write, I discovered to my surprise that in spite of my assumptions, there was no coherent story there. Not yet. Only the bones of it. The set pieces were self-contained, but the links needed between them had as yet no substance, no plausible characterisation which would help the audience identify with the characters and work to move the story forward. The truth was that we had no filled-out idea about who all these people were, what they were like, where they had come from. They had no back stories. That was even true of King Kong himself. Did I really know him? And it was true too of the chorus – the group of washerwomen onstage during the overture and at the end. The music existed, but what were these women going to say? Why were they going to say it? Who were they? And how would the built-in subtext signal the quality of the characters' lives, which were so much affected by the oppressive regime they lived under?

Suddenly the task wasn't quite as straightforward as it had seemed. I was confronted with the need to tell the story from the inside, so that it held together and made coherent sense to me. One step had to lead to the next: I needed to think the whole thing through from scratch. Indeed, I would have to go away and actually learn how a script was written.

'How do you write a play?' I asked an educated, literary friend. 'One based on a true story which ended in tragedy.' He said: 'You establish your hero. You get him higher and higher up a tall tree, and then bit by bit you shake the branches until he falls right back down to the bottom.'

That started me thinking. I wanted to understand how the life of the extraordinary Zulu man Ezekiel Dhlamini, known to one and all as King Kong, could be told in that way. I began to puzzle out the steps up the tree and down again, peering through the mists of my imagination to see how the story was unfolding. One thing I was sure of was the ending. As in the stories that had enchanted me from early childhood, King Kong was a larger-than-life hero. His story had captured the imagination of all who knew him or knew about him. At the end, it needed to find its way into the world of myth and legend.

And here, I think, I need to explain both my huge reverence for books and stories, and how various early events in my youth affect the story I am telling here, leaving me with no further education after the age of fifteen, an astounding (though well-hidden) ignorance about practically everything, a huge hunger for knowledge, and a lack of confidence in the company of anyone who seemed sure of themselves.

I grew up in a house in which I remember only three books: a cookbook, a tattered detective paperback, and an unused book of common prayer. But crowded into my bedroom I had scores of my own, bought over the years with every penny of my pocket money. I was getting no help from my family or those around me, my thinking went, even school didn't seem to be interested in answering the questions that clamoured within me, so maybe there were books which would throw a light on, help me get the hang of, what I was supposed to be doing in this strange and confusing planet, what life here was about, what I was *for*. Any book which looked as if it might hold part of the secret claimed my money.

From the age of about nine I was gutting books for

clues: thoughtful novels, a little history, popular science, and later on a few others that my school headmistress considered shocking, like the works of Oscar Wilde and a biography of Annie Besant. And then the others which made my mind soar! Korzybski's *Science and Sanity*, published soon after I was born, was pre-eminent among them. I was fifteen when I came across the words inside it, 'the map is not the territory', and it was as if I'd been released from chains. That book became a talisman. So, a few years later, did Eric Hoffer's *The True Believer*, which showed me, as Korzybski's had done, but from a different perspective, that all kinds of behaviours and beliefs which, to the people around me, seemed set in stone as immutable truths, were automatic and predictable. I began to see that in spite of what my parents and others 'older and wiser' than me insisted was the fixed and only possible outlook on life, the real truth of things lay underneath their training and their mechanics and their maps. And from another direction, again like a body blow, came the other treasured book – Homer's *Odyssey*. I read it enthralled – it opened itself up and I fell straight into it, drenched in the endlessness of its metaphors, even though I didn't yet know what a metaphor, or a myth, actually *was*. The transitory nature of states of mind I was noticing in myself and others seemed in a way analogous to each of the islands Odysseus visited. The objective was not to be trapped on any of them but simply to experience them, then get safely away, and continue the journey, searching for whatever one thought of as 'home'.

But even though I was a precocious reader, and books were the exit door to a wider, more real world, what I read remained in some sort of mental air pocket that rarely intersected with my dealing with others, or with the realities of daily life. I was leading two lives, searching for meaning and understanding in the hidden, unspoken one, and outwardly, in the 'performance life', conforming as much as I possibly could to the way others behaved, so that I wouldn't stand out as 'different'.

My father, however, was not a reader of anything, except the occasional detective story. Life had cut short his education, and he saw books and learning as the enemy. He was by nature a kind and mild man, but I think he must have been burned out and exhausted by the events of his early teenage years. He was born in England, in the slums of Birmingham, into a Jewish family, the oldest boy of eight siblings. The family had little money, nor any prospect of change. In desperation, his mother Paulina dispatched her husband to South Africa to find work, make a place ready for her and the children, and when all that was done, send for them.

They waited a year or so, but no word came. So finally Paulina sent my father Harry, then only fourteen, to go and find his father. It must have taken enormous courage and determination to do so, and entailed a great deal of hardship, but he actually managed to track him down. Somehow he traced his path, first to the squalid euphoria of the diamond-mining camps of Kimberly, and then on to the gold-mining camps of Johannesburg, where he had been living it up in the rip-roaring world of gold prospecting, fortune hunting, illicit liquor and loose women – the stereotypes of that time and milieu. To his father's credit, with his dutiful teenage son knocking at the door of his conscience, he sobered up, shouldered his responsibilities, and made the necessary arrangements to import the whole family from England.

I never knew this grandfather, or even his name. But I have a very small photograph of him, in middle age, staring out of round rimless specs and looking like a model citizen – stern, serious and solidly respectable, though with a somewhat raffish moustache.

The experience of hunting down a father in foreign parts would surely have been too much for almost any boy, and so it was for Harry. The adventure and ordeal must have exhausted his inner resources. And whatever still remained would have subsequently been burned out in World War I, during which he was a private in the army. I can only guess that it was a time spent in hell, in spite of the comradeship, because like most foot soldiers in that war, he would never, even when pressed, say anything at all about it. All I know is that he returned to South Africa, met and married my mother – love at first sight, he said – worked for a cousin in the textile business, and in due course ended up as manager of a small dress factory. He worked hard and long, until his final illness and his death at eighty, and was constantly worried about money. We were always 'comfortable', so I thought, but by white South African standards he was nowhere near what could be called well-off.

I think it unlikely he had any more education after he left Birmingham to seek his father. That, in my opinion, together with all the other demanding experiences and responsibilities experienced so early, may be why he subsequently had so little tolerance of anything unfamiliar. The unknown was always a threat. He reacted violently against anything he didn't understand, or from which he felt excluded. His innate affability would be hijacked by sudden explosive rages. Almost anything could set it off – if my neckline were too low, for instance, once I'd reached my teens. If my friends were not sufficiently polite. If a black servant was what he decided was 'cheeky'.

There was never any conversation or real communication in our house, about ideas, or books, or current events, or even what we were thinking about. My father felt snubbed and excluded from the common fund of knowledge, and rather than looking for that knowledge for himself, simply barricaded himself against it. What seemed to matter most to him, and to my mother as well, was keeping up appearances in public. At home, particularly at the dinner table, there were only silences, or else bickering or nagging, and reproaches aimed at me.

My father was also ashamed and worried sick, in equal parts, I think, about my mother and her permanently doped state. She had become so habituated that she often took a dozen or so barbiturates a day, I was later told – unaware, I assume, of how risky this was, given that the lethal dose is very close to the 'normal' one. But my father would never acknowledge that there was anything wrong. When I was younger, I would ask: 'Daddy, why is Mummy bumping into the furniture?' 'Shut up,' he would snap, 'she isn't.' Or: 'Why are her words coming out all slurred and funny?' 'Shut up, they aren't.' Our GP visited at one point because my mother hadn't been out of bed for days, suffering from the euphemism known in our house as her 'liver complaint'. When the doctor said she needed hospital treatment for the drugs – and he meant mental hospital treatment – my father exploded and threw him out of the house.

In what turned out to be my last year at school, when I was fifteen, he was beginning to lose control of me and 'my ideas', as he called them, and this enraged him further. He stopped me seeing my friends, and sometimes even followed me when I went out. One day, trying to please him, really, I showed him a poem I had written which expressed a yearning for, and a sensing towards, something greater in life than the everyday. Though the word was unknown to me then, it could have been labelled a 'mystical' poem. My dad read it, and as I stood there awaiting praise – I did think I'd done it rather well – he suddenly boiled into rage.

'That's filth, you've written,' he yelled. 'Utter filth.'

He was trembling with fury. But in my innocence, I had no idea why. The ecstasy evoked in the poem was, to me, about something mysterious, towering way beyond the physical.

'I don't know where you get all your ideas from,' he shouted. 'It must be these,' and he kicked at the books piled up on the floor of my bedroom, and pulled at the volumes jammed into the bookcases, hurling them onto the floor. 'I'm going to burn them all tomorrow,' he raged. 'Burn every single damn one of them!'

However, when tomorrow came I woke terribly ill, close to death for several days, and was tended at home by day and night nurses. The illness was diagnosed as viral pneumonia, but I knew then, and know even more profoundly now, that it was a response from my deepest being to an attack on the essence of myself from the father I trusted. He was going to destroy the most important things in my life, my treasured sources of learning and understanding, not only of the mysteries of the world but the mysteries of myself. They were the only means I had yet found of searching for what would enable me not only to feel but to know, and after that, perhaps, to *be*. It was as if he was saying that I was, in his eyes, invalid, unreal. And if that were really so, I knew I would be unsecured and utterly unsafe. Indeed, could I even exist?

But the illness was also a deliverance. When the crisis had passed and I had begun to recover, my father's sisters, three stout, full-bosomed aunts who had been watching with concern from afar, sailed into our apartment like battleships. They announced that I was not getting adequate nurturing or attention, and for my own survival they were removing me. They sent me a thousand miles away to Cape Town, to stay with my cousin and her family, and I am eternally grateful to them for the readiness and generosity with which they took me in. I had a shot at going on to university, but at barely sixteen, I seemed to have no way of getting my bearings, so after two months I left.

At about that time, my father had a breakdown, from which he somehow put himself together again. And while he was struggling, my mother was removed to a mental hospital.

This has been a long diversion, but I think a necessary one to explain some of what happened next. It also explains why I was so unconfident and throughout my life ran away from success. The core of me was bright and optimistic, but I was sufficiently affected by my childhood to be run, much of the time, by patterns printed in me from the templates of my parents' difficulties. Appearances, of primary importance to both my parents, became so for me. Like my father's, my formal education stopped very early. And for much of my life, again like my father, I too felt at a disadvantage – useless, paralysed, utterly unable to stand up for myself when I encountered confident, articulate, well-educated people who opposed or in some way put me down.

Out of necessity I became a diplomat, playing my cards close to my chest, so that the mismatch between my deeper perceptions and my outward behaviour would not be spotted. But this strategy worked only when I was not challenged by difficulties or threats of aggression. Such challenges triggered a sense of powerlessness, of utter nothingness, and a feeling of life-threatening danger. All of this would play a part in the confrontation with Harry Bloom which lay ahead.

★

As I continued working on the script, I began to see how callow I was. I could sound knowledgeable with most people I knew, nearly all of whom were white, but was uncomfortably aware that, in spite of my deeper feelings, what I actually said only skated over the surface. It didn't occur to me that this might have been true of many others too. But as I came to know some of the cast of *King Kong*, I began to see, as I mentioned earlier, that no matter how intensely people like me felt, or how intellectual we tried to be, or how serious we thought we were, for the majority of us, our white, privileged and carefully protected lives kept us in an invisible prison and made us soft – 'spoiled', in the literal meaning of that word. We were also hedged in by the fear of black violence on the streets. My father, for instance, forbade me to go for a walk, or take a bus on my own, even in my teens.

But there was also something else at work within the *King Kong* creative team. Although my father had come from England, most of the other Jews I knew were first- or second-generation immigrants from countries where their families had been oppressed, or later exterminated in the World War II death camps. In South Africa, however, they were saved by their white skins. Some even worried about getting too sunburned, in case they began to look 'Indian'. My parents, too, were carefully not making trouble. When I voiced anger at the regime they would admonish me: 'Keep quiet – this time it's not us.'

It's easy to see my parents' point of view, one widely held in the Jewish community. During World War II the Nationalist Party, later the government but in those days still in opposition, openly backed the Nazis, even though South African troops 'up north' were fighting them. Prominent Afrikaner Nationalists would announce publicly that when the war was won – by the Germans, of course – then the Jews in South Africa would be 'dealt with'. And now the Nationalists were in power. Little wonder that the majority of the Jewish community were apprehensive. A ghastly joke circulated about two Jews facing a firing squad. As they stood with their backs to the wall, one of them asks for a blindfold. The other nudges him and mutters under his breath: 'For God's sake, don't make trouble.'

However, a significant minority of Jews, not all of them young, were prepared to risk 'making trouble'. The centuries of oppression of Jews within the ghettos of Europe and Russia, seemed to them very similar to the plight of the black population in South Africa. As Nelson Mandela pointed out,[1] the Nationalist regime thought of his people as animals, or even lower than animals. The pattern was identical, I could see, to what had happened in the Nazi regime in Germany, when people with Jewish blood were regarded as 'rats'.

So while the majority of Jews gave thanks that 'this time it's not us', a large minority, of which I was one, instinctively identified with the victims of oppression. We were driven, wordlessly and almost unaware, to fight against it, to some extent at least, wherever we found it, and in whatever form it took. So in a way it is not really surprising that the creative team for *King Kong* – the Menells, Goldreich, Bloom and myself, and then later Gluckman and Glasser, the stage director and the orchestrator of the music respectively, and Ian Bernhardt, the producer, though thoroughly secular in belief and lifestyle, were all of Jewish origin. The only exception was Arnold Dover, the choreographer, who was neither black nor Jewish. He had been born in Sheffield in 1914 and emigrated to South Africa in the mid-1930s.

My friends and I were a whole generation away from persecution, some of us two or three generations away, and because of our skin colour were living within the gift of easy material privilege. But I began to see that the black people I was now meeting had a far more valuable gift, because hard-won – a depth and maturity born of having to find ways round life's obstacles or confront them full on, every day. Even if, in the urban townships, the people were on the whole cut off from their tribal roots, they were not disconnected from the knowledge of them, which was bred in the bone. Most township people had strong family ties and a traditional culture wiser and deeper than anything I was brought up with, or was aware of. What is more, oppression, privation and difficulty had taught most of them to embrace life fiercely.

*

Why on earth had I imagined that I couldn't be a real writer just because I didn't have a university degree? Evidence to the contrary was all round me. The material that was beginning to come out of the townships from the black writers, of whom Todd was one, was energetic, immediate, vibrant and uninhibited. And few, if any, graduates among them! These people, frequently published in *Drum* magazine, spoke in their own voices, directly, with zest and humour and insight into life's hardships and joys. This was not the oblique literary style that I was more used to in my own circles and strove to imitate, nor was it to be found in the fashionable novels I read, where, on the whole (in those days), nastiness and strife (and sexual detail, of course) were hidden behind closed doors or high style. But the township writers transposed raw life and energy and humanity directly, authentically, and somehow like jazz, onto the page.

Above all, they understood the glory and power of metaphor. The beauty and endless simplicity of Todd's two

Xhosa lyrics for *King Kong* were like a call from a harsher but richer world than the one in which I dwelt. For instance, in a handful of words Todd, composer and poet both, was able to say in his overture, to all who had ears to hear, that the abomination of apartheid would not last: *The beauty of this world is like a blossom. It cannot be hidden by weeds, nor destroyed by ignorance.*

My parents and their friends, insulated within their received feelings of superiority, would have jeered indignantly if I had been able somehow to tell them the truth – that every one of my African friends and colleagues could express themselves more sincerely, and was more of a *mensch*,[2] than most of our lot were. The world, I began to think, is truly upside down, reflections in a deep lake.

*

King Kong himself, my imagined reality of the man, was growing in my mind as I sought to know him in order to write about him. I came to see there was something 'different' about him. Wild, unpolished, but with speed and stamina and furious strength, he began to be thought of as unbeatable – but I gather he had probably only half a dozen official fights in his ten-year career. It was hard to find opponents, and it was only in his final official fight that he became heavyweight boxing champion of black South Africa. For the rest, it was challenges in small Reef mining towns on Sunday afternoons, where he would fight all-comers, bare-fisted.

He was also dangerous. He held grudges. He would fight someone in the ring and then invite them to come outside and fight again in the street. Someone who was there told me about an incident when he was followed by a gang of killers – 'he doesn't look round, and they don't touch him, so in the end he forces them to be like they are his escorts all the way home to Sophiatown'. He could be a big-mouthed bully, but in spite of it the crowds loved him. Something about him was special. He was the greatest, the strongest, the unbeatable one. Top of the tree. The tree whose branches I had to shake until he fell.

In fact he lived out precisely that classic tragic dramatic arc in real life. Because there were so few fights at his weight, it was suggested that he shed some pounds and begin to fight as a middleweight. At the first such fight, with a weight advantage of a stone,[3] after some desultory exchanges he pranced around the ring, Zulu war-dance style, taunting the smaller boxer, 'Greb' Mthimkulu. But in the third round Greb landed a left on King Kong's jaw. It laid him out cold, and he was counted out. There was a stunned silence. Greb himself could hardly believe it. Indeed, after just one more fight, which he lost, Greb, suddenly a celebrity now, retired to live on the accolade of being 'the man who had knocked out King Kong'.

King Kong's identity had been invested in being unbeatable, being 'The Greatest', as Muhammad Ali would later say about himself. The humiliation of Greb's knockout punch changed him. He became a figure of fun, paranoid, smarting with humiliation. If anyone laughed in his presence, even someone in the street whom he suspected had done so, he beat them up. When he was thrown into a crowded cell for a night by a scrawny jailer because he was without his pass, again perhaps because of

61

the humiliation, he beat up everyone else in the cell (including a future member of the *King Kong* cast, in the cell for the same offence). At some point – it may have been at this time, or perhaps earlier – he became a bouncer again, at a dance hall known for its violence. One night, while removing a gangster armed with a knife, he fatally stabbed him. In court he pleaded self-defence, and was acquitted of murder.

Ezekiel Dhlamini was also showy. He would often wear a green or purple suit, for instance, as he strode through the township. I tried to capture that flamboyance and confidence in the very first song he sings:

> King Kong, brave as a lion
> No one can hold
> King Kong champ without trying
> That's me! I'm him! King Kong!
>
> King Kong bigger than Cape Town
> King Kong harder than gold
> King Kong knock any ape down
> That's me! I'm him! King Kong!

He genuinely didn't seem to need to have a girl on his arm just as an ornament, even though women were drawn to him, and even though, according to the writer and activist Don Mattera, who knew him, he was very gentle with women. I have seen this more sensitive side of him reflected in a photograph I found of him on, of all things, the cover of a knitting pattern for a man's sweater. The sweater certainly suited his physique. And the young Ezekiel himself was beautiful – strong and manly, yes, but with the face of a lost, wistful boy, almost like the young Marlon Brando. He was perhaps no more than twenty at the time of the photo, and above all, and in spite of everything, he looked like an innocent.

I've heard of only one serious girlfriend, Maria Miya, of whom he was, apparently, obsessively suspicious and jealous. She left him for a member of the Spoilers Gang, the toughest and most feared gangsters of the day. This was what finally brought him down from the top. When his emotions were raw and aroused, anything could set off his fury. It landed on Maria one weekend when she was talking with another man, flirting very probably, at a social gathering at the Adult Education Centre run by Johannesburg Council's Social Welfare Department, which doubled as a social club at weekends. There was a quarrel, and Ezekiel stabbed Maria to death. Now he was truly on the ropes. Everything finished for him.

That was the real-life story. In our musical, Maria was morphed into Joyce, *shebeen* queen at Back of the Moon, and girlfriend of the gangster's leader Lucky – until she leaves him for King Kong. But later in our story, she is drawn back to Lucky – and King Kong, in a jealous rage, strangles her at the wedding of his trainer, Jack.

However it happened, in real life, as in our show, there was a final, redemptive chapter. With the knife still in his hand, King Kong called for the police. They shot him three times in an effort to get him to drop the knife – though police in those days were so trigger happy that I can't believe they made much effort to talk him out of it. In the event, it was reported that the bullets passed through his body and wounded two policemen standing behind him. After a brief hospital stay he was considered able to stand trial, where – this is what catapulted him into 'white' attention – he virtually ordered the judge to sentence him to death.

No transcript would have been kept, of course, even if one had been made, so my imagination is free. I see him telling the judge that he, King Kong, must be sentenced to death as an example to others not to live as he has done, and in particular as a lesson to the young. Indeed that was my memory from reading the newspaper at the time. It struck me then, as it struck many others I think, that this man was more than just another criminal and murderer. His story had echoes of the legend of the swan, which, when facing its death, finally finds its voice and sings its heart out. King Kong's speech to the judge was his swan song.

But few white men in those days, and certainly not one of status, would stand for being told what to do by anyone with a black skin. The judge silenced him and then sentenced him to fourteen years' hard labour on a prison farm. I imagine the urgent, if jumbled, thoughts within his sad, tired head. Crying for justice and yearning to become a beacon for those who came after him, a warning beacon if not a heroic one, again he asked for the death sentence. Impatiently the judge rebuked him and reiterated his sentence.

Ezekiel was sent to a prison farm a few miles north of Johannesburg. Within the fortnight he had drowned himself in a nearby dam. Two days later his body was found and hauled from the dam. When I came to write this scene in my original book for the musical, I changed what really happened and made it that his body was never found, thus turning him into the legend he has indeed become. At the end of the show, as the township slows into the rhythms of the night, the washerwomen in my script are talking about King Kong:

> Lena: Ay ay . . . that man. Never been one like him.
> Pauline: Sometimes I think (quick, frightened) . . . I see him!
> Nancy: Maybe he didn't die that day, and he's here . . .
> Lena: Could be. They never found him. Maybe he's going to come back. One day . . .
> Pauline: Maybe he quickly went to England like he always wanted, and just never told anybody.
> Nancy: Ja, or maybe he's here. Now. Watching all of us . . .
> Severally: Hmmm, maybe, could be, maybe . . .

I was delighted to discover, so apposite was my invention, so much the way it should have been in the *really* real world of story, myth and metaphor, that when I was lunching with Irene Menell many years later, she spoke about how fitting it was that in real life King Kong's body had never been found, and how important that was for the story. She had unconsciously absorbed the metaphor which encapsulated the essence of the event – and stripped of its externals, was more truly real than the outward reality – and was giving it back to me as fact.

★

I was already aware of King Kong before the musical was even mooted, because I worked on the *Rand Daily Mail*, in which his story had been so surprisingly, though briefly, covered. But what has taken me by surprise is that even today, nearly sixty years after his death, and in spite of never having boxed outside his own country, as he had so wanted to do, the details of Ezekiel Dhlamini, boxer, known as King Kong, are actually present on the World Wide Web.

The information, though, is sparse and inaccurate. One website I found gave his nationality as Vryheid, Natal (actually that's the town of his birth). He was rated as a heavyweight, and his thirty-six years on earth noted: from 1921.01.01 to 1957.04.03. Yet his age was given as ninety-two – which is what he would have been had he survived, I suppose, at the time I read the entry. Sadly, the fields designed to contain all the boxer's physical details, such as height and reach, world ranking, and the names of trainer and manager, were all blank. And there were different blanks in yet another boxing website, including the place where a biography and a photograph should have been.

It is a sad irony. The fact that King Kong is recorded internationally, and so long after his death, would have delighted Ezekiel. But with so many empty spaces where his details and achievements should have been! That would have hurt him terribly – because they make manifest all the obstacles that he could not overcome. At the core of his tragic story lies the fact that he could never find out how good he really was. Heavyweight champion of black South Africa, yes – for what that was worth. But he was never allowed to test himself in his prime by fighting a white man in his own country, because black boxers and white boxers were not allowed by law to fight each other. They could, however, spar together. I heard a story that before the final fight with Greb there was an informal occasion, during the period of his decline, when that happened, and his sparring partner was definitely superior.

Nevertheless, the real source of King Kong's tragedy, I think, was that while still at the height of his powers he was never allowed to go overseas to fight, even though there had been a few invitations. Vryheid, his birthplace, means 'Freedom' in Afrikaans. Another irony.

I did my best to track his story. In his teens Ezekiel worked briefly in Vryheid as a gardener for a white family. Then the trail goes cold, and picks up later in Durban, where he fought a bit, had some success, and obviously began to get a taste for it. A little later he travelled to Egoli, the Zulu name for the big city, the city of gold, Johannesburg, magnet for the young, hopeful or desperate, just as London is for the British young today, and just as dangerous for those who disappear from their families and try their chances in the metropolis. Many of them, as in London, end up in crime or on the streets. And for black youths in Johannesburg at that time, living under the shadow of the implacable race laws, there was also gambling and dicing, and hanging around dance halls and *shebeens*. Ezekiel did all that, but he also found his way to the Bantu Men's Social Centre in Polly Street.

'Bantu', the word, simply means 'the people' or 'humans'. It is a general label for hundreds of ethnic groups, and hundreds of millions of African people, speakers of the Bantu languages from the Cameroons to Central and East Africa, as well as down in the south. In fact the Bantu family is fragmented into hundreds of individual groups, the largest – some ten million – being the Zulus, Ezekiel Dhlamini's people. But because of the apartheid regime's use of the word on official documents, and because of official mouths spitting it out with contempt, in South Africa, the word Bantu acquired pejorative and degrading associations.

Nevertheless, the Social Centre itself, founded by an American missionary, was a dynamic and welcoming place, providing education and recreation for black adults and children. It hosted choirs and bands; and also offered boxing, judo and ballroom dancing. It was run by Cecil Skotnes, one of South Africa's great painters and the son of a missionary himself. I felt lucky to count him and his wife Thelma among my friends. When Cecil took the job, there was only one art student enrolled, yet today, as a result of his work and influence, Polly Street is remembered mostly as an art school. However, in the late fifties it was jumping, a lively, noisy, rowdy place. I remember Cecil telling me that they needed strong men for bouncers at the door, which is why at one point he employed Ezekiel Dhlamini.

Indeed, this is where the record picks him up next – not as a bouncer, though, but in the gym at the Social Centre. He had encountered the boxers and had been jeering at them, taunting them for fighting with 'cushions' round their fists, challenging them to fight, to fight *him*, with or without the cushions. So he was invited into the ring – and quickly flattened.

Ezekiel was a man of huge and angry pride, quick to explode with rage, but he had a drive to stand out, knew what he needed, and saw a potential teacher in the trainer, William 'Baby Batter' Mbatha. So he asked for lessons, learned quickly, and soon was flooring all contenders, night after night.

He had a genius, said those who saw him, for raw boxing. And soon he was a real professional, wearing in the ring a maroon and blue dressing gown he had seen in a shop window, with 'Spy Smasher' written on it. He was beginning to pull in the crowds. But it took some hard persuasion before his trainer persuaded him to abandon the alluring fantasy of being he who smashed the spies and become, instead, King Kong, the mighty ape.

We know all this from recorded or remembered events. But what, I wondered, were the other influences, born within him, perhaps, or shaped within childhood, which made him react in his own particular way to the political cruelties and obstacles he encountered, and which made him such a loner, so troubled and so aggressive? As I worked my way towards him in my imagination while writing the script, I began to get a feel for the sensitivity of the man, the integrity of an individual who would at all costs be himself, not the creature of a regime which denied people like him the right to vote, and passed laws prohibiting them from living where they chose or working in anything other than unskilled jobs. Whether that was the truth about Ezekiel Dhlamini I had no idea. But it was true, it seemed to me, in a larger sense. King Kong stood as a symbol of the damage that could be done to others by ignorance manifesting as hatred, brutality and greed for power, and encapsulated the experiences and life trajectories of many Ezekiels.

I've already mentioned Don Mattera, the poet and activist, son of an Italian father and Xhosa mother. I knew him only slightly, but liked and admired him enormously. Recently I found an interview with him, published in 1986, which confirmed my intuitive sense of Ezekiel Dhlamini, the man inside the boxer.[4] Don himself suffered appallingly from the constraints of apartheid, and reacted to the endemic violence of Sophiatown, the township where he lived until it was torn down, with violence of his own. In his youth, circumstances turned this man with the heart of a poet and the mind of a reformer and visionary into a thug and a murderer: the record shows he was arrested 202 times, and spent twelve years in jail during the apartheid years. But his later experiences transformed him. He grew through them and today is the author of several fine books of both poetry and prose, and an honoured leader of his community. He has created educational organisations, as well as homes and institutions, to take care of the disadvantaged and vulnerable. Don met Ezekiel when he was in prison in 1955, on his first murder charge, and says he 'liked him as a person'. He describes him as 'an ugly man, powerful, very large teeth, I remember. And very cold.' He also said something which would have been helpful to have known at the time I was writing the script, about the way he was with women and children – about 'his gentleness with women, the way he looked after them, which I think the "King Kong" play didn't really bring out; the way he loved children – he used to sit and talk to kids, encourage them. And there was a "philosophy" about him, about the way he was – strong but gentle inside. But it was gentleness he did not want to show.'[5] Although I wish I'd come across these words at the time, I sensed and implied some of this in my script, particularly about the way King Kong was with children.

As I worked on, living each day with Ezekiel Dhlamini and understanding him better, daily life outside the *King Kong* bubble continued to demand my time and energy. I had a full-time job, a typical well-off doctor's-wife-cum-journalist's high-end social life – dinner parties and so on – and also a family life with its attendant necessities, and all too often fraught with emotional tensions. So the only possible time I found to devote to *King Kong* was at four a.m. each day. I would creep out from the bedroom into the adjacent study and think about, visualise the story, and then write until just after six. Then Joe would rise and get ready for the long drive to a hospital in Springs, on the Far East Rand, where he was the consultant physician and cardiologist. Some time after, I would drive to work, singing.

While I was still busy with the script, an evening was organised to raise money for the show, at which some of the songs would be performed to potential backers in Ciro's, the fashionable downtown night club. (Several optimistic *King Kong* musicians who had heard about the coming event without realising its purpose, hoped we might have been organising some sort of hedonistic Bacchus evening.) Representatives from Coca-Cola were there, I remember, as well as representatives from Anglo-American, and other potential sponsors. Agents from the South African branch

71

of Bayer, the makers of Aspirin, were – I think – there too. The musicians played, Miriam Makeba and the Manhattan Brothers sang, drawings and paintings of Arthur's sets were on display, tables of booze and elaborate snacks were laid on, speeches were made. I remember part of a speech made by Myrtle Berman, one of the organisers, a petite, vivacious and immensely attractive woman whom I would come to admire and respect enormously. She had risked a lot because of her political commitments and would later end up in prison. Compared to her fierce courage and spirit I knew myself to be faint-hearted and puny, barely in 'the struggle' at all.

She started her speech with the words: 'We who do culture work among the Africans . . .', and then went on to explain that 'we culture workers' think *King Kong* would be a Good Thing for the people present to invest in. I began to feel uncomfortable. Were we really doing culture work among the Africans? Culture work? That wasn't what I thought I was doing. Looking back, and knowing Myrtle as I do now, I imagine that this was her way of trying to raise money for the show; that she would have been deliberately trimming her speech to circumvent the audience's prejudices. But at the time I took exception to the words. My take on what we were doing was very different. I had simply thought we were just a bunch of people trying to get a musical on and have fun doing so, plus there was the extra exhilaration which I always experienced when breaking laws and barriers. No patronage, no concept of 'culture work' existed among those of us who were busy with the *actual* work. Not a trace of it.

I left abruptly, going outside just to rid myself of these

negative emotions at this plush assembly. And to my surprise, I found Todd hanging about in the corridor outside.

'Hello Toddy. What are you doing out here?'

A wry smile. 'They won't let me in', he said.

'What? *Really?*'

Oh, but of course they wouldn't. Black skin may be acceptable for culture work, but not in a white night club, with free drinks on offer, and Todd there not as a working musician but as part of the audience. The fact that he happened to be the composer of the heart-lifting music they were listening to and obviously enjoying cut no ice. I tried to have a word with the nightclub manager and get Todd in. Not a chance. He was not even interested in the irony of the situation. So for most of the rest of the event I remained outside with Todd, hearing the music through the closed door, the two of us chatting and giggling. Later, though, common sense finally prevailed. A door opened, and we were called in. A small victory.

*

I handed the script in on the promised date, an unfinished first draft, with blanks here and there, places marked 'this speech to come' and so on. I wasn't too worried about that, because the man who would be our stage director, Leon Gluckman, was without doubt the best theatre director in the country and would be able, I was sure, to realise its potential. Leon was a handsome, charming and sensitive man with a brilliant theatrical track record and a prodigious talent as both actor and director. He had already spent several extremely successful years in British theatre, an immensely promising start to what clearly would have become an illustrious career there, had he stayed. I was confident he would be able to see what I had written for what it was, and what it could become. The hard thinking had been done. The structure held. The characters and motivations made sense. Some of the writing was good, and the rest was good enough, I thought, for this first stage. I imagined we would develop it the rest of the way between us. Even the gaps I'd left described in note form the content I envisaged. It was a sincere and honest piece of work, in which I had pushed my thinking towards the furthest edges of my capacity. Given the limitations of my experience, the result was the best I could possibly have managed to do.

But it didn't work out as I had hoped. Leon was in Cape Town, working on two productions there. Harry Bloom was a friend of his, and I can now see that the two of them must have been conferring about *King Kong*. The first note of disquiet came early on, although I didn't recognise it, when Leon sent a message telling me, while I was still busy writing, that he wanted a ceremonial funeral scene (rather as in his earlier production of *Hamlet*, which I had seen) where King Kong could be carried across the stage like a prince, and mourned by the crowds. I said that a funeral scene of that kind was too grand, out of context in the story as I had conceived it. I thought that what he had suggested and what I had replied were the beginning of a conversation, and that we'd have time to talk it through.

I didn't expect what came next.

Not long after I had sent the finished script to Leon, Harry informed Irene Menell that he was coming up to

Johannesburg, and required a meeting about the script. My version was no good, he said. Leon found it unworkable and he himself found it puerile. I felt utterly crushed. It also seemed to me as if, in addition to what well might be justifiable criticisms, Harry was determined to be back in the driving seat of the show that he had left, and that was now shaping up so well. So Irene, Harry and I met in the Menells' studio one late afternoon, the day after he arrived, to find out what his specific objections were.

I remember the scene very clearly. The lovely room, the striped curtains, the artefacts, the comfort, so different from the formal angular, draughty interiors I'd grown up with. Like the garden outside, Clive and Irene's studio had a texture, a cohesion – the materials worked together . . . the word I find I must use, as I have done again and again in this story, is harmony.

But now the harmony we'd felt between us was disrupted. Irene and I listened as Harry explained why my script was amateurish and unplayable. Hating confrontation as I did, I was agitated and apprehensive. I had bought a pair of mirrored sunglasses that morning, I remember, to wear during the meeting, so that no one could see the tears that would no doubt come into my eyes. I remember also Irene asking me rather sharply to remove them.

'About the script,' she said to Harry. 'Can you give us examples of your objections?'

Surprisingly, when it came to it, there seemed very little. Some trivial details, easily fixed. I was greatly relieved. If that was all, then there wasn't much of a problem. Why all the fuss?

In a recent conversation, Irene filled in the details for

my husband David: 'When I asked for specifics, there were only a few small things Harry could point out, and in discussion we agreed that these could be easily dealt with. I remember that the meeting ended surprisingly quickly because there was so little to do, and I left Harry and Pat to work together, there and then, to make those adjustments. As far as I was concerned, that was all there was to it. My memory has always been that Harry's role in the script was very minor, and I have continued to think so over all the years. Looking back now, though, I realise he must have returned to Cape Town, and probably worked closely on the script with Leon. But even so, it is based on Pat's work.'

Looking back, I wonder if Leon and Harry had agreed in advance that they would work together in this way, once Harry had returned to Cape Town. If that was the case, then the few flimsy objections he came up with at our meeting could have been merely a necessary charade.

But of course word got around that there were script problems, and some of the reports and monographs and academic theses and studies of *King Kong* that are still knocking around mention that I had written *four* scripts. How do these rumours start? There was only the single first draft that I'd hoped could be worked up in collaboration with Leon. But the collaboration was not to be with me.

Leon possessed a genius for theatre. He came from a privileged and cultured background, his father had been Minister of Health in the somewhat less racist United Party government, which ruled before the Nationalists came to power. He was good-looking, socially assured, and very likeable. Harry was a celebrated novelist, and also one of a number of courageous human rights lawyers, as they'd be called today, who were prepared to defend black clients. Both were clever and worldly, both had reputations on the side of the angels, both were older than I was – and both were men.

Hard to believe these days, but it seems to me, looking back, that this actually had a bearing. Leon and Harry could be blokes together, they were already friends, extremely confident, exceptionally successful in their work, and skilful at swimming in social waters. I was young, female, unsure of myself, unpredictable, not on their wavelength, inexperienced in theatre, and, from their point of view, annoyingly precious and stubborn. After all, I had not given Leon the funeral scene he wanted. Normally so unconfrontational, so loath to create scenes, so compliant, in this particular case I was totally refusing to give an inch, because I felt it would falsify what I had written.

But of course I had doubts. Maybe Harry, the well-known novelist, and Leon, the experienced and celebrated stage director, were right about what I'd written. What did I really know about theatre? The script could obviously have been greatly improved, yes – it was a first draft after all, and I had been looking forward to working with and learning from Leon, to amplify and complete it between us. The only thing I was sure of was that I had done my honourable best. So although the greater part of me was deeply wounded – and also ashamed that with no discussion at all the script was so summarily taken away from me – at some deeper level the criticism didn't really find its mark.

But when I saw the final working manuscript, I was embarrassed. It was jaunty, clever, professional and very playable, I could see that. It certainly 'worked'. But it seemed to me that even so, something of the freshness and truth of the story had been replaced by a rather patronising tone, a kind of knowing, benevolent condescension. I knew then, and know still, that had the final result, given all its many virtues, been in my eyes less shallow, I would have been glad, and the first to offer my congratulations.

And indeed, although I couldn't know it at the time, my greenness and naivety when writing the script were not necessarily disadvantages. I later learned that in the judgement of two experienced and respected members of the theatre world, my script in fact had a lot to recommend it. Their opinion lifted off my shoulders the burden of doubt and shame that I had been carrying for years. But that was nearly half a century later.

*

Harry Bloom's new version of the script built upon some of my ideas and used many of my lines, but he also made definite improvements. Where Joyce, for instance, was simply a girl in the *shebeen* in my version, she was promoted to *shebeen* 'queen' in Harry's – a very good idea. But whereas I had tried to work from the inside out for the sake of truth and understanding, Harry, it seemed to me, had worked from the outside in, for effect, which had resulted at times in the shallowness I have mentioned. I veered from one point of view to another. Given the prevailing attitudes in our country at the time, maybe our musical required that slickness and simplification to reach the stage at all? But I squirmed at what seemed to me the patronising 'Uncle Tom'-ism, and the way the characters were at times rendered virtual caricatures. I also now had the extra, irksome task of rewriting already finished lyrics to fit new scenes and situations.

And yes, predictably, there *was* now an elaborate and theatrically very effective funeral scene.

★

After our strange little script meeting, Harry returned to Cape Town, and Irene and I heard no more. Communication from him and Leon ceased. Perhaps what ended up happening had been intended from the moment I had objected to a grand funeral scene. In her book, Mona Glasser puts it briskly: Leon 'received the script and asked Harry to work on it once more'. And some sentences later: 'the revised plan necessitated additional work for Pat Williams, who had already completed many of the lyrics, working in close collaboration with the composer.' 'Fortunately,' she added, 'she worked fast'.

From that point on, Harry has always been on record as the sole writer of King Kong. My contribution to the script was never acknowledged. Indeed, he was unwilling to share a credit for the script or even recognise my contribution in some way, when asked by the Menells if he would do so. So Arthur, Irene and Clive decided between them to give Todd and myself a joint extra credit, for what was called 'musical conception'. It was a way of indicating that my contribution to the libretto had been more substantial than writing the lyrics. And that extra credit was a necessary further acknowledgement for Todd as well – because his situation turned out to be very similar to my own.

Round about the time that Harry had come up to Johannesburg to take back the script and 'save the show', Todd was simultaneously having to swallow what, to him, were the unhappy results of Spike Glasser's orchestration. Spike had spent some years studying composition in Europe, and was in his final year studying orchestration at King's College, Cambridge when Leon, a friend from childhood, had asked if he would come back and orchestrate the *King Kong* music. Spike was very talented indeed, I had heard, but I was beginning to hear stories that he seemed in some way to have taken the music over. I heard from a reliable source close to Todd that he had been 'pushed out', not allowed near the orchestration, and that he was 'very angry'. Moreover, Todd told me himself, the final sound didn't have any of the depth and richness he had heard in his mind when he was writing the music. So the extra 'musical conception' credit was as much for Todd as for me.

Indigenous South African music of the time was spun out of three influences – African music bred in the bone, 1930s jazz from America, and church music, which had originally arrived with the missionaries. Todd's music, was drenched in the spirit of all of these, and also expressed, in a way that no words ever could, the energy and sadness of human existence in the time and place in which he found himself. But even to my musically uneducated ears, the final orchestration had turned his glorious music, into rather tame Europeanised 'swing'. This did not of course, diminish the beauty of Todd's melodies themselves. The result still caught wonderfully at both body and heart, just as the essence of a poem manages to survive almost any translation into a foreign tongue. But compared with what could have been . . . No wonder Todd felt angry and disappointed that he had not even been consulted about the orchestration.

Stories circulated that Todd was incapable of orchestrating his own music, so it had to be handed over to someone who had the skills, just as word spread that I hadn't been capable of doing the script, so it had to be passed on to Harry. What surprised and hurt both of us further, however, was that we were both simply ignored in the production process thereafter. I had no idea what was happening to the script, and Todd, I gathered, didn't hear much more about what was happening to the music. I think a predictable territorial aspect of human (or, more accurately, animal) nature had manifested itself. Just as Harry came to think he had written the whole script, so I heard that Spike felt the success of the music was largely down to him. And having worked long and hard on the score, and equally intensely with the musicians, he had come to think that his work had 'made' Todd's music. The reliable source close to Todd, whom I mentioned earlier, commented: 'I think Spike got away with much more than he deserved.'

When people devote their time and attention and creativity to something, the work they've put in and their familiarity with the material tend to make them feel it's completely theirs. Awareness of other helping hands or collaborators is liable to fade. Looking back, I can see that we were like children fighting over a toy. 'It's mine!' 'No, it's mine!' 'I had it first!' 'Yes, but I've got it now!' And so on. Of course the time and thought I had put in, the creative journey I had gone on, made me feel that to a great extent the final script was still mine, in spite of the changes it had undergone. I imagine Todd felt exactly the same, even more justifiably, about the orchestration of his music. At one of the rehearsals, I overheard a couple of the musicians talking: 'Spike is very good, man, he's trained in music, and all that time in London. He's good to work with too, but he's not Todd Matshikiza. But sometimes he thinks he wrote the music himself.' And then someone else: 'Ja, I heard Harry Bloom also used Pat's work, and thinks it's all down to him.'

I hadn't realised that of course gossip was flying around the townships too.

Before the show got as far as auditions, Todd and I dropped our bombshell. We felt that the show had been spoiled. It was not what we had originally conceived. So we composed a letter to the press saying that because of artistic disagreements we were walking away. We would leave our work but wanted our names removed from the credits, and dissociated ourselves from the production.

And having done that, we told Eddie Joseph. Eddie was a well-connected businessman who had played a large part in raising the funds to put the show on. (The backers' evening at Ciro's, sadly, hadn't raised nearly enough.) Eddie, we felt, was solid, reliable and fair. He pleaded with the two of us to change our minds. 'If you walk out, I will have to pay out large sums from my own pocket, because much of the money we have already received from our guarantors has been spent.' I still don't know whether that was true, or a tactful way of reining us in, but Eddie was a man of integrity and generosity. Without telling anyone, for instance, some months later he gave Miriam Makeba, star of our show, the money she needed to get to America. His daughter, Jessica Strang, told me that she heard about it from Miriam only years later, 'at the time she returned all the money to my brother Michael'.

Our rebellion ran out of steam very quickly. We decided we couldn't allow Eddie to pay. So we pulled back the press release – though too late for the biggest morning paper, the *Rand Daily Mail*, which printed it with a large picture of me.

And perhaps this final – in our eyes adulterated – version of *King Kong* was all that was possible. Black and white were still living in separate universes, corralled there by harshly applied laws. The raw truth would have been hard to put on the stage, particularly in a musical. Perhaps the mental landscape couldn't accommodate what Todd and I had wanted, because our more edgy perception of the story and its music wasn't yet sufficiently saleable. Those who had the know-how, muscle and skills to get the show funded, launched and on stage, called the tune. Todd and I were dreamers, not capable of, or even that interested in, organising the nuts and bolts of a production or paying too much attention to market realities. Certainly what none of us could have known at the time was how successful – in spite of all the flaws – the finished *King Kong* would be.

But the pain remained with us both. We felt ignored, our work thoughtlessly and peremptorily brushed aside. Over the years Todd would repeatedly speak resentfully of 'the heavy white hand' that had descended on his music. And when I think now of what I have since learned about Todd's considerable musical knowledge and abilities and qualifications, I wonder why the orchestration *wasn't* more of a collaboration. Even if Todd had no experience of writing parts for different instruments in the band, surely he could have been drawn into the process? For many years, too, I would wince whenever I read or heard someone say that Harry Bloom was the author of *King Kong*, clearly without any knowledge that my work was in there too, absorbed without even a nod. The record has Harry as the source and sole writer of the show in all the published references, and for years, as I imagine perhaps Todd also did, I nursed and stoked my hurt and grievance, quite unable to let them go.

I know that it is true for most people, as it certainly is for me, that in any creative effort, after spending time dwelling deeply inside the imagination, pushing at the horizons of thought and perception, one feels extremely raw and exposed. And until that rawness settles, any criticism, unless very gently and carefully couched, is likely – deeply and disproportionately – to wound. The imaginary world that one has conceived and built is always as real as real can be to the individual who has dwelt and worked there, and to harshly deny its validity while that rawness exists is like bombing someone's internal citadel.

But why, in my case, had that citadel's fires continued to burn for so long? Years later I realised that having my sincere efforts so casually discarded, my hard work so ignored, matched the pattern of my father's attack on my aspirations when he threatened to burn my books. In both cases I felt utterly unsafe, the ground gone from under my feet: something crucial, from the core of me, ridden roughshod over, treated as of absolutely no value. I had not yet come to understand that certain things can never be taken away from one, and that my essential self, along with all my talents and resources, was, and always would be, perfectly safe.

As far as outsiders were concerned, of course, all the fuss and hurt could be summed up in three dismissive words – that's show business.

★

We were nearly three months into the project now, and the mood of our *King Kong* enterprise was changing. From what had been such an easy and open-hearted beginning, egos had begun to intrude, in the company of their close companions, ambition and greed. In the case of Harry and myself, the atmosphere became so tense that as a precaution against future litigation, Irene gave my original script to a lawyer, to be sealed and locked away for safekeeping. And there it remained for decades.

Looking back from this distance, it is clear to me that Harry was utterly single-minded and possessive about *King Kong*. Even though he'd hardly been around at the beginning, now he was back he was not going to be a team player. His attitude, that the script was all his, and only his, and so was the glory, became clearer when the contract was drawn up, and laughably clear again on the opening night.

And just as Harry had his tendencies and limitations by reason of his own character and past difficulties, I of course had tendencies of my own. 'What about me?

Can't you see me? You're making me invisible!' my wounded and exaggerated emotions silently raged at Harry – and also, more crucially, at home, at my husband Joe.

3

The mind, I sometimes think, is a bit like a large hotel, accommodating diverse visitors arriving from all over the place – an analogy which can perhaps explain how I coped with my hurt over the script. So much was happening in my marriage, at work and with *King Kong*, that I simply put the hurt in one of my mental hotel rooms and closed the door. If I went back into that room I felt upset all over again, so most of the time I just didn't go there. Indeed, I think the human capacity to switch from one 'room' to another is what enables us to perform effectively – in life as in the theatre.

And far too much else was going on. What had been cooked up between the five of us in the warmth and friendship of the Menells' upstairs studio was now taking its first step towards fleshed-out reality.

From the time we had started working together, Irene and Clive's plan had been to involve Ian Bernhardt, impresario and producer, as the obvious person to bring our show to the stage. He was a large, bulky man with twinkling eyes, an unexpectedly high voice, and, at twenty-nine, older than many of us. For someone who loved the theatre, his demeanour was utterly untheatrical. I saw him as more like a benign, rather shrewd vicar – something to do with his jolliness, his air of private enjoyment, and the amiable way he regarded me from on high – unavoidable really, given how tall and heavy he was. The 'vicar' persona was my private joke – his family's origins were in the ghettos of Lithuania.

He was also political, passionate about fairness and justice, though I don't remember him ever haranguing anyone on the subject. As a member of the Congress of Democrats, he was just about as far left as you could go without being a member of the Communist party – and his two allegiances, political and theatrical, threaded through everything he did. He had also chosen to be self-employed (publishing trade magazines) so that his time was his own. And one of the things he had recently started to do with that time was to put black jazz musicians onstage in front of white audiences – a brave and very new development. So the choice of Ian as our producer was no choice at all. Who else could it have been?

★

One must always choose to begin a story *somewhere*, even though there is always so much more behind that story than can be known or told. An invisible chain across time and space, people and events, intentions and emotions, lies hidden underneath the outward sequence of the story itself. When I hear professional storytellers acknowledging the provenance of their tale – 'I got this from so and so, who heard it from so and so', they might say, going back as far as they can, 'and it was doubtless told well before being written down by so-and-so in the twelfth century' – that telling of the 'story of the story' always feels right and important to me. Nothing stands in isolation. A 'real' story, is actually an organism. And in the case of *King Kong*, many unseen, forgotten or submerged connections and sources from the past had flowed into it, far too many to name here.

But one unforgettable influence, in varying degrees affecting everyone connected with the show, was a single peerless man – Father Trevor Huddleston, member of the Anglican Community of the Resurrection. He had arrived from Britain to become Provincial of that community in Johannesburg, and had left South Africa nine years before our *King Kong* musical was even dreamed of. But for the thirteen years before that he had lived, worked in and been in charge of the Anglican Community's Sophiatown and Orlando Mission. He was also Superintendent of St Peter's Community School in Sophiatown, the freest and most integrated of the townships, situated just south of Johannesburg. All races, including some white people, lived there together.

There was no one else quite like Trevor Huddleston – and in this case those words are not a platitude. Even those who knew of him only by report, of whom I was one, were touched by him as if by contagion. A constant thorn in the flesh of the government, he was also – to the black community and to sympathetic whites – an unparalleled beacon and exemplar of courage and humanity. 'He was able to pick out the gems of South Africa, the best people, and not only in Sophiatown, and was keen to elevate people's lives,' musician Hugh Masekela told me recently. 'He was an inspiration to all of us.'

As well as his priestly duties and teaching at St Peter's School, Huddleston watched out for his parishioners' welfare, fighting the brutality of the apartheid regime at every turn. He initiated a feeding scheme for black children, even raised money for a township swimming pool in Orlando. And crucially for *King Kong*, he developed a community of outstanding black musicians, and also encouraged a handful of young white people, Ian Bernhardt among them, to look after their professional welfare. Bit by bit, and in the teeth of the law, all that led to the formation of a trade union. The Union of Southern African Artists, as it became in 1951, was sorely needed to protect and fight for the rights of black musicians and entertainers, who in those days were often ruthlessly exploited. And it was under the banner of that union, by the time Ian had become its director, that *King Kong* was produced. I was told by his daughter Linda that he had found himself running a trade union, which didn't really interest him, so moved its focus towards his great love, the performing arts. In any case, the Industrial Conciliation Act of 1956 had legislated against multi-racial trade unions, so it was no longer possible to employ black staff within their own union.

Even though Trevor Huddleston had left South Africa nine years before our musical was even born, I wonder whether *King Kong* could ever have happened without him. Over the thirteen years he lived in South Africa, in addition to his many other activities, he fostered and nurtured the exceptional musical talent pulsing through his students at St Peter's School, as indeed it did throughout the townships. He saw that music brought his students to life and that music also kept them alive. So he solicited donations from organisations and individuals, and begged, bargained for, or himself bought various musical instruments and gave them to those students he knew had a great talent. And then, when the time came that there were enough enthusiastic and practised young players, the Huddleston Jazz Band was born. The band gave its musicians experience of working together, playing gigs, becoming professional in their outlook and developing their musical skills.

To give you a flavour of what those instruments meant to the schoolboys, I will tell the most obvious of the many inspiring stories that circulated – that of Hugh Masekela – because at one point in it there was an act of such unexpected generosity that the event was even reported in the white press.

At the age of eight, Hugh was already so difficult and disruptive in school that he had to repeat his second year there – more or less, he believed, as a punishment. Even he, looking back, has described his behaviour at the time as 'despicable'. He didn't care much about anything. Only music had any meaning for him. And when he saw Kirk Douglas as Bix Beiderbecke in the film *Young Man with a Horn*, he was determined that *somehow* he would become a trumpet player himself. Early in the school year that he had needed to repeat, he came down with flu, and while lying sick in bed, Huddleston came to his bedside with a big smile on his face.

'Hugh, what would make you well? What do you really want to do with your life when you grow up?' he asked him.

Sensing that he was in a generous mood, Hugh said, 'Father, if you could get me a trumpet, I won't bother anybody any more.' Huddleston asked: 'Are you sure that's what you want, little creature?"[1] ('Creature' was an affectionate word he used a lot.)

Hugh's vigorous assurance must have told him all he needed to know. So he bought him a second-hand trumpet from Polliacks, Johannesburg's specialist music store. It cost him far more than he had reckoned on paying, but the trumpet transformed the young boy so substantially that by the time he was thirteen, his remarkable development as a musician and single-minded devotion to his instrument were unmistakable.

While on a trip to the United States that same year, Huddleston went backstage to see Louis Armstrong before one of his concerts. He told him Hugh's story and asked if he would be willing to donate a new trumpet. Of course Armstrong agreed – but then, with characteristic understanding and warmth, told Huddleston that rather than give him a new trumpet he would send him one of his own. If he had played it himself it would mean far more to Hugh.

Thus the connection was made, across thousands of miles – and it was literally mouth to mouth, and heart to heart. When the trumpet was put in his hands, Hugh literally leaped for joy, high in the air – there's a photograph of him doing so. It was another of those moments when the barriers of time and space collapsed, as they would on that unforgettable day, still waiting in the future, when in the Menells' small studio room, Doris Fisher astounded us by playing her father's song, *Chicago*. Hugh was there that day too. By then, still in his teens, he was one of the team of *King Kong* musicians copying the orchestral parts of the score, and playing third trumpet in the band.

Jazz, the ability to play it and sing it and *live* it, was both symbol and fact of the links between black Americans and South Africans. Although living in different countries, they shared their origins from centuries before – and, sadly, had shared destinies too, in terms of being subjected to dehumanising forces and prejudice. When the slave-traders tricked, stole or bought free men and women to be sold as slaves in America, their victims took with them on their dangerous journeys only what could never be taken away from them: their spirit, their talent, their minds, their music – their essential selves, in fact. Now, by the mid-twentieth century, the music – transmuted over time into jazz – had returned from America to Africa, and was speaking directly to the hearts of the young in the townships.

(And suddenly I ask myself: do I need to say what a township actually was? Perhaps I do: so much has changed. Townships were shanty towns, with row upon row of government-designed identical matchbox houses, often with electricity and water only in the streets, deliberately separated by many miles from the white heart of Johannesburg, and ringed by roads wide enough to accommodate an army tank. White people, other than the police, needed a permit to enter a township, otherwise it was illegal, and if caught they might be arrested.)

*

Without Father Huddleston preparing the ground, there wouldn't have been a pool of skilled musicians and performers, or a union to actively protect them, or later, a building in which to house that union. There might not even have been an Ian Bernhardt ready and waiting, or a Robert Loder, the high-powered enabler of the show in both South Africa and London, because Loder, who at the time of *King Kong* was working for the powerful Anglo-American mining and industrial organisation, had originally come to South Africa from London to work with Father Huddleston. And there certainly wouldn't have been a network of experienced musicians and groups, all familiar with each other, and enthusiastic, able and ready. There might not even have been a King Kong.

I have often thought how much pleasure the show would have given Trevor Huddleston, had he been able to remain in Johannesburg. But as the years went by, apartheid's screws were turning ever tighter, and the political climate was growing increasingly dark. Just four miles south of Johannesburg, so virtually a suburb of that city, Sophiatown had originally been a suburb built for whites, but when few of them wanted to move there, the suburb's owner opened the area to 'blacks and coloureds'. The diverse population made for a vibrant culture of the arts – musicians, writers, and (beginning to develop, in my day) a colony of painters, all thrived there. Some people even built and owned their own houses. In spite of the gangsters and the poverty, the essential quality of life was higher than what apartheid deemed sufficient for non-white people. However, Sophiatown's mixture of races was a thorn in the regime's ideology, and also 'dangerously' close to Johannesburg's city centre. So in the early 1950s the government decided to remove the township's entire community of 60,000, and bulldoze it out of existence.

This forced removal, over many weeks, by 2,000 armed police, brought Father Huddleston into direct conflict with the police and other authorities almost daily. He stormed into meetings, calmed near-riots, spoke up against the removals, and incident by incident, to the best of his ability, protected his 'dear creatures'. His lack of fear in confronting the police as he fought against all the injustice and oppression had earned him in the townships the nickname *Makhalipile* (Dauntless One). Whether motivated by respect or shame or fear or caution, even the most brutal cop backed off in his presence.

In 1953, the passing of the Bantu Education Act further intensified the obstacles non-white people had to bear, by rigidly restricting what black children could be taught at school. Reading lessons and arithmetic were to stop at roughly eight or nine-year-old level. What more was required, given that black children needed to be educated only to the level of servants or labourers? Certainly not the enriching mix of other conventional school subjects. It was an appalling time, but it also prompted the ingenious creation of 'secret' schools-without-books, which I was lucky enough to observe in action a few times, but whose whereabouts, to their credit, members of the press never revealed. It was in this context, after a great deal of thought and prayer, and with immense sadness, that Huddleston decided he would have to close St Peter's. Better that than handing it over to government control and thus abandoning his students to 'education for servitude'. The following year, shortly after the school was closed, he was recalled to England.

It was a bolt from the blue, a source of disbelief and distress to those who knew, or knew of, this strong, humane, much-loved priest, so unusual, such a beacon of sanity in the struggle. I remember trying to work it out at the time, as shocked as everyone else. Why should this man be called away when he and his work were so crucial, when we all so badly needed him, both for his practical help, and for his example, his advice and, yes, his inspiration? Didn't the Church exist, among other reasons, to develop good men[2] to be of service to their fellow human beings? Why then, when a shining example, a rare man like Huddleston, makes an appearance, and is so essential where he is, does the organisation tidy him away – even if they say it is for his own safety? Surely his removal was simply a gift to the enemies of humanity against whom he so honourably fought? I've often wondered how the story would have unfolded had he stayed.

In Huddleston's honour, the citizens of the townships organised a farewell concert. It was held at the Bantu Men's Social Centre, and was called *The Stars are Weeping*. Ian Bernhardt produced it, and Todd Matshikiza wrote a heart-breaking farewell lament – 'one of his most beautiful choral works', Hugh Masekela told me nearly sixty years later, the wonder still in his voice as he remembered it. I couldn't be there, though when I was told what had transpired that night, I smiled as if my heart would burst, idiotically happy at such an outpouring of love. It had been an unforgettable night – even to those who, like me, only heard about it. It seems to have been one of those rare and special times when an event seems somehow to have intersected with another dimension, when there is something extra in the air, a sense of time suspended. More than 200 people performed, and the programme became wonderfully disorganised in a truly black South African way, in which timetables become elastic, yielding spontaneously to the demands of the moment. Throughout the evening, as word spread, I was told, more and more artists arrived, including a sixty-voice choir; and then more and more, some having walked many miles, just turning up, wanting to play, or sing, or dance, to honour and pay tribute to Father Huddleston. It all ended, finally, sometime after 2.00 a.m.

And then the aftermath, the unexpected gift! According to Hugh Masekela, the concert netted the equivalent of more than 4,000 US dollars for the newly formed Union of Southern African Artists, and thus, as if by magic, it became possible to find premises for the union – and in central Johannesburg itself, not miles away in a township. A former textile factory, Dorkay House, was acquired – a run-down four-storey building for rent at the shabby end of Eloff Street (Johannesburg's posh main shopping street of grand cafés and department stores), where it petered out into factories, dilapidated repair garages, car cemeteries, scrub and waste land. It was about fifty yards up from the Bantu Men's Social Centre, in fact – where King Kong had learned to box.

Dorkay House quickly became a name to conjure with – a haven for musicians and performers. The union had its admin offices on the top floor, and the other floors were virtually a club and social centre, a place to hang out, with rehearsal and working space for the 600 members. The windows were cracked and stuffed with paper, but the place was jumping. Even the external iron fire escape at the rear served as practice space for groups of three or four musicians. They now had their very own territory, where they could meet, work, practise, learn from each other, form groups, rehearse or socialise – and it was also somewhere they could get to easily after work. From time to time, visiting European artists would come and perform there too, and sometimes give masterclasses. I remember, for instance, hearing Johnny Dankworth at Dorkay House. He had contracted to do several concerts in South Africa, but once he arrived and discovered that the concerts were for white audiences only, he refused to perform at all unless an equivalent number of concerts were organised for black audiences too.

★

Once there was a Union, musicians' original work and recorded performances could to some extent be protected. But try as I might, I find the intricacies of the subject impossible to master. I gather that a group of four musicians, such as the top-ranking Manhattan Brothers, who were to play leading roles in King Kong, might sometimes receive only £5.00 between them as a one-off fee – for records which sold in tens of thousands. I have been told, too, both that it was against the law in those days to pay royalties to black people, and also that the black producers employed by the record companies often took the credit and royalties for themselves, leaving the unsuspecting musicians with virtually nothing. Sometimes, too, musicians were asked to choose between a fee or a royalty, and unaware of the potential earnings, usually took the meagre cash in hand. A very tangled situation. My memory is that Ian Bernhardt and his colleagues at the union were from time to time able to get back *something*, at least, of what the artists should have earned. Solomon Linda, for example, who in 1939 wrote the melody and Zulu lyrics for what later became famous as 'Wimoweh', or 'The Lion Sleeps Tonight', hadn't seen any royalties when his song became a number-one hit in America. He didn't even know it had happened. The union fought for him, to the extent that it could, given that no contracts were ever signed. It also arranged royalty payments for musician and song-writer Mackay Davashe, later to be the conductor and band leader for *King Kong*.

It was at Dorkay House too, under the auspices of the union, that Ian initiated a programme to find, train and present African musical performers to white audiences, and where, in years to come, the boycott by British Equity of all segregated shows in South Africa was engineered.

Most of this had happened in the five years before Irene handed our script to Ian, which meant that by the time we were casting *King Kong*, we knew exactly where our band and the majority of our performers would come from. Dorkay House.

*

I had no say in the casting, of course. My job was done. But occasionally I'd sit in at auditions, and though still smarting over the events surrounding the script, found the hurt annealed by the sheer pleasure and excitement of listening to each new candidate. I was absorbed and enchanted. The sounds of their glorious voices, each one different from, yet in its individual way as beautiful as the last, uplifted my spirits. I remember in particular a soft-spoken 14-year-old schoolgirl who had turned up in her gymslip and timidly asked whether she could audition too. As she started to sing we held our breath. The room was electrified with the enormous sound that poured from her small frame, resonant with strength, passion and truth. The moment remains unforgettable. 'Do you remember the day Letta auditioned?', I've been asked more than once over the years, when reminiscing with friends about the show. Known affectionately from that moment on as 'little Letta', she was our youngest cast member. She fell in love with Caiphus, a Huddleston-schooled lad a few years older than her. He appears in the original programme's cast list as one of the 'people of the township' and an 'extra' – though in fact he was already a remarkable musician.

Fast forward just a few years: Letta Mbulu and Caiphas Semenya are launched on their international careers – married, living in self-imposed exile in Los Angeles, working with, among other American stars, Quincy Jones, Cannonball Adderley, Nina Simone and Harry Belafonte. On that day of Letta's audition, who could have dreamed . . .?

A handful of performers needed no audition. It was generally understood from the start that they would be cast in the main roles because of their experience, professionalism and star quality, and with the bonus that they could handle the English language with ease and confidence. Pre-eminent were the four Manhattan Brothers, Nathan Mdledle, Joe Mogotsi, Ronnie Sehume and Rufus Khoza, the most famous of all the South African black entertainers, and the extraordinary Miriam Makeba, whose untrammelled voice, endless and timeless, seemed to pour from her very depths. Her sound – joyful, fierce, sweet, dark, pure, all adjectives for great voices apply – was like no other I'd heard. The parts were doled out between them, just as we had visualised: Miriam as Joyce the *shebeen* queen, Nathan as King Kong, Joe as Lucky the gangster whose girlfriend is stolen by King Kong, and Rufus and Ronnie as members of Lucky's gang, the Prowlers, who were modelled in our story on a real-life gang of township thugs called the Spoilers.

The Manhattans had been in show business since their schooldays. Joe had first appeared on stage when he was six, in church performances organised by his bandleader father. When he was ten, he formed the Manhattan Brothers, together with Nathan and Rufus. Because they had no formal training, they learnt by listening to records and watching films, and were deeply influenced by black American jazz singers. Their role models were Paul Robeson, Ella Fitzgerald, Billie Holiday, Louis Armstrong, Sammy Davis Junior and Nat King Cole. Whenever they could find the money, or once a month at free outdoor 'bioscopes[3] for black people', they watched American films, picked up ideas from them, and adapted them to their own styles and rhythms.

One of their favourite films was my own great favourite too – the 1941 surrealistic *Hellzapoppin'*, starring Ole Olsen and Chic Johnson, which introduced them to jitterbugging and tap dancing. The four of them had no money to buy tap shoes, so to get the right sound for the tap, Joe told me, they held Coca-Cola tops between their toes and tap danced barefoot on the pavements.

'What?' I gasped in amazement and admiration. 'It must have hurt like hell!'

'Yes, it was excruciating, we couldn't do it too long at a time,' he said. 'But the sound just wasn't right when we tried to stick the bottle tops on the soles of our shoes. And we could manage to tap dance for just long enough at a time to be able to include it in our repertoire.'

They also earned extra money by busking on street corners in the centre of Johannesburg, constantly harassed by police threatening to arrest them, but bringing in enough cash in the end to buy proper tap shoes. 'We got them from a shop in town which reduced the price if we would give them a private show, and dance for them,' Joe remembered. They also busked in the townships. 'We would rush home from school to do our homework, so we could go out and sing on the streets by the time most people were coming home from work,' Joe explained. 'They would always stop and listen to us, and it gave us confidence.'

Busking brought them more than just attention. It brought bookings – even (virtually unthinkable in those days) from countries outside South Africa. Few people would have credited the possibility that four black school-boys (Joe, for instance, was just fourteen at this point) would be able to organise travelling that far, given the legal and practical restrictions on movement and opportunities. How they managed the paperwork, let alone the rest of it, I can't imagine. They travelled to Botswana, a country larger than France, moving about in borrowed lorries and horse-drawn carts. They went to Swaziland, Basutoland, even as far as what today is Zimbabwe, where they learned to their surprise that black people in that country were in some ways worse off than their brothers and sisters in South Africa. To most white eyes, the four members of the Manhattan Brothers may simply have seemed to be part of the great mass of the downtrodden, but wherever they played, at home or beyond South Africa's borders, they were greeted as celebrities. Indeed, outside South Africa, as word spread, they were received and royally entertained, sometimes literally so. In Swaziland, a rich farming country, King Sobhuza invited them to the royal palace. And in Botswana they were entertained by Seretse Khama, born into one of Botswana's royal families, and later to become Sir Seretse, that country's first president.

As a result of these trips, they earned enough to acquire their own public address system, and accumulated a bit of capital as well. And at the end of each of these tours, they had to rush back to Johannesburg in time to get to school on Monday mornings. They didn't always make it, which meant the cane.

The schoolboys soon established themselves as a group of national standing, and became – and remained – the biggest stars of their day. Their sound was initially modelled, I suppose, on the African–American pop vocal group the Ink Spots, but it was also very South African, and very much their own. They recorded scores of their own songs, as well as covers of others. Solomon Linda, for instance, had composed the song 'Mbube' in 1939, and recorded it *a cappella* with his group the Evening Birds. But it was the Manhattans' rearrangement of it nearly twenty years later, using harmonicas – 'an idea we got from Larry Adler', said Joe – that made it famous as 'Wimoweh', or 'The Lion Sleeps Tonight', first at home, and then in America.[4] With all their songs and recordings, the Brothers should probably have become millionaires. Gallo Africa produced their discs for many years, but according to Joe Mogotsi, it was in some ways a heartless association, typical of the times. Given that they were the golden boys of music, selling to a population of 13,000,000 non-white people, their records must have sold in tens, perhaps hundreds, of thousands. 'We'd walked into the lion's mouth,' Joe wrote many years later. 'We knew nothing of copyright or royalty entitlements.' Joe alleged that they handed over all the rights to their compositions and recordings – 'at the same time delighting in all the publicity we were getting'.

It took many years of negotiation, but in 1999 the past was finally wiped out. The Manhattan Brothers signed a new agreement with Gallo. They were also paid a mutually agreed sum of money. That same year, Gallo brought Joe and Rufus out from London, and at a grand reception launched a CD of the Manhattan brothers' greatest hits.

The four of them. Tall, handsome Nathan, with his honeyed bass-baritone voice and good looks, was the star. He was dignified, charming, and soft-spoken, with a small Clark Gable-style moustache. He negotiated many of the group's contracts and business matters. Rufus favoured a convincing American accent, swagger and style – a very useful alter ego, sometimes, when faced with the police: 'But officer, I am a tourist from the United States.'

Ronnie, a tailor by trade, looked after the group's wardrobe. He was a terrific dancer and the group's choreographer. All of them became my friends, and we met from time to time through the decades we all lived in London, but it was Joe, the extraordinary Joe, whom over the course of my life I came to love beyond words. He was an exceptional character, a man of unquestionable integrity and outstanding quality, kind and humorous and strong, utterly 'together', with a powerful bass voice and an extraordinary presence – and devoted, in his own words, 'to music and to the Brothers'. It was he who was the Brothers' enabler, holding their whole enterprise together, catching balls before they landed, noticing and dealing with whatever was necessary, from the biggest crisis to the smallest detail.

By 1946, with their many records all selling well, the effect of the Manhattans on black audiences in South Africa was rather like the effect of the Beatles on Britain fifteen years later. During a tour to the Orange Free State,[5] for instance, a vast mass of people crowded round them, all trying to touch them, girls screaming and fainting, and so many people stampeding to get into the already overbooked theatre that extra shows had to be arranged. At this time, the Brothers also started to raise funds for the African National Congress, and entertain the crowds at ANC rallies. *King Kong* composer Todd Matshikiza often played piano for them, and composed some of their songs.

Their career soared, success upon success. They were at the summit of what was a stupendously rich musical landscape, populated by many other exceptionally talented groups, but in a special spotlight of their own. Seven years later, in 1953, the government of what was then Southern Rhodesia invited them to perform at the Rhodes Centenary celebrations, a vast jamboree and international trade fair covering sixty acres, at which the Queen Mother, who came with Princess Margaret, was guest of honour. I was there too. As a young newspaper reporter, I had been sent to cover the events.

By that time I was fully aware of the Manhattan Brothers and their music, and later would often put one of their discs on the record player, and dance about to their sound with my baby son Dan in my arms. Indeed, I still have some of their 78rpm recordings. To buy them, I had been taken by Ian Bernhardt into unfamiliar streets far from my usual haunts, to a shop which sold African music. However, when I went to the Manhattan Brothers' concert at the Rhodesian celebrations, unaware of what the future would bring, I didn't meet or have reason to interview them. The *Rand Daily Mail*, the newspaper I worked for, though liberal by the day's standards, had not yet started publishing 'black' human interest stories or reviewing 'black' music It took Ezekiel Dhlamini to change all that.

*

Joe actually contributed a new word to the English language. It's in general use now, and included in the *Oxford English Dictionary*. I still revel in the story, which just slipped out in conversation one day. Joe was always smart and stylish, and tended to be the one who paid most attention to what the Brothers wore on stage. Quite early in their career, he told me, he bought cloth for trousers for the four of them, with a distinct style in mind.

106

'I asked my sister Lydia to make us very narrow trousers. I told her I wanted them to fit extremely tightly,' he said. 'And very soon those narrow trousers became our trademark' – more than a decade before the Teddy Boy fashion for stovepipe trousers in Britain, I might add – 'and then the township's leading gangsters, who always came to our shows, began to copy our style.' From there, it caught on with other gangsters and would-be gangsters, and soon tight, narrow trousers signalled that the wearer was probably a gangster. 'Lydia called the trousers "*tsotsis*" – "Here are your *tsotsis*," she said to me when she finished making them. *Tsotsi* just means "very narrow" – so that's what we also called them, and what other people began to call the gangsters who had taken the up the style and were wearing them too.'[6] The *Oxford English Dictionary*'s definition of *tsotsi* is accurate enough: 'a young black urban criminal. (origin, South Africa, 1940)'. But the derivation it offers – 'a Sotho corruption of *zoot suit*' – is wide of the mark.

*

Gangsters. They were part of township life, always to be reckoned with. Thieves, robbers, burglars, thugs, all violent, many of them killers. Wherever they went, they threw their weight around, and people had to learn to live with it. They preyed on the poor as well as the rich, on black people as well as white. But on the other hand, the underworld was for decades the only thing that blacks, to a certain extent, controlled. In Hugh Masekela's words,[7] 'It was heroic for a black person to be good at theft, drinking, burglary, bank robbery, bootlegging, selling drugs, and being in a gang whose speciality was robbing white people.

Diamond smugglers, numbers runners [for the Chinese lottery] and street muggers who targeted white folks were township heroes.'

But what made life particularly difficult for the Manhattan Brothers was that their concerts attracted the gangsters, who could on occasion dangerously interfere with performances. Nathan said he thought it was because 'they see a glamour and excitement about our lives and keep trying to muscle in on us'. On the whole, gangsters admired the musicians and to a great extent left them alone, but they also admired their women, which could make for terrifying moments. If a gangster wanted a woman, she could be dragged off and taken by force. Miriam Makeba was a frequent target. There had been more than one violent attempt to abduct her. On one occasion in the middle of a song, the Brothers, realising that this was happening backstage and out of sight, broke off their performance, and in the ensuing fracas, Nathan – who showed conspicuous courage – was stabbed.

The Brothers recognised that somehow they would have to learn how to stand up to these dangerous men while trying at the same time to keep performing. So they took up body-building under the tutelage of a professional boxer and trainer, and often actually sent a gangster packing with an explosion of blows from one or another of the four of them. On one occasion, at a big anniversary concert at the Bantu Men's Social Centre, a gang member called Boykie, who for weeks had been stalking Miriam from concert to concert, sent a henchman backstage to bring her to him. Word spread of trouble brewing, and the Brothers quickly decided to form a protective wall round

Miriam. But before they could do so, they saw that the gang leader was already pointing a .38 revolver at her and shoving her towards his car.

Nathan deliberately put himself between them.

'If you stay there,' said the gangster, 'I'm still going to shoot and the bullets can go through you to her.'

Then out of the blue another group of gangsters appeared, also carrying guns. One had a big, rusty sawn-off .45. They pushed Nathan aside and started taunting Miriam's attacker. 'You want to be a big guy, Boykie, and shoot? Come on . . . do it now!'[8]

A bloody fight ensued, knives flashing everywhere. The Brothers quickly surrounded Miriam, shouldered their way to the back entrance, pushed her into the car and made off as fast as they could.

Joe, who told me the story, said that was just about the worst shooting they'd ever seen, blood and gore spattered everywhere. But it was far from the only occasion.

During rehearsals, I used to worry about Nathan's safety. If I was driving past, I would occasionally catch sight of him, at night, shadow-boxing his way up Jeppe Street, immersed in the character of King Kong, and would hope, apprehensively, both that he would be safe from the police, and also that some *tsotsi* would not misread his behaviour and slug him. As it was, Nathan lost himself so much in the role of King Kong, the violent bruiser, that during one performance he flung Miriam across the stage as dictated by the script, but so furiously that she broke her foot.

At one point during rehearsals, the Spoilers, Alexandra township's most feared and vicious gangsters and killers, heard that part of the story we were telling onstage was modelled on them, and decided to stop us. They didn't like the prospect of their beans being spilled and the police finding out. So first they threatened Todd, telling him they would burn his house, burn his car, twist his neck, rape his wife. The police, Todd said bitterly, were no protection. Then one afternoon soon after that, they turned up at Ian Bernhardt's office. If he didn't remove all signs of their presence from the show, they told him – and out came the revolver and the knives – people would be cut or shot, starting with Ian himself.

Ian told me later how surprised he was that he managed to keep such a calm head. He was terrified, but held steady. Then an inspired idea 'just came' to him. 'Why don't you wait?' he suggested, seeming quite relaxed, but with his heart thudding and his head dizzy with fright. 'Come and see the show first. I'll give you complimentary seats for the first night. See what you think.' He paused for effect. Then: 'You actually come out of it very well.' They bought it. I imagine them snarling as they left: 'We want the *best* seats, *jou*,[9] understand?'

The story ended happily. The Spoilers approved of their prominent role and the way they were portrayed, realised their secrets were safe, and came night after night to see the show, demanding their free seats, wearing their *tsotsis*, and wandering in and out of performances as if they owned the theatre.

★

I felt a little shy turning up at rehearsals, but also loved every minute I was there, even though feeling superfluous and somewhat diffident among all the brilliant performers and musicians. It was a golden age of music in the townships, and being in the company of these gifted musicians was, I felt, a privilege and a wonder, like being invited to the best possible party, jam-packed with so much talent that you felt really lucky to be there too. The musicians were an exceptional generation who fed and fertilised each other; they were sophisticated, and they had listened to and learned from all the jazz records they could get their hands on. As Joe Mogotsi dryly remarked, white visitors from abroad often expressed surprise that South African blacks could perform an international musical repertoire while the Boers[10] seemed limited to what was called *tiekie-draai* (literally, turning on a threepenny bit), a very simple form of folk music.

*

At this point I am struggling to control my unwieldy story. I want to introduce the flavour, at least, of each musician, singer and dancer, to communicate their remarkable individuality, but there were just so many of them, the majority of whom I knew only to greet and smile at. So I will try to give an impression of some of those I knew best, hoping that the general atmosphere of vitality, spontaneous creativity and friendship among all concerned, will ride out with it.

For a start, there were the children, all already members of groups with wonderfully jaunty names. They would become members of the chorus, part of the township crowds, dancers when needed, and sometimes also solo players. Caiphus and Letta were among them. When they were called on stage during rehearsals it was reminiscent of a cumulative carol: 'Calling the five Jazz Whistlers, four Swanky Spots, the Saints, the Katzenjammer Kids, the Crazy Folks and the Queens Pa-a-age Boys!'

The adult groups had great names too. They all knew each other, and were sometimes related. Big bands like the Harlem Swingsters; the Merry Blackbirds, modelled on Glenn Miller and his orchestra; the influential and ground-breaking Jazz Maniacs; the superb Jazz Epistles, comprising Kippie Moeketsi, Hugh Masekela, Jonas Gwanga, and pianist and composer Dollar Brand,[11] and a proliferation of smaller groups as well.

And suddenly, having evoked these bands in my imagination, the musicians – all of them male in those days – come jostling back, a whole cavalcade of legends crowding out from the caverns of memory and into present time. Kippie Moeketsi, venerated as 'the father of South African jazz', self-taught genius on the clarinet and alto sax, with an extraordinary mind which at one point flew too high to hold his sanity; saxophonist Dudu Pukwana, small in build, dedicated to his music, seeming to me always impish and mischievous, whatever his private troubles; grave-faced, beautiful Mackay Davashe, composer and saxophonist, leader of the *King Kong* band, with his air of utter stillness and focus; Hugh's cousin Jonas Gwangwa, superb trombonist whose instrument also came from his schooldays with Father Huddleston, and who electrified the Sophiatown music scene until the government declared him a 'banned person', making it illegal for him to 'congregate' with more than one person at a time; and pianist Sol Klaaste, for whom I had immense affection – the first black South African to attend the University of the Witwatersrand in Johannesburg, and who became the Manhattan Brothers' permanent pianist after *King Kong* closed.

These were the people I knew best. But I see other faces too, listen to their greetings, smile at their broad smiles. Although some of us barely knew each other, our shared endeavour made us light up with pleasure whenever we met. And now here come the women, actresses, singers and dancers. I have plundered my memory (and also the various autobiographies and academic works about these artists) for the flavour and spirit of these women, all so vital, so physically beautiful and so generous, each one of them. Beautiful Abigail Kubeka, with her warm smoky voice, for instance, whom I adore to this day, as I do 'little Letta', whose voice Quincy Jones would later describe as 'projecting a sophistication and warmth which stirs hope for attaining pure love, beauty, and unity in the world'.

In fact, every single one of our singers and dancers had an unaffected, individual beauty and a blazing talent as joyful and natural as breathing. For instance, I couldn't take my eyes off Thandi Klaasen when she was onstage. In the years ahead she would become a star entertainer, both singer and dancer, and utterly magnetic. But in *King Kong*, what I remember most clearly is Thandi, carefully placed in the front row of the group dance in the *shebeen* scene, moving with the grace and danger of a panther. I still see her gyrations in my mind's eye as I type these words.

And then, of course, Miriam Makeba herself. Electric, astonishing, memorable Miriam. Born with a talent lodged

113

not only in her vocal cords but in her very being. Her exceptional voice was utterly free, I think, because it arose from the core of that being. Even in childhood her voice was recognised as exceptional.

When she and I were both in our mid-teens, King George VI and Queen Elizabeth, together with their young daughters, Princess Elizabeth and Princess Margaret, came to visit South Africa. A big public event was organised for Johannesburg schoolchildren. We all sat in the spectator stands of (I think) the Wanderer's Sports Grounds, in pouring rain, watching the royal family take tea and cake under a canopy erected for them in the centre of the arena. A child from each of the various white schools had been chosen to make up the team of waitresses serving them. And Miriam had been chosen by the teachers at her Methodist school to sing. Possibly her first public performance. Sitting with my friends, all wearing our ungainly school *djibbah*s (inspired by the dress of North African tribesmen), I saw and heard her, not dreaming our paths would ever, *could* ever, cross.

Seven or eight years before *King Kong*, Miriam had asked to be introduced to the Manhattan Brothers. They listened to her singing, and immediately fell in love with what Nathan called her 'plaintive' voice. From that moment on, without hesitation, they wanted Miriam as their female vocalist. But they had to talk her into it, Nathan told me, because to start with she flatly refused to join them. She was afraid! This strong, formidable woman, destined to become renowned internationally as the great Mama Africa, was, by nature, she herself admitted, often timid, soft-spoken and shy – unless she was actually singing, when she was taken over by the spirit of song. And when that happened, as she herself said on more than one occasion, '*Watch out!*'

However, according to Miriam[12] there was no hesitation – immediately the Manhattans asked her, she jumped at the chance, and toured with them until 1957. It was not only the chance to sing, and sing for a living, but a way out of a parade of sickeningly awful and underpaid jobs that were undermining her sense of herself.

She'd had as tough a start as any. As a young girl she had the usual round of 'black girl' jobs – nursemaid, domestic servant, that sort of thing. And she had, as well, the all-too-frequent experiences of exploitation, with white employers paying a pittance and then taking whatever further advantage they liked. One employer, for instance, paid Miriam as a nursemaid for the first month, then said she couldn't afford to pay for the second month (Miriam obligingly said she'd wait), and in the third month planted her husband's watch under the pillow in the outhouse where Miriam slept. Then she loudly denounced Miriam as a thief and called the police. Fortunately for Miriam, the police were already wise to this woman's tricks – she had done the same with several previous employees – getting three months' work out of them for one month's pay, then firing them and starting again.

Of course, with a black skin there was often no way of avoiding prison. I imagine only a lucky minority would not have seen the inside of a jail at some point in their lives. By the time Miriam left South Africa for the United States, which was shortly before the *King Kong* cast left for London, she had been in jail more times than she could remember. It had begun when she was an infant, too small to be taken from her mother, who spent six months in prison for brewing liquor.

In adulthood, Miriam would find herself in prison for stupid, random things. On one occasion, for instance, on her way to give a concert, an unclaimed gun found on the bus she was travelling in landed all the passengers in jail for a week, with no one knowing where they had disappeared to. It goes almost without saying that black entertainers were mistreated and deliberately humiliated. When Miriam was touring with the Manhattans, the five of them were frequently stopped, their story of being musicians returning from a gig ignored, and all of them thrown into prison. It was worse if it were a Friday, Miriam told me, because you had to wait until Monday before you could get to court and pay the fine. Your family, of course, would not know what had happened, or where you were.

But at the same time as she was working at a succession of demeaning jobs, Miriam was singing. Quiet and demure in ordinary daily life, when the songs poured out of her, so did her spirit, and she soared. She sang at home, in the school choir, with friends, and while still in her teens, with a cousin who formed an amateur group called the Cuban Boys. Her mother was a *sangoma*, a traditional herbalist and healer, who had a wide acquaintance with the unseen ancestral spirits – known, I learned from Miriam, as the *Amadlozi*.[13] A whole variety of these would possess her and speak and heal through her.

Apparently, if the *Amadlozi* inhabit an individual they will not leave them alone. They trouble and disrupt their hosts' lives until they finally acknowledge them, bow to the inevitable, and submit to the strenuous training to become a *sangoma*. Miriam's mother was sure Miriam had *Amadlozi* within her, and would wonder how it came to be that they so seldom troubled her. So did Miriam, until many years later she decided that she was serving them already, through song. In ordinary life she might be happy to be almost invisible much of the time, but put her in front of an audience, and when she opened her mouth the *Amadlozi* took over, threw her into a virtual trance and possessed her. She was wild and free, her voice almost unearthly. In her later years, singing all over the world, there were many times, she said, when she could not even remember her performance a moment after it was finished.

There were many female singers at the time with gorgeous voices, a number of whom, like Letta Mbulu, with her beautiful sound and thrilling sensitivity, had accomplished and very successful careers. But there was something about Miriam that set her apart, as if the elixir of life itself poured through her as she sang. Within a few weeks of arriving in America she had taken the country by storm, and as the years went by she became a huge international icon. Perhaps it was indeed the power of the *Amadlozi*. Certainly that's one valid way of talking about a power and energy well beyond words.

After six years singing and touring with the Manhattan Brothers, Gallo Africa suggested to Miriam that she should form her own group, so that they could record her as a solo artist. Nathan used to describe her as 'the African Skylark' when introducing her at concerts, and so she called her group the Skylarks. She also toured for eighteen months with a musical extravaganza, *African Jazz*

117

and Variety, and began giving solo concerts. In 1956, she recorded her signature song, '*Pata Pata*', which in 1967 became a major American hit.

During rehearsals, I watched Miriam with fascination. Whenever she was present it was impossible not to be aware of her. Young and slender, the flavour of the earth-mother she would become, the legendary singer with equally legendary generosity, was in fact already there. In spite of her shy demeanour, the vivid life that glowed in her eyes spoke of huge reserves of vivacity, strength and passion. She shone when she entered a room, no matter how demurely.

I heard a story of her generosity from the enchantingly pretty Abigail Kubeka. She had been cast as one of *shebeen*-queen Joyce's girls – that is to say, Miriam's girls – and in fact was one of Miriam's Skylarks, along with Letta Mbulu. We were chatting in a corner of the rehearsal room. Abby's parents, she told me, had refused to give their permission for her to be in *King Kong*. They wanted her to become a nurse, one of the professions which brought respect and was an upward step for black girls – the equivalent, I suppose, of the Jewish parents' dream of a 'my son the doctor'. As Abby was still in her teens, what her parents said went.

But Abby was desperate. All around her people she knew were being cast in *King Kong*, and she, with beauty, charm, a thick, richly textured singing voice and the offer of a part in the show, longed to be among them. She poured her heart out to Miriam. 'Let me talk to them,' said Miriam. 'Maybe I can help.' At first the parents wouldn't budge. But neither would Miriam. In the end, she suggested that Abby should come and live with her during rehearsals and the show's run: she would be like a mother to her, seeing she ate well and slept well and worked hard. Furthermore, Miriam told Abby's parents, she would be directly answerable to them. They were won over.

I heard also, here and there, rumours of Miriam's vile temper when aroused. Hugh Masekela described her anger as being as sharp and dangerous as an icepick. Over several years the two of them had been deeply drawn to each other, no matter that Hugh was seven years younger and, I think, no matter who else either or both of them happened to be seeing at the time. In any case, scandal never bothered Miriam. 'She was brazen and acerbic with anyone who tried to get in her business,' said Hugh.[14] 'This was probably why the press never wrote about her affairs. No journalist wanted to feel the wrath of Miriam Makeba.' She was a woman of huge appetites, it seems, open to fully experiencing the whole range of emotions. Was it the *Amadlozi* again?

One of the early songs that made Miriam famous was known as the 'click' song[15] – the clicks being sharp, explosive sounds, rather like corks pulled from bottles. The Xhosa language, her language, is full of them. I remember a time when Miriam was visiting me, and was talking about how easy it was to make the Xhosa clicks. I was doing my daft and incompetent best to copy her, pushing my tongue into the correct places, but even so finding it almost impossible to come up with anything close to the various sounds. 'It's *easy*, Pat,' she said. 'Honestly. Even a child can do it.' At that very moment my young son Dan, who had been lying quietly on the bed, started making all the clicks that Miriam had been demonstrating, one after another, absolutely naturally. We stared at him in amazement, then fell about with laughter. So many ideas, perceptions and capacities are literally child's play early on. As Einstein said: 'The pursuit of truth and beauty is a sphere of activity in which we are permitted to remain children all our lives.' And I think that one of the things that made *King Kong* so special was that the exuberant fun we were all having working together was indeed something like the innocent fun of children playing, even though we were in what was, in its way, a war zone.

Miriam and the Manhattan Brothers were easy casting for the five main parts in *King Kong* because Leon Gluckman, the stage director, knew they were experienced performers, comfortable onstage and able to handle the English language. But we were aiming for a large cast, which in the end turned out to be seventy, including the musicians. Stunningly talented people were surfacing in the auditions, but few had ever been near a stage or an audience, English was not usually their first language and their enunciation needed a lot of work. They were fascinating people, all of them, to watch and hear, with marvellous voices and bodies that danced as easily as they walked. They were, in fact, part of the staggeringly large pool of gifted township singers, dancers and musicians. Among them, some were 'nice-time girls' (as they were called), others domestic servants, clerks, teachers or messengers. They would arrive straight after work, and then give themselves to rehearsals, solidly, wholeheartedly, without a break (and until Clive and Irene were able to arrange refreshments, without food

120

either), and then struggle back over long distances, risking being picked up or harassed by the police and arriving home well after curfew.

I would drop in to rehearsals for an hour or two whenever I could manage it. They took place in a huge empty factory warehouse close to Dorkay House, but further towards the edge of town. It was a desolate area, with waste ground all around, but very soon a *shebeen* had established itself *somewhere*, and for a long time nobody, except its grateful customers, could find out where. Ian Bernhardt was baffled, and worried about police raids, but its whereabouts remained a mystery until the factory owner himself found an enormous pile of empty gin and brandy bottles in an unused, unvisited corner of the vast space. Ian had to take gentle, regretful action against the enterprising young man who ran the *shebeen*, fearing consequences which could have stopped the show. The police would have been only too pleased to find a reason.

Inside the warehouse, immediately known by one and all as 'the Dungeon', there was a lot of space for dance rehearsals, as well as room for rehearsals in small groups and a blocked-off area which served as a stage. Spread about at random were trestle tables, paper and clipboards, empty soft-drink bottles, scattered chairs. It was here, in this unadorned space, that, as I watched and listened, I began to get a growing sense of the spirit of our musicians and performers and the potential of the show.

Down in the Dungeon, as some of the cast rehearsed and others sat about waiting, I was taking steps into new friendships – with Joe Mogotsi in particular, and also with

Gwigwi Mrwebi, who played alto sax and clarinet in the band and had a speaking part in the township scenes. He was a considerable musician, creator of an influential group, the Harlem Swingsters, along with Todd Matshikiza. Books by historians and scholars confirm the important part Gwigwi played in the history of South African jazz – Lindelwa Dalamba acknowledges him in her dissertation on South African Jazz in England during the apartheid years as 'a crucial protagonist in South Africa's jazz creation myth'. He was also a founding member, along with Ian Bernhardt and others, of the Union of Southern African Artists, but that lasted only until it was forbidden by law to continue being 'inter-racial'.

Gwi had been a soldier 'up north' during World War II, a sergeant in charge of the unit which entertained Allied troops all over North Africa. He also turned his hand (and feet) to whatever was required: singing, tap dancing, filling in backstage, onstage, in the orchestra pit. To me, he seemed a true eccentric, by turns lugubrious, comical, thoughtful, wry, philosophical and satirical. I found something deeply tragic about him as well. After the war he'd had many jobs – among others, a shop assistant, Sophiatown Boys' Club secretary and assistant circulation manager of *Drum*, the massively popular magazine that focused on black urban culture. He fitted the Harlem Swingsters around whatever else he was doing, and wrote songs too, including one huge hit, 'Fish and Chips', which, try as I might, I can find no trace of now.

At parties, he was known for a number of routines, including one in which he energetically demonstrated how King Kong fought, with characteristically vigorous balletic antics in the ring. In another, he demonstrated how African soldiers were drilled up north, with much emphasis on the guns they were allowed to carry – that is to say, *wooden* guns.

He was also a deeply serious man. I found I could speak to him easily, and the two of us would talk intensely in a corner in the rehearsal breaks, sipping our soft drinks as we did so. He talked of his ambition, his wish – like most of the others – to get out of the country, go to America maybe. And we'd talk about friendship. I found it good to have a friend like him, with so little common background but an instinctive rapport. He also told me of a different kind of friendship, created through the unbreakable bonds of tribal initiation.

'Jesus, Pat,' he said. 'Once you've been through that you are joined to your brother-initiates for life. We can call on each other, we belong to each other, in a way we *are* each other. It's the deepest bond you can imagine. *Deeper* than you can imagine.'

'Tell me, Gwi. I'd be really very interested to know. What happens? What was asked of you?'

His face became impassive, a blank wall. 'I can't tell you anything, Pat.'

'Really? Truly?' Wheedling tones.

'No. Not possible.'

Again the gulf. I felt it occasionally with Todd too. Each of us retreating into our familiar cultural privacy when the abyss of difference and cultural experience seemed too deep to bridge.

But I could tell from what rode out in Gwi's voice, his body and his whole demeanour just how profound the experience had been. I thought wistfully what an essential human experience my own Jewish people had lost. When a boy says at the end of his bar mitzvah, 'Today I am a man,' it is an almost empty statement, nothing like the deep-rooted experience of an initiation, the unsayable flavour of which I'd had a whiff of, riding out on Gwigwi's words. I began to glimpse the meaning of initiation, or so it seemed to me. The traditional experience is dangerous and demanding, I sensed, I hope correctly, because that is the point of it – to handle the experience and survive requires all the candidate's inner resources to be hauled out, including some he didn't even know he had. After it's over, the candidates can truthfully say: 'Today I am a man.' It is like first steps taken into a new life, I thought as I mused on it – a life to be lived with changed strength and consciousness, not so much an end in itself, but a *beginning*. I vaguely wondered whether the *King Kong* experience we were all sharing was in its own less gruelling way also an initiation of sorts. So much demanded of us that we had never done or thought of before. Whatever its effect on us individually, the experience, I thought, might just hold us together after it was all over.

On a Sunday afternoon in mid-January, three weeks before opening night, we came together for the first complete run-through of the show. Up till this point the set pieces had been rehearsed in separate blocks, and in different parts of the Dungeon, with no regard for sequence. Now they were to be joined together into the complete story. It was summer, hot outside, and here we were, some of us sitting on boxes and others on the cold cement floor.

Todd and Esmé, Clive and Irene, Arthur, photographer Ian Berry, who had been taking pictures of the rehearsals for *Drum* magazine, the prop men, those making the costumes – black, white, young, old, among all of us in the warehouse that day, as we waited, excitement and tension were building. We were one organism, one whole. What would it be like? No one knew what to expect, and we hardly dared hope it would be OK. The bare cement of the 'stage' was outlined in chalk and set only with two small side rostrums and one large one across the back, from which a ramp led down. On the far wall leaned the sets which were being painted by Arthur Goldreich and a team of helpers. In a partitioned area other members of the cast were trying on costumes so they could be fitted there and then, and at the same time were watching through the windows to see that they did not miss their cue.[16]

In such unpromising surroundings the band began playing the overture and the township came to life, washerwomen, children, preachers, penny-whistlers, hawkers, the bus queue . . . The shabby rehearsal room receded, we were taken by surprise, utterly absorbed into this other time and place, this waking township. We had almost begun to accept as a given the talent of our musicians, singers and dancers, but seeing the whole put together for the very first time that afternoon, their capacity as individuals and as a group was a revelation. It was one of the most astonishing and emotional afternoons that I and the others had ever experienced, as we told each other again and again. As the final note of the last lone penny whistle faded on the still township night, we sat there stunned. I was acutely aware that the script and ideas were not all mine, not at all, but some of it was, and some other parts were based on my work, and in the end it was the work of all of us, and boy, forget the flaws, it was *something*, something we didn't even know was possible. Our Phenomenon was beginning to manifest. It was like an unexpected dream. After the stunned silence came our excited applause and loud calls of praise to one and all. Though we didn't know it yet, this was a pre-echo of what the response would be on the opening night.

And then, workmanlike and full of purpose, Leon called for the rehearsal to continue.

★

Since those days, experience has shown me that sometimes life or any stretch of time really, can play out as if it were a dream – as if waking life itself is answering some deeply needed, unexpressed, sometimes even unrecognised question, attempting through events themselves to manifest the answer into consciousness. The day of that first run-through rehearsal was the first time I saw that a waking event could be read in this way, as a dream presenting itself for attention and divination.

The rehearsal had been a high point of amazement, joy and happiness for all of us, as we saw what had been brought about – the result of talent, skill, sincerity, cooperation and the setting aside of both prejudice and a preoccupation with self. That on its own was enough to make the day memorable, and was at the heart of this strange waking dream.

But the rehearsal was framed by two other events which stretched from the day before the rehearsal to the hours immediately after. As dreams often do, cut to a scene which had taken place the previous afternoon. I had been at work at the *Rand Daily Mail*. A large extended family group of black Africans, men, women, and children, from a region possibly hundreds of miles away, had walked to Johannesburg, and in desperation had come to the newspaper office and asked for me. They had been given my name as someone who could possibly help them, a last resort if all else failed. I imagine my name was known in that way, as someone on an influential newspaper who would certainly be friendly, and with luck might just, sometimes, be marginally useful.

I don't remember all the details, but the broad strokes stand out. The Group Areas Act, which had been first promulgated in 1950, meant, in effect, that a bureaucrat could pick up a pencil and draw a line on a map and in a split second transform a former black area into an exclusively white one. This had happened to the people standing in front of me. They had been summarily turned off their land at a pencil stroke, and now were homeless, placeless and helpless. They had sought advice from one agency after another, and had then been advised to come to Johannesburg, to the offices of the Department of Native Affairs, to see what could be done for them there. They had carefully drawn up an awkwardly handwritten document describing their predicament in great detail, ending with a desperate written question to officialdom: 'Can you help us? Please can you tell us where we can go?' They had handed the document in, and then waited, I don't know whether for days or weeks, sitting patiently each day at the department. Finally they were called in. An official handed their document back to the leader. 'Here!'

he said. The written answer was staggering – and was the reason they had come to me in desperation. I could hardly believe it. Scrawled in careless handwriting at the bottom of the page in red ink, in answer to their question, was the official's response: 'You can go to hell for all I care.'

Then the waking dream cuts past the *King Kong* run-through, and the amazement and delight we all felt there, to my cardiologist husband, usually so detached and impassive, returning from the hospital in an utterly incendiary state. He could hardly speak for rage. A colleague, a consultant gynaecologist, had been operating on black patients and told him, in casual conversation over coffee: 'Whenever I get one of their women on the table, no matter what else I do medically, I always tie the bastards' tubes so they won't breed.' Joe reported him, just as I reported to my newspaper the tale of the group told to 'go to hell'. Both of us suspected at the time that it would make no difference, and both of us were right.

Thus the sequences of my waking dream, the answer to my unspoken question, laid out in front of me to read and understand. The central experience, the dress rehearsal, showed me that a great deal was possible when ordinary human beings were working together, tolerant of others, doing their best. And then wrapping around all that, the ugliness – depravity almost – of self-serving human behaviour. I began to see that people doing their almost-best could emerge from the very same soil as humans at their almost-worst. It was a pattern of understanding I took with me into the future.

★

I'm presenting just about everything that I can personally remember in this memoir — my luminous memories of events, scenes, visual moments, brief exchanges, instants and instances. But something else needs to be communicated – the pervading *atmosphere* of the time, in which our work was contained and from which it emerged. It was the sounds hanging in the air, the flavour of what was happening in the rough-and-tumble of friendship and jostle and vivid life and inevitable violence of the townships – and above all, it was the music, so much music, together with the harmonies of spontaneous song. It was like an elixir. When I saw Hugh Masekela many years later, his words crystallised it:

> There was music *everywhere*. Sophiatown was the most cosmopolitan of the townships. It also had electricity. There were musicians of every kind, and migrant labourers from all the neighbouring countries had brought with them their own instruments and music too. All weekend, from Friday evening till Sunday evening, the place was alive with unsponsored and unplanned carnivals – you heard drums everywhere, and church bells, and big bands, and children singing. There was no TV then. At Odin's cinema every Monday night there were variety shows, and sometimes jazz concerts. Everyone had a gramophone. We heard and played all kinds of music – jazz, and also the other music coming from America. If there was a wedding coming up, for instance, there would be six weeks of rehearsals, where we played Victor Sylvester–style waltzes. We didn't think in categories.

We loved it all, the Andrew Sisters, the Mills brothers, Louis Armstrong, Glenn Miller, all of them. We knew and sang their songs. You know, I've been all over the world, but with perhaps the exception of Cuba, I have never been anywhere where there was music *all* the time.[17]

Here and there, a thread of that music spilled over into my white world. I would sometimes decide to walk from the apartment where we lived to the Johannesburg General Hospital, a few blocks away, in order to stand outside the building where the laundry and kitchens were, and listen to the people working there, their voices raised together in song. The rich sounds provided a nourishment both to them, I'm sure, and to me eavesdropping outside, dimensions beyond the food being prepared and the laundry being done.

Then, too, there were the men walking down the pavements of the quiet white suburbs intently making music on the *mbira*, a wooden board on which staggered metal keys were fastened, as if it were a hand piano. And above all, the hoarse sound of the penny whistle, played on city street corners by little boys, on their own or in small groups. A few of these children had won themselves fame and fans of their own – in particular, Spokes Mashiyane and Lemmy 'Special' Mabaso, who had made popular recordings of their music, both on their own and with Miriam and the Manhattan Brothers. Unfortunately Spokes, at fourteen or fifteen, was now a bit too big to be a 'boy' in our cast, so Lemmy, slight and wiry and twelve years old, became *King Kong*'s lead penny-whistler.

During rehearsals, lateness and absences were facts of life. There could be no blame or reprimand. The lives of our cast were fraught with obstacles: transport, illness, sudden responsibilities at home after a long day's work, and endless brushes with the police. Rehearsals in the Dungeon would sometimes have to be held up while a missing person was tracked down and bailed from jail, having been picked up by police without his pass. One night, I remember, it was Joe Mogotsi, together with Norman Martin, one of the drummers. They had been working late on a couple of scenes, and decided to stop in on some girls they knew in Johannesburg before they went home to the township. They were caught by the police on the city streets at about midnight without their passes, instantly arrested, and next morning were transported thirty miles away to join a labouring gang on a farm near the gold-mining town of Randfontein.

When they didn't show up the following night Irene sat phoning prisons, using her powerful charm and energy and knowledge of the law to get them released immediately. In the end she and Clive arranged special 'King Kong passes', but even these didn't always work. The police were often as much a hazard for our theatre cast as the gangsters. The only difference between the two was that the police had the law on their side.

Years later, in London, Molefe Pheto, a member of the cast, told me how on his way home after rehearsals he had been stopped over and over again, in spite of the special pass. It may have legally protected him from arrest, but not from being harassed and deliberately delayed. The cops could always find some way to impose their power. More than once, he said, he had to endure long, threatening rants about how, if he knew what was good for him, *and he'd better,* he would have no more to do with this *King Kong* thing, or with any of the whites he was working with. We were '*kafferboeties*'[18] and 'Communist Liberalists', the lot of us, and it would only be a matter of time before he would be in deep trouble. They would, they warned Molefe, be watching.

Even the merest trivialities were fair game for police on the prowl. On one occasion the trigger was nothing more than a box of chocolates. It was a big box, sent to me by a PR man to thank me for the good review I'd given the film he was promoting. (I'd praised it not because of his efforts, but because I liked the film.) If the box was anything to go by, the chocolates looked as if they would be delicious, and I decided I wanted Todd's wife Esmé to have them. So at rehearsals that night I gave them to Todd, initiating a sequence of events I had no knowledge of for about two years.

At nearly one in the morning, Todd was waiting for the bus specially chartered to take everybody home from rehearsals. It was due in fifteen minutes, and the rest of the cast were still inside the Dungeon singing. He was waiting alone on the corner of the badly lit street, so as to be first in the bus when it arrived. He described in his book *Chocolates for My Wife*[19] how he saw headlights approaching in the distance, which turned out to be not the bus but a police pick-up van.

He was well aware that if he tried to get back into the Dungeon, the police, seeing him carrying a large box, would think he was running away. Better to stay where he was, he thought. The police van stopped, and Todd heard the voice of the African nightwatchman, speaking to him in the threatening tones such watchmen put on when they were about to beat someone up – beating them even harder when they saw the white police coming. Such preliminary beating up made it easier for the cops to arrest someone without too much struggle – an interesting insight into police tactics.

'Please Mkhulu don't hit me, God of my father.'

'What is it then? You standing outside while the others are singing inside. Explain.'

Todd wrote that he was wondering how to explain that he was on the brink of a nervous collapse, having been listening to his music and watching it go 'from black to white and now purple' – a reference, I have always imagined, to his raw pain and emotional unhappiness on hearing his music taken over, distorted and watered down to 'white man's "swing"'.

Then six armed, uniformed police poured out of the van and towards Todd. One demanded: 'Declare your damned self, Jong.' But Todd just stood there in his shapeless, crumpled, discoloured overcoat, thoughts of all the many things they could get him for racing through his head. Silence being the least incriminating option, he took one hand off the large chocolate box and fished out the small blue card saying 'Bearer is a member of the *King Kong* cast. Members of the South African Police are kindly asked to allow him to go home after rehearsals, which usually stop about one a.m. Thank you.'

Todd evoked vividly what happened next, in all its awfulness:

'Oh Ghod, this one of the King Kong kaffirs. Okay an' what's that you got in the parcel, Jong?'

'It's choc'lats, baas, choc'lats for my wife. I jus' got them now from a friend'

'Oho, Jesus, Piet, listen to this one. Of all my night shifts I never met a baboon like this one.' They gathered around me.

'Please, baas, don' break the box.'

'Ha, ha, ha . . . Caw . . . Caw . . . Caw . . ., ha, ha, ha,' until they split their sides with laughter.

'The monkey got choc'lats for his wife . . .'

'The maid is now called wife, caw, caw, caw, an' choc'lat's for her!'[20]

It is this incident which clinches it. As they lie in bed that night, I learned from Todd's book, he and Esmé make a decision. It is enough. They must take their children and leave South Africa – somehow, for somewhere. 'Anywhere else is better than here,' they say.

From my position today, all these years later, I can look down from on high (as I imagine the *djinns* of Arabian Nights tales do) and see the whole story spread out beneath me. Todd and Esmé, down below, cannot dream of what is coming, so clear from up here – that the Matshikiza family *will* leave South Africa, and be flown 6,000 miles away, riding on the phenomenal energy of *King Kong*. And Todd, at present subject to the insults and brutalities of idiots, will be meeting British royalty and having his photograph all over the British press, including in the society magazine *Tatler*. In themselves, such surface events mean very little, of course. But they are the outward expression of an optimistic new start in a country which is a stranger to oppression and legalised racial discrimination. But not, it later transpires, to indifference.

Looking back now over the weeks of rehearsal, I realise how intensely difficult it must often have been for cast and musicians even to get to the Dungeon each night – difficulties I was barely aware of and couldn't begin to imagine. I didn't even know what befell Todd with those chocolates until I read his book. He was too much of a gentleman to tell me. But members of our cast were carrying the heavy baggage of risk and humiliation and hardship on top of their daily work and time-consuming nightly rehearsals – one a.m. night after night, and then a dawn start to catch the crowded township bus to work in Johannesburg next day. Somehow – *but how?* I ask myself, looking back – everyone swam or struggled through it, and managed to enjoy themselves most of the time as well. I had my own personal difficulties too, wounded by the way the script had been hijacked, unhappy in my marriage and secretly planning to leave it.

Yet as far as *King Kong* was concerned, our eyes were on our goal, not on the obstructions. Difficulties, as they arose, were no more than stumbling blocks in our ground-breaking and utterly absorbing obstacle race. We just needed to get past those obstacles with as little fuss as possible, limiting the drama to the script and the stage. Everybody consciously held the lid firmly on their personal differences and difficulties and kept going forward, step by step, tolerating or solving their personal logistics and the practical problems of the show as efficiently as they could.

And we made mistakes. Of course we did. We were young, none of us were very experienced, and few of us were professional. One of those mistakes, as Irene pointed out later when we were talking about the script difficulties, was that when the creative team handed my finished book and lyrics over to Ian, the process passed out of our hands and we lost control of the content. But of course it had never occurred to us that any such control would be necessary.

4

As opening night approached, Irene was doing her best to get a contract written and signed. 'Oh we don't need one!' Todd and I said in surprise. 'We'll just divide the proceeds and give most of it away.' Neither of us had given a thought to legal agreements and assumed – in the teeth of the evidence of Harry's behaviour – that we'd good-naturedly just share out anything that came in. In other words, Todd and I were impractical and naive, as musicians and creative dreamers tend to be, particularly when young.

Irene explained that we had to know ahead of time how we were going to divide any profits. She'd worked out what she thought was fair, and asked if we would sign it. No problem there. And we had already agreed in principle, early on, that we wanted a large proportion of the profits to go to the African Medical Students' Trust Fund. The fund had been born in Johannesburg ten years earlier, when a mass meeting of university students decided to impose a voluntary levy of ten shillings per student per year after the government withdrew bursaries to black students. A similar decision quickly followed from Cape Town University and then from academic circles round the world. By the time *King Kong* opened, enough money had already been collected to train twenty doctors.

But our plan depended, of course, on whether we made any money at all.

Todd, Arthur and I were happy with the contract Irene had suggested, but it was necessary for Harry to agree too – and he was still in Cape Town. Even so, it should have been simple enough to sort the contract out with an exchange of letters and documents. But Harry was not responding, and as time passed, Irene was getting more and more worried. Without him, she couldn't finalise the contract. Then, less than a week before the show was due to open, he came up to Johannesburg, ready to meet Irene. He had not been present at that memorable first full-length run-through, but by this time there was a real buzz building up around the show. Our press officer, Margot Bryant, had been doing her work brilliantly. Rumours of what had happened at that rehearsal had built up interest and expectation. And here, thank goodness, was Harry, who was probably aware of all the interest, ready at last to sign.

But it became clear very quickly that he was prepared to do so only on his own terms. There was no give in him. Irene recalls that he demanded a larger share of the royalties and profits than she thought was fair. It was out of proportion to his contribution, she told me later, not at all in the spirit of what we'd been doing. But he was intransigent. Take it or leave it was his attitude.

At that point, I think, Irene was probably unaware that Harry had been working on the script in Cape Town with Leon. She was under the impression that he and I had sorted out his few objections the evening after the three of us had met, and oddly enough, Harry didn't tell her about his subsequent work. So Irene genuinely believed that he had contributed very little indeed to the show – especially as he had not been present at any of our creative sessions.

'I remember that day so well,' Irene told me when we met recently in Johannesburg. 'Even though I had a law degree, I was young and inexperienced, and found it incredibly difficult to know what to do for the best. My particular aim was to ensure that Todd would get something out of what might be earned, because he needed it more than the rest of us. But what transpired with Harry to a great extent blew that possibility away. When we finally got together to talk about the contract, opening night was four days away. And there was Harry, just like Captain Queeg, that ghastly captain in the film of the Caine Mutiny, jingling the money in his pocket, refusing to budge, blanking me 'broken record' style, stubbornly standing his ground, repeating what he wanted, no matter what I said. He was adamant. He knew he had us over a barrel. In the end I decided that the rest of us were more interested in the show's success than in the money and prestige, and that all I could really do was accept the inevitable. The deadline left no more time for negotiation.'

His terms were met. The profits were shared out, in what proportions I no longer know, between Harry, Todd, myself, the African Medical Students' Fund, and Arthur. Arthur had contributed so much to the visualisation of the show that it was decided he should have a share of the royalties, and to protect Todd's income, that share came out of my royalties for the lyrics.

And even though Todd's and my personal royalties amounted only to a small part of the show's total income, they still added up to considerably more than the £60 we had fantasised about that day in the café in Fordsburg.

★

The final weeks before the show was due to open, everything was coming to a head at once – the last rehearsals, Harry's repossession of the script, and my plan to leave my marriage. It was a bleak time. I could feel only coldness from Joe: there was no connection between us. At one point, when he had been particularly unresponsive about something I had said (whatever it was has fled), I freaked out and started beating at him with my fists in frustration, almost experimentally really, beating at him without cease, not hard, I wasn't that strong, but just trying to get *some* response out of him. He stood impassive, a statue, unmoved, staring straight ahead until I wore my emotion out and stopped. Then he moved on quite casually to his desk, behaving as if that weird little scene was nothing but an irrelevant interruption. Once again, I felt I was being treated as if I wasn't real; once again I experienced something of the buried terror of that abandoned three-day-old baby on the verandah. At that moment I had a sudden, clear vision that living without any love or responsiveness from my husband would drive me to a breakdown, or even suicide – two things most children including, I feared, my son, would find hard to forgive a parent. That vision of suicide made my escape from my marriage imperative. I knew that for my own survival I would somehow have to get Joe to see that we needed to part.

There had been heavy pressure on me to marry – marry

almost anyone! – from my parents, who, by the time I was twenty, considered me already 'on the shelf'. So when Joe and I first met, at a dinner party, I had been immensely relieved and interested to find someone very different from the ordinary run of rather boring young men my parents favoured – someone who had been out in the wider world and thought in ways beyond the confines of South Africa. In World War II, newly qualified as a doctor, Joe had learned Japanese and then been sent first to Burma and then to the Far East, to interrogate Japanese prisoners. His stories of that time fascinated me. 'Was it hard doing those interrogations?' I remember asking. 'How did you go about it?' But the job, he said without a trace of irony, was unexpectedly easy. Most of the Japanese tried to commit *hari-kiri* when facing the prospect of being captured. Which meant that those who actually fell into the hands of the Allies felt utterly dishonoured and tended to pour out everything they knew without restraint, almost without being asked.

But Joe's interests, and his experiences outside South Africa which so fascinated me, were not enough to sustain a marriage in which, it turned out, there would never be any closeness. He was eighteen years older than me, and life with him was like living with a remote, elderly uncle. In those days, premarital sex was not the norm, not officially, anyway, and I really believed, in my innocence, that everything would come right on the wedding night. But sadly, I soon found I was living in an empty land. Years later David, my second husband, said to me that even though many first marriages don't work, perhaps they happen because there are children waiting to be born. I liked that

141

idea, and decided that was certainly true in the case of Joe, me and our treasured son, Dan.

Early on, when I asked Joe why he had wanted to marry me, he said I was the first woman who had never bored him. I was too smitten and inexperienced at that stage for warning bells to have sounded. But as time went by, I was becoming unbearably lonely. I was also growing and changing.

'Joe, we must talk to a lawyer and sort out some kind of separation. You know this can't go on,' was the preface to what would turn out to be several hours of confrontation I'd reluctantly gear myself up to have with him from time to time over the years. The next day, after these marathons, I would be emotionally exhausted, while Joe's behaviour would be unchanged, as though nothing had been said or even happened. Later I understood that this was not deliberate or in any way his fault. His intelligence was wide ranging, but he was to a great extent detached from emotion and empathy. Indeed, I think that it was because of this very detachment that, as a physician, he was known for a number of what those concerned described as 'miracle cures', after all other doctors had given up.

Knowing that nothing would happen, that we'd go round in circles unless I took action, in about March of 1959 I asked a lawyer I knew if she would come to our house and try and talk to us about a divorce. But the conversation went nowhere. She tried to discuss how we would separate our assets, saying to my astonishment that I 'deserved' some financial compensation, having given Joe the best and most marriageable years of my life. 'It won't be easy for her to find another husband,' she said. (*What?* I thought. *This is weird!*) But Joe was not open to negotiation. He was emphatic. 'If Pat leaves, I see no reason why I should give her anything.'

The night after the lawyer left, I said in desperation, 'Look Joe, if we can't do this in a civilised way, then' – wildly plucking a date out of the air many months ahead – 'come February 2nd next year I won't be here. You'll find a note pinned to your pillow, and I'll be gone.'

'Oh no you won't,' he said. 'You like your comforts too much.'

'Yes I do like my comforts. But they are not top of the list. There are things I value far more.'

Word for word, that conversation is burned into my memory.

I had made my plans and, convinced that when I did leave my marriage I would need to leave South Africa too, I applied for a passport in plenty of time. As the weeks went by and I heard nothing, I thought there must just be some petty bureaucratic delay. I wasn't bothered about politics being a problem because I didn't have any, nor did I belong to any political group. I loathed the contortions of theory and dogma in which I saw my communist friends caught up. Couldn't they see they had put themselves in a straitjacket? Yet at the same time I admired and respected these committed people, and was in awe of their courage. Many white people active in the struggle, Arthur Goldreich among them, lived comfortably, high on the hog, but at the same time did not rest on their privilege. They took huge risks, and some of them spent time, even many years, in prison. Yet others gave their lives, or rather, their lives were taken, by agents of BOSS – the self-congratulatory acronym of the Bureau of State Security. Of these, Ruth First was the one I knew best, and therefore the one I personally mourned most.

Part of me wished I could be more like Ruth. Whenever we met, I felt guilty that I was not as committed and focused as she, wholeheartedly and actively fighting against the repressive regime. But I knew the best I could manage was simply to try and live as if I were free. I made a vow to myself to strive to do so whenever I could. I don't remember ever consciously breaking that vow, though I must have fooled myself on scores of occasions.

I would not seek to break laws for the sake of breaking them, my decision went, but if a law was in the way of my freedom, then I would do my best to behave as if it wasn't there. I would see the people I wanted to see no matter their colour, visit them, when necessary, if they lived in the townships (out of bounds to whites), hide a document or a person if asked (as I did in the former case but was never required to do in the latter) and would try to stay invisible.

In many ways my husband Joe seemed very conventional, but he had no time for racism either. Two of his good friends were classified as non-whites, so the law was willy-nilly broken whenever we met them. One of these was Yusuf Dadoo, leader of the Indian National Congress, whom I mentioned earlier. The other was Mr Yensen – I never knew his first name – a wealthy Chinese merchant who was also a member of Chinese leader Chiang Kai-shek's government-in-exile. It was at Mr Yensen's house, with his family, at a huge square mahogany table groaning with dishes, that I first tasted authentic Chinese food, a whole world away from what was on offer in the Chinese restaurants. We visited him and his family regularly. I suspect that Joe may have had business dealings with him, as well as being his doctor. This was before the time, some years later, when Chinese people were reclassified from being 'non-white' (that is to say, lumped within the parcel of 'Indians, coloureds and blacks, etc.') and became, as the Japanese had a little earlier, no longer 'yellow' but 'honorary whites'. The chance to make money had a truly magical effect on the apartheid government's perception of skin colour. How easy it is to change, I saw, when the people you have been opposing or oppressing suddenly have something you want or need. Some years after that, Iranians were given 'honorary white' status too. But not Afghans. There was no visible profit to be gained from Afghans.

But Joe, though without racial prejudice, was also for a quiet life. When, for instance, within the space of a fortnight, three political groups representing left, centre and racist right points of view came canvassing for money for their cause, he donated the same sum to each.

I wasn't too bothered about my passport at first. I just assumed there was some sort of bureaucratic bottleneck. Our crime reporter had 'cordial relations' with the police (something of a euphemism, given that he would sometimes ride in the back of a police van during night raids on the townships, ostensibly 'getting the story', but with a rifle in his hand and taking potshots, for 'fun' I assume, at scurrying township 'miscreants'). He offered to find out what was happening to my passport. And I was flabbergasted when he came back with the message that I would need a police interview.

Thus it was that I ended up face to face with the notorious and implacable inquisitor, the Chief of Police, Colonel Theunis Jacobus Swanepoel of whom many terrible and terrifying stories circulated, accounts of behaviour which became ever more brutal and inhuman as the years went by.

I can't now remember much about the interview with him, except thinking how stupid his first question was. 'Are you a communist?' *Well, nobody would admit that*, I thought, as I answered truthfully that I was not. But it was a shock to see that he had in front of him a very thick police file – and it was mine. I couldn't believe I'd warrant any sort of file at all. Yet there it was – but surely in the most harmless category of all, I presumed, sympathetic to the struggle, unpolitical, not directly an activist though she spends time with them, probably could be manipulated. I had no inkling that my living invisibly had been noticed at all – but nearly every trivial incident of friendship, fun and occasional helpfulness must have been observed and recorded. I was asked about some incidents, and people I knew, but thankfully couldn't and didn't give Swanepoel anything he wanted. The tension drained away. In the end both of us seemed quite bored. I think I would have made a really good spy.

Soon after, again with some nudging and more enthusiastic vouching by our crime reporter, my passport came through.

As rehearsals proceeded and opening night grew closer, there were some worrying injuries and accidents. Rufus was on crutches for nearly a month after a dramatic fall while practising the gangsters' fast and furious Knife Dance. He had suddenly stopped, spun around, clutched himself, and dropped to the floor, flat on his back. At first it was thought he had been accidentally knifed and killed, but in fact he had fainted from the pain of a very badly sprained ankle. One of the children had an injured foot, but was allowed to go on stage with his bandage, which later a reviewer picked up as a nice touch. One of the chorus sustained multiple bruises after a car crash. Most nerve-racking of all from the point of view of the production was the fact that at the final dress rehearsal there was a crack on the stage floor which everyone except for Miriam stepped either on or over. But she was wearing very high heels, one of which caught in the crack. She fell forward, and within minutes her ankle, badly sprained, swelled (as she later described it) to the size of a football. Joe Teeger, doctor for the cast, was hurriedly called, and injected her foot with painkiller, while someone dashed out to buy a larger pair of shoes. On opening night she wore, perforce, one regular shoe and one several sizes larger. Goodness knows how much pain she was in, but nobody would have guessed, or even noticed – not even, Miriam said later, her own mother.

But on the other hand, when Miriam's mother, who had never been to the theatre before, saw her daughter being strangled on stage, she let out a horrified cry, and her frantic screams of 'My child! my child!' rang through the auditorium, piercing the dramatic silence.

The week before *King Kong* was due to open, anticipation had grown into an excited awareness that something new in everybody's experience was looming. Our publicist had done a great job, and word of mouth seemed to be doing the rest. Even formerly sceptical friends who had lectured me on my foolish involvement all bought tickets for the opening, and turned up dressed to the nines for a posh night out.

Our friend Robert Loder, who had excellent contacts and organising skills, had explored where *King Kong* might actually play in front of an unsegregated audience, and the best – in fact the only possible – choice was the Great Hall at Witwatersrand University. The university itself was 'multiracial' in the sense that it had always taken in a small proportion of non-white students, and so the hall was unsegregated. But because this performance was for the public, not students, it had been deemed necessary to rope off areas to separate the different skin colours. When the first night finally arrived, all 1,200 seats had been booked, and the atmosphere in the Hall fizzed with excitement and expectation. There was some construction work going on across half the Hall's wide front steps, so people dressed up in their party best had to pick their way through a thicket of wooden barriers which determined the route to the entrance. Nelson Mandela, a keen boxer himself, was there with his wife Winnie, sitting a few rows behind Todd and Esmé. Years later I heard that he saw the show four times.

And oh what a reception it got! Beyond all expectations and all imagination. There was a timelessness, a 'something extra', in the air that night, a product of more than all the many elements coming together perfectly, and more even than the marriage of all our aspirations and hard work. Joe Mogotsi called it 'a miracle'. Certainly its manifold effects, stretching over many years and in all directions, were as far-reaching as one might expect when a miracle manifests.

What moved and aroused the audience to such an unprecedented degree may have been that they were watching the cast on the stage not so much acting as living out their own familiar experiences. That is what breathed life into every minute of it. Along, of course, with Todd's beautiful melodies. In Joe Mogotsi's words, 'King Kong was ours. We had known him in the townships. We had seen gangsters, so we knew how to inject the glowing viciousness with which they terrorised the townships. Many of us had had to do manual labour at some time in our lives, so the scene featuring a road gang at work benefited from personal experience.'[1] And illegal *shebeens*, of course, were part of the cast's everyday life. Even though *King Kong* never totally met accepted professional standards for a musical, I doubt whether any of its shortcomings were even noticed on that triumphant night, and indeed were seldom noticed thereafter. Criticism was wiped away by the glorious music and the joy and spontaneity of every single performer on the stage.

That first night, members of the audience sat holding their breath almost in disbelief, falling in love with the songs, the dancing, the story, the cast, the *life*. Who would have imagined that the melodies would dart straight into heart and mind and stay there for ever? As I've already mentioned, more than half a century later people are still singing me the songs, word perfect. Who would have expected the perfect pace and timing, the humour, the pathos? Director Leon Gluckman's patience and determination and skill had built a brilliant ensemble cast of players. Yet these were people who had, with few exceptions, never been on a stage before, or even in a theatre, and who didn't know, really, what 'acting' was, exactly. What is more, they played from start to finish without a single hitch. Miriam was wearing odd shoes, moving, and even dancing, with a hugely swollen ankle. Who would have known? Rufus had only been given the all-clear to put down his crutches the day before the opening. Who could tell? At the final curtain there was a stunned silence in the crowded theatre, followed by a thunder of stamping and shouting and roaring, and a storm of applause that went on and on, and then on and on again, seemingly endlessly. When an obviously exhausted Leon Gluckman finally appeared on stage, he stood quietly in front of the audience for a moment, acknowledging the applause. Then, turning his back to them, he bowed low to his actors.

Only after an uncountable number of curtain calls, with audience and cast applauding each other seemingly non-stop, many with tears running down their faces, a rustling near-silence finally fell. And as it did so . . . *then*, from the orchestra pit, the musicians suddenly let rip. They played their bursting hearts out in a wild, triumphant version of *Kwela Kong* – the uninhibited dance in the *shebeen* scene. Members of the audience converged on the band, crowding closer and closer to listen, and somehow be part of it. Below, in the orchestra pit – they called it the Devil's Pit – were the exhausted but wildly happy musicians, most of them stripped of their jackets, and some without their shirts or even their vests. It was a hot night, the emotional temperature was even hotter, and the pit had boiled into an oven.

And nobody would go home! Well after midnight the astonished cast and many of the audience were still there, embracing, laughing, weeping; intoxicated by relief, excitement, and the joy of seeing ordinary life in South Africa safely enacted, for the very first time, in song and dance and story . . . without the skies falling in! It joined ordinary people together in friendship and celebration, black with white – and that was new and wonderful. Just as our dress rehearsal had been the precursor of this opening night, so this opening night, I truly believe, was the precursor and first sounding note, the faintest foreshadowing taste, of the sequence of events which – after all the decades of pain and struggle – werc to follow nearly forty years later: those jubilant days when the new South Africa would finally be achieved and everyone, *everyone*, whatever their colour, went out, ready to queue for many hours in the hot sun to cast their precious vote. I really think the atmosphere of those few hours of our opening night was a signal and portent, a pre-echo, of those miraculous days so far in the future and, in the days of our *King Kong* musical, so utterly inconceivable.

That first performance had also not been without its moment of backstage farce. Todd was refusing to go on stage at the end of the show, both because, Irene told me, he was adamant that he didn't want to share a stage with Harry, and even more so because he was so upset about what had happened to his music. The pain was something I well understood, because of my own experience. I imagine the phrase going round and round in his head: his music gone, as he had written, 'from black' where it started, deeply, with him, 'to white', its fate in the orchestration, 'to purple', bruised, bruised, no longer his.

But Irene was determined that when the curtain calls began, Todd should be there, and should also be the one who led the team onto the stage. How could it be anybody else? The whole show rested on the genius of his music. She was also aware, knowing Harry as she did, that he would want to be the first on stage himself. Finally, before the applause began to thunder in the auditorium, Irene managed to persuade Todd to go on stage – but only, he insisted, if she was there with him. The wings where they waited were very cramped, so Irene got the waiting creative team to hold hands in a ring, with Todd, and her next to him, in position to go on first. Harry was further away, but did his best to yank the circle round so that he could manage to be first himself.

But Irene, powerful and utterly determined (while at the same time heartily amused by these manoeuvres), tugged the ring back again, so that she and Todd were best placed. The ring heaved and strained this way and that, as Harry tried to move himself nearer the stage entrance. But whenever he succeeded, Irene heaved the human circle in the other direction, and Todd was back in place once more. And then the moment came, and cries for 'author' began. Harry moved fast and almost made it. But Irene moved faster, blocked him with her body, and at the same time pushed Todd forward.

And thus it was that Todd, handsome and dapper in his bow tie and dinner jacket, stood on stage, at the head of the line-up, thunderous applause falling on his small shoulders, taking his well-deserved bow. Todd, that man of smiles and sadness, whose music was the beating heart of the African jazz opera, *King Kong*.

What a hilarious and inspiring scene! One I have re-lived many times in my imagination, and also with Irene, always with laughter.

And then one final irony. The joyful first-night party for the exhausted, exhilarated cast, thrown by Monty and Myrtle Berman, was raided by the police.

★

I have read and heard various accounts of *King Kong* on stage, but it is the memories of the Paris-based writer Denis Hirson, kindly written for this memoir, that in my opinion best communicate the musical's flavour and impact. Denis is the author of the book *I Remember King Kong (the Boxer)*,[2] an evocative collection of triggers-to-memory, described by a reviewer as 'a homage to the place of his youth, and a kind of ode to memory itself'. He was a boy, wide open to the experience, when he saw *King Kong* in Johannesburg, and what he has written vividly evokes his astonishment, and the lasting impression it made on him:

> The second thing I remember about the *King Kong* performance in 1959, was the sky above the stage. It was blue and soft and deep as a summer morning and this was strange because I could have sworn that when we had arrived it was night-time. I knew that the silhouettes of shacks and crooked chimneys on the stage weren't real because you didn't get those in Jo-

153

hannesburg, and I knew we were in Johannesburg because this was the university where my father worked, just as I knew that there were lots of steps and Roman pillars outside and I was seven and a half years old, but that still didn't explain the pure blue sky up there. It had definitely been dark when my father drove my mother and me through the streets of the city to get to the theatre in our little grey Morris Minor under the streaming lamplight.

The first thing I remember about the performance when we entered the Great Hall was the audience in the plush seats because there were black people alongside white people and they weren't wearing aprons or overalls either, they weren't working or anything but just sitting there like we were, dressed as smartly as when they went to church on Thursdays; and I had never seen such a thing in my short life before.

Then the curtain went up or perhaps there wasn't a curtain but very soon everything else disappeared, the whole of Johannesburg and the audience including me, there was so much seeing and listening to do, such a slow rush of singing and dancing to take in, and everyone on the stage was black which was also entirely new but after half a breath it was just how it was. And once it had all started I didn't want it ever to end because, because, because, well there wasn't any reason but this was simply how everything should always be.

Not anything in particular at first but just the freshness of those people up there, all unwrapping their presence one by one: they weren't wearing the cloak of obscurity that made them sink into their servant half-lives on ordinary days. And then there was the singing. The women with the mournful swaying voices at the bus stop near the beginning of what was happening up there on the stage were not the women I would see waiting in their blankets for the dirty-bottomed murky-windowed PUTCO bus lopsided with cramped up crowds on Louis Botha Avenue. I had never heard women singing so sadly, altogether giving out their voices, while the ones I used to see were only waiting and resigned, and still waiting when our white busses went past just about empty and twice as high. There was the sadness and the singing and the waves of sound in the voices that changed the sadness into a long rolling song.

Then everything turned into a story. A boxer called King Kong appeared and sang that he was bigger than Cape Town and his manager arrived too. Soon there was trouble, and later a wedding but not just a wedding, a whole exclamation of a celebration with presents and cakes and drinks and speaking voices and jazz music and more songs, words going up like balloons and exploding in capital letters, IT'S A WEDDING.

Which was all very well but there was also a gangster whose name was Lucky though it should have been Unlucky. He looked like a real gangster, how could anyone be sure he wasn't a real gangster? King Kong had to look out because the whole world went blood red — sky, floorboards, the lot — and Lucky came in singing that he wanted to kill King Kong but

King Kong wasn't there to hear him so something terrible was going to happen. And it did.

But not the way I expected because King Kong didn't die, or maybe he did later. But anyway the woman he loved didn't love him back even though I wanted her to, how could she prefer Lucky and sing a song with him about the back of the moon? Didn't she realize he was a gangster? And then King Kong killed her. She wasn't wearing a doek[3] and she had a beautiful voice and then he killed her, just like that.

Later there were lots of policemen on the stage wearing khaki policemen's uniforms with pith helmets to match. King Kong looked up at the judge and sang in his deep voice that he wanted to die, how could anyone sing that? The policemen stood in a ring around him chanting 'King' and then 'Kong' and the song was even sadder than the one of the women in the bus queue at the beginning.

Where did they get all those policemen from? It didn't matter, because soon everyone was together on the stage, the slender woman wasn't dead, she was smiling, and the audience was clapping like the biggest, longest hailstorm on a tin roof. Afterwards, no one wanted to leave. We all just stayed there because even though the stage was empty and the sky had been switched off, the air was still jiving with all that life.

★

Now it's more than fifty-five years later but it is not difficult to still be seven and a half years old in the Great Hall because I had never before been so entirely

entranced, *King Kong* opened up a new space of wonder inside me. I found the record in its red and black
sleeve at the tip of my bed when I woke up on my
eighth birthday, it was from my uncle and aunt, the
first LP I ever owned. I read through the programme
of the play over and over, looking at the photos of the
people who had been in the performance and put it
together, saying their names to myself like a lineage
that needed to be repeated, because they were real
people in the same world as I was and look what they
had done.

We knew Monty Berman and Arnold Dover but
we didn't know any of the others. Pat Williams was
a black and white photograph at the top of a glossy
page until I met her in London at the end of 2011.
We sat down in her house and talked and talked until
the atmosphere between us was considerably warmer
than tea and *King Kong* came out of the wings of the
conversation for an encore.

What had happened on the stage did not stop happening in my mind when we walked down the steps
of the Great Hall in 1959. But the years passed and
the scales of apartheid grew over all our skins, a great
comfortable dullness settled over the suburbs of Johannesburg, while out of sight there was the Sharpeville massacre, marches, shootings, meetings, states of
emergency, tortuously terrible deaths, distant news
of blood that hardened in an instant and took on the
texture of a scab against the skin of amnesia of the
suburban air.

I can imagine an epic written about the white

157

life of those years which would have only a single sentence repeated from beginning to end, over and over, only one set of words: Never was a black family, mother, father and children, once seen all together walking down a suburban street in the midst of our Johannesburg lives.

Not all the protests, the courage of those who went underground, the literature, the theories of revolution, the student discussions and resolutions, the clear and sturdy words of churchmen, were able to remedy this. And what could the artists do? In one way or another, they could go on bringing back into play the life that apartheid managed to cover over, at least in part, with its deathly cloak.

It was 1959, then it was the next year and the next, I put on the *King Kong* LP and brought the play to mind all over again. There came the voices and the dancing, the jiggle of penny whistles, the sweet boom and oomph of jazz. There was Miriam Makeba singing her slinky way to a shebeen called *Back of the Moon* where people were 'being what they please'.

'Come on Lucky, let's go!' she called out and the whole place shook with his laughter as they were off, diving into the night, into the story of their lives. Don't forget such stories, the play said as the apartheid years dragged on, don't forget the bursting fullness of those characters, the love and the dark parts and the colours and the music. Though it sometimes seemed as if nothing would ever change, there was the irrepressible exuberance still stretching out from the play, way beyond the magic planks of the stage.

★

The days and weeks after opening night confirmed how supremely our Phenomenon had achieved itself. Rave reviews in the newspapers. The booking office, Show Service, run by Percy Tucker, was overwhelmed with calls. Queues wound round the arcade in which Percy's office was sited, along Johannesburg's main street, Eloff Street, where further down, at the shabby end, stood Dorkay House. And then the queue wound still further, round the corner into a side street, Jeppe Street, where I had more than once spotted Nathan shadow-boxing at night, as he walked on his own to I know not what destination. Johannesburg, with a population of two million, had seen nothing like these huge queues, this demand. More than five thousand people booked seats by post. Telephone bookings were made from as far as a thousand miles away and from every part of South Africa. It was unheard of. *King Kong* fever raged across the whole country. Special buses were hired by groups who travelled from towns within a radius of three miles. Johannesburg cinema managers were phoning Show Service to ask when *King Kong* was to end, as their attendance figures were being affected. Even the Post Office complained several times about congestion on Show Service's telephone lines.

Within a week there was not a single seat left for any of the performances, and people were being turned away. Anyone connected with the show had constantly to field phone calls from people they barely knew, or even from 'friends of friends', asking if they could get them tickets.

'You won't remember me, but . . .' or 'I waited in a queue for six hours, but . . .' It was a vast explosion of energy. The biggest hit song of all, everyone singing or whistling it, was 'Back of the Moon'. And Todd's melodies were everywhere, blaring from music shops and over the transmission services of the green 'African' buses. They penetrated every back alley and all the servants' quarters in every town. People whistled the melodies as they worked. A reporter from the black *Zonk!* magazine wrote: 'Funny, now that King Kong has come back to life via a great new stage show, guys who crossed to the other side of the street if they saw him in real life, are walking around bragging that the late thug was their mate . . .'

And then what *Private Eye* would today call 'Desperate Marketing', or 'King Kong Balls', started. The ads proliferated: *King Kong* cast members 'wear X brand berets', 'smoke Y brand cigarettes', 'drink Z Brand tea'. A correspondence college advertisement in which one of the teachers was a one-time boxer added to its status by describing him as 'a contemporary of King Kong'.

The *Star*, Johannesburg's quality English-language afternoon newspaper, 'liberal' by reputation but actually ultra-cautious, never ran 'black' news or, as far as I could see, took any chances on behalf of the black people. But even so, its review by South Africa's premier theatre critic, Oliver Walker, spanned three columns, topped by the headline '*King Kong* is greatest thrill in 20 years of South African theatre-going'. He felt the need to qualify this, though, by adding, with truth, that 'this abounding vitality from the other side of the tracks would have meant nothing without the glitter and polish of Leon Gluckman's direction'. And on the Saturday after opening night, the *Star* came out with an entire page of pictures headlined: 'They call it Jazz Opera – Scintillating King Kong'.

The *Rand Daily Mail*'s full page of pictures was headed 'Here's the Township Spirit! For the first time African talent has been used in a constructive way – not merely to show Africans doing tricks, but to express African life and experience.' That kind of coverage – indeed, any interest at all in a black show – would have been inconceivable even a week before.

And on it went. The *Sunday Express* (8 February): 'King Kong: You've never seen anything so real on the S.A. stage before.'

'It's King Size!' said the *Sunday Times,* in a king-size review by its drama critic.

The black press loved it too. *Golden City Post*: 'King Kong IS GREAT!' The March issue of *Drum* carried four pages of pictures headed 'Black and White sweat together to make King Kong a SMASH HIT.' And *Zonk!* (March 1959): 'King Kong – a milestone in African theatre.'

Todd wrote in his column in *Drum* magazine: 'What's it like to be in King Kong?'

It's like dreaming all your life, 'one day I'll be important an' useful an' happy.' Then suddenly that dream comes true an' you're singing an' acting an' passing important ideas to over a thousand people in the University Great Hall. The lights are bright, the handclaps loud. There are bow ties an' mink. It's delirious but not dementing.

But boyo, let's take a peep into the headaches department.

And he lists just a few: Rufus's mad knee ('it gets crazy and shifts out of place and he has to dance'), Miriam's sprained ankle ('when she has to move about "monroe-ely"'), a chorus girl fainting, the cast's doctor called several times for emergencies, another girl threatened with death for alleged double dealing in love, musical instruments pinched . . .' And on and on.

The review that touched me most personally was of the *King Kong* LP written by Bloke Modisane, journalist and writer on *Drum* magazine. I quote a substantial part of it here because his words so clearly negated those criticisms from Harry that had hurt me so, and made me feel both vindicated and absurdly pleased – especially because he was writing for an almost totally black readership:

> Usually, when the music is good, lyrics are so-so, but not so here. Lyricist Pat Williams belongs up there in the major league. 'Oh those marvellous muscles' and 'King Kong' are a joy. The music is catchy and the lyrics outstanding. 'King Kong' must be the best tune in the show, a definite hit-parade winner.
>
> Winners both, with 'Back of the Moon', perhaps the one that get closest to portraying the illicit fun behind the shanties. Pat Williams achieved real brilliance with her lyrics:
> *right behind the shanties*
> *is the back of the moon*
> *though the floor starts shaking . . .*

The lyrics get so close to the real thing one can almost smell the shebeen – the cold sweat, the stench of stale liquor. And 'Quickly in love' is as good a pop as any, nothing to do with anything except two birdies in love.

One can see, feel the townships with 'In the Queue' . . . the open gutters, the gangsters, the hunger, the long bus queues. It's beautiful. This is the one most people believe is the only authentic African.[4] Hogwash, I say. The Death Song is the commitment song. It realises the philosophy of the African mentality. Africans are committed to reputations, family tradition, personal vanity. King Kong was committed to his name, his strength. These motivated him to acts which to some seem insignificant. He sings

'I'd kill that girl again
And show other men
I'm Kong'
This is lyricist Pat Williams' greatest triumph.

We had wondered whether we'd get a hostile Afrikaans press, but needn't have worried. They raved, while at the same time managing to hold their ideological line. *Die Vaderland*, the venerable afternoon newspaper in Johannesburg, the first Afrikaans daily, founded in 1934 and ardent supporter of the National Party, was surprisingly and magisterially approving: 'Impressive use was made of the contrasts inherent in the story to reveal the tremendous emotional depth of the life-struggle of the Native. In addition this was one of the best mounted and rounded-off productions (imported or local) seen on the Johannesburg stage for a long time.'

And the magazine *Dagbreek* said: 'We ought to send presentations like this to the Paris Drama Festival or the Edinburgh Festival because it is a rare opportunity to show the outside world an essential aspect of South African Bantu culture . . .' That was interesting and revealing. *Dagbreek* was clearly smarting under the bad publicity South Africa was just beginning to gather in the 'outside world', as we called it.

Our Phenomenon was manifest now, for all to see and experience. The intensely human, essentially forgiving *King Kong* jazz opera – in the programme's words, that 'co-operation between all races' had exploded in the most human of ways – in song, dance and story – bursting through official hatred and brutality. The reaction caught everyone almost totally by surprise.

I only realise now, looking back, that our show was in some ways a watershed. There were the beginnings of a visible shift, because of it, at the margins of the colour line, and it had nothing to do with politics. It was a small social breach, but an indicator of change to come. It sounds so crazy these days to be saying something like this, but the secret was now out, and publicly. Many white people began to think a bit differently after *King Kong* had happened. The city dwellers of Johannesburg, some of them at least, and in time many of the others who saw the show, or read about it, were being nudged towards recognising the possibility of a rather different way of seeing things. How could people go on pretending that the black people in our country were totally different and utterly inferior to the white? Gosh! No difference at all, beyond the differences of personality and character and capacity that exist between all human beings, and of course interesting differences of culture. The realisation was dawning, in some quarters, at least: *These people, black and white, who made the show, have worked together, and have created something beautiful between them. And see, the black cast are talented, disciplined, focused, quick learners, delightful, attractive people. They are humans, after all. If we prick them do they not bleed?* I think it started lot of people thinking about all the pinpricks, and all the malignancy greater than pinpricks, which had been taking place. And I think this was seminal. The genie was out of the bottle for some people at least, who previously hadn't thought of black people as anything other than servants, creatures with a different smell, shabby presences on the pavements, and an amorphous threat. It began to dawn on quite a lot of individuals, I was sensing, that they would have to think again.

I go through some of the *King Kong* cuttings and find this realisation between the lines, in no way revolutionary, but there, in cautious phrases such as 'it deserves to run for a year and indeed a propaganda-wise government should subsidise such a venture'. And 'where in the cast was there any real weakness? When we consider this talent, we must acknowledge the genius of these people, whose creative greatness is yet to flower.' And then, at greater length, Father Martin Jarrett-Kerr, C.R. (who had succeeded Father Huddleston) wrote: 'I think the long-term significance of King Kong's immense success . . . will not be lost upon the thoughtful citizen . . . no amount of talk about "separate development", about "Bantustans" and "Balkanisation" can conceal the fact that the urban African, on the stage and in the audience, walking the streets with us, his mother working in our back yard, his brother making tea in the office, is now a "westernised" person. He will not and cannot go "back to the reserves". And he matters. He is going to matter more and more.'

To me, it seemed there was a simpler truth: these people were part of our *family*, as magnificent in potential, and often in realisation too, as any other human beings on earth. All they needed was to be given half a chance, and even without it, many were already role models one could learn from.

★

There was also a more immediate, quite unexpected side effect to *King Kong*'s success. It was the first time that black musicians had white groupies. Hardly surprising, given the charm and attractiveness of all the players: Nathan, with his tall, film-star good looks and magnificent baritone voice; Joe, exuding energy, charisma and a kind of palpable 'wholeness', exploding like a firecracker when he sang, and danced to, Lucky's ferocious 'Knife Song' of vengeance against King Kong; Miriam, svelte, lithe and sinuous, an electric presence, her body monroeing (Todd's brilliant word) her way through the story, and her voice, powered by the *Amadlozi* as she believed it to be, touching all who heard it. Who could not be attracted to these highly charged presences, these great intelligences, or to the allure of the music and the men who played it, or to any or all of the members of the cast, in fact, and their memorable singing and dancing, their generous spirit, their physicality and their exuberance. Now that they had been seen and heard, now that the show had generated such giddy emotions, the cast *of course* had fans and followers. The young, in particular, were immediately responsive.

★

Within days of the opening night, Princess Margaret had somehow heard about *King Kong*, and asked to be sent several LPs of the show. We were informed that she had loved the music. In that same week, enquiries started coming in from overseas managements, asking for options on the show. Chief of these was one from the impresario Jack Hylton in London and another from the renowned dancer-director Jerome Robbins in New York. Robbins had staged the original versions of brilliant shows like *The King and I* and *West Side Story*, and on the surface his was incomparably the more attractive offer, But Hylton had already put money on the table. So Ian Bernhardt grasped the bird in the hand.

There was gnashing of teeth in some quarters, including mine, when we first heard about the loss of Robbins. But Ian may well have been right. I have heard since what a harsh taskmaster Robbins was, and how difficult to work with. And in spite of various serious offers over the years, including the one suggesting Muhammad Ali as King Kong, the show never made it to the USA. We wouldn't have been such a novelty there, of course. They had polished black shows of their own. *King Kong*, in my opinion, could have seemed amateurish in the light of the American musical tradition, Gershwin's *Porgy and*

Bess in particular. There were obvious fault lines in our book, certainly compensated for by the exuberant talent and marvellous unfettered glee and energy in the performances, but *King Kong* was entirely without the contained slickness and well-made-ness that US audiences expected.

*

It had become obvious even before the show was bought for London that *King Kong* could run in South Africa for as long as it could find a place to play. Ian was frantically looking for other suitable stages, because the university was reluctant to have the show on stage during term time, when it would need the Great Hall for its own purposes. There were clear disadvantages in moving the venue – in particular, that no other available stage in Johannesburg was big enough to cope with the mammoth sets and cast, still less with the complications of the lighting plot. Finally, however, the university made an exception and Ian was able to announce after the last curtain call on 18 March that the production had been granted another week's run in April. Thus far, there had been thirty-seven performances to audiences totalling 40,000 people.

But Ian still had to fill the few weeks between the coming April reopening and the closing down of the show in March. A season had been arranged in Southern Rhodesia, but had to be cancelled because political troubles had flared there. However, Ian and Leon did not want to let the cast disperse, afraid – and it was a realistic fear – that they might not be able to collect them together again. Too much could intervene. There was also an obligation to keep the cast on the payroll while they were not working, so it made sense to keep everyone employed. Many had been given leave from their 'day jobs', or had given up their jobs entirely, when full-time rehearsal-pay had begun.

The obvious step seemed to be to take the show to Pretoria. Only thirty-five miles from Johannesburg, it was sufficiently near to warrant striking the set and moving everything and everyone there until the Johannesburg run could be resumed three or so weeks later. Pretoria, however, was – and still is – the administrative capital of the government, from which all the oppressive racist laws emerged. There was not the same constituency of 'liberal' people there as could be found in Johannesburg. But still, given the excitement of *King Kong*'s reputation and pulling power, it was worth a try. So Ian applied to Pretoria City Council for permission to use the City Hall – and was refused. He then tried the University of Pretoria – and was refused. Indeed, in a letter to the *Star* dated 20 February, the Afrikaanse Kultuurraad (Board of Culture) expressed its appreciation of the firm step taken by Pretoria's City Council and university. It added that it 'did not want in any way to stand in the path of the Bantu in the development of his culture – if (in the instance concerned) it could even be called "culture"'.

This attitude had been reflected in perhaps the most extraordinary review of *King Kong*, certainly the most hilarious, which had come from the morning newspaper *Die Burger*, the biggest Afrikaans newspaper and the mouthpiece of the government. Leon had asked Spike Glasser to write some music to fill the space after King Kong murders Joyce, in order to cover the actors leaving the stage

169

– and in keeping with the dark mood of the scene, Spike had written a sombre series of drumbeats. The *Die Burger* writer had found in that drumbeat the 'dot dot dot dash' of the Morse code, and 'with a shock' recognised this as the V for Victory signal of underground wartime movements 'from the fjords of Norway to the caves of Sicily'. And now here was the same ominous beat in *King Kong*, he said, sending a message 'which sounds through the strike of midnight, like a voice which calls for the red of a new morning. And red is the colour of blood.'

The barring of the doors, the refusals to accommodate the show and the crazy review in *Die Burger* illustrated between them the free-floating fear, guilt and apprehension of the citizens of Pretoria and supporters of the government, most of them Afrikaners, which must have been lying just under the surface of their oppressive hatred.

But never was that fear exposed more clearly than in the farcical event which erupted during Leon's next production, in which Joe Mogotsi played the lead.

Eugene O'Neill's *Emperor Jones* was a play which Leon had long wanted to do. So once the *King Kong* tour was over, and while Ian was busy organising the paperwork for the cast's passports, Leon thought of *Emperor Jones* as a good way of keeping the principals – that is, the Manhattan Brothers – working. The play is about a resourceful American railway porter, Brutus Jones, who having killed a friend in a dice game, is jailed, escapes, and flees to a remote island, where he sets himself up as emperor and finally goes mad. Leon cast Joe Mogotsi as the emperor, a part which Paul Robeson had played in the first production in

America. But Joe was a musician, not an actor. He didn't know anything, really, about plays, and had absolutely no experience of dramatic theatre. Leon, however, saw clearly the unusual power and potential in him, and talked him into taking the role, explaining that he would work with him every step of the way, and also hire a tutor to help him with the English and explain what the words meant.

Emperor Jones opened also at the Witwatersrand University Great Hall, once more with sets by Arthur Goldreich. The play, though so sombre, was a resounding success, and Joe's astonishing performance earned him enthusiastic ovations. He was the centre of the play, the only character who spoke, while the other three Manhattan Brothers were silent, shadowy figures in the landscape. It was a huge challenge for Joe, and a landmark in more than his career, he said, though in that too. The experience of doing this play, he told me, is what taught him that with determination and concentration one could achieve the apparently impossible. It was a determination he would need to call on again and again in future years in Britain.

As I write I look at a photograph, unposed – a 'snap' – of Joe in the role of Emperor Jones, and I can see why all who saw it reckoned it extraordinary – the picture is not really of Joe. He has disappeared totally into this other character: all one can see is the horror and agony in his face, burning through from deep within him. He must have saturated himself in that part, rather than just acting it. The reviews, when they came, rejoiced in his extraordinary talent.

When the Johannesburg run came to an end, Leon booked *Emperor Jones* into the Great Hall at the university of Pretoria. I can't imagine why. He must have understood how dodgy it would be, knowing that *King Kong* itself had not been able to find a venue there that would accept it. But, surprisingly, the booking *was* accepted. It was only when Leon and the four Manhattans arrived with the crew that, in spite of the confirmed booking, they were refused entrance to the Hall.

Leon, characteristically determined and resourceful, decided they would just have to perform outside then, in the open air. The weather was warm, there was no threat of rain. And in spite of posters hanging on nearby trees, saying 'Kaffirs go climb trees' and 'Get the natives out of here', word spread and the alfresco 'auditorium' was packed.

'Those posters were really frightening,' said Joe later, laughing at the memory of what transpired. 'But it turned out the audience were more frightened than we were, even though we had more reason to be. At one point in the play Emperor Jones takes out his gun and starts firing at all the phantoms and ghostly images he imagines are crowding round him. And suddenly, Pat, it all went crazy. Absolute pandemonium!' Joe rocked with deep, hoarse laughter as he remembered it. 'The terrified audience just took to their heels and ran away!'

I'm laughing too at this point, so much I can barely get my words out. 'Wow! And then, Joe? What then? Where did they go? Was that the end of the performance? Did you just pack up?'

'No no, we just gently led them all back to their seats, and picked up the play from where we left off, as if nothing at all had happened!'[5]

There were about eighteen months to be filled between the end of the *King Kong* tour and the cast leaving for London. During the waiting period, the lives of the cast and musicians were already changing. Everyone's thoughts and dreams were now of London, of the prospect of new experiences, and perhaps, for some, even the possibility of being able to stay and make a new life in a new country.

During this period the Manhattan Brothers were in as much demand as ever. After *Emperor Jones* closed, the passport paperwork was still not finalised, so they went back on the road, appearing in shows around the country, keeping themselves occupied and earning. But now, from time to time, they were also meeting – as equals and colleagues – visiting theatrical personalities who, for one reason or another, would turn up from London, either on private visits or to work professionally. Actress Dame Sybil Thorndike, for instance, saw *King Kong* and assured Joe, who was wondering what to expect out there in the big world of international theatre, that in her opinion London would welcome it warmly. And harmonica virtuoso Larry Adler, who gave a recital at the Bantu Men's Social Centre, offered to give the Brothers an informal workshop in the rudiments of harmonica playing. They absorbed as much as they could from him – and with practice found they were able to add some harmonica playing to their shows. It made a noticeable difference for the better, Joe told me, particularly in their rendering of 'Wimoweh'.

★

Miriam Makeba had already left South Africa. Her departure was sudden and secret, accomplished before anyone realised. It had happened in the waiting period, well before the rest of the *King Kong* cast finally left for London.

Her destiny was propelling her in a different direction. Before and during the period we were making and rehearsing *King Kong*, American documentary film maker Lionel Rogosin, famous for a notable film, *On the Bowery*, had been in Johannesburg secretly shooting a feature-length documentary to be called *Come Back Africa*. It would be a far more authentic picture of life in black South Africa than the official version which was sold as the truth to the white world, both at home and overseas. Rogosin shot his film mainly in Johannesburg and Sophiatown, and had a simple scripted storyline largely improvised with his non-professional actors. He was in constant fear of discovery – the film would have been confiscated and he would have been instantly deported – so the cover story was that Rogosin was making a commercial musical. Secrets, however, can sometimes be pretty open. Our network of *King Kong* friends were well aware of Lionel's project, and that he had been in Johannesburg for months, getting to know the place and the people, shaping the story line, and selecting his 'street actors' around whom to improvise the simple script.

His film was about a defenceless young Zulu who leaves his famine-stricken district to work in Johannesburg's gold mines, finds a place to stay in a township, and stumbles into South Africa's brutal tangle of laws and restrictions on the one hand, and the atrocities of gangsters and hoodlums on the other. It is a bleak and terrible tale, but redeemed both by the resilient humour and humanity of the actors, often playing out events of their own lives, and also by the background music of street jazz and penny whistle, featuring both Spokes Mashiyane and Lemme Special. Miriam Makeba, glowing with life, sang two songs in a brief scene set in a *shebeen*.

Rogosin arranged to present *Come Back Africa* at the 1959 Venice Film Festival, and wanted Miriam to be there with him. So plans were laid to smuggle her out of the country. Only Miriam's mother, her daughter Bongi, Hugh and Ian were aware of his intentions. Ian felt that if too many people knew, word could get out and the film could be seized. So very shortly before the *King Kong* cast was due to leave for London, Miriam slipped out of the country. Rogosin had bribed the necessary officials to get her a passport, assuring them, by posting a bond, that she would return very soon. In fact, he had quite different plans for her. And – yet another irony – though officialdom was eager to secure her immediate return, as her fame grew and she became more outspoken, the South African government, furious at her 'disappearance', as well as at the subversive film made right under their noses, revoked her passport and banned her from the country – and thus, painfully, from her family – for what turned out to be decades.

Those who had seen *Come Back Africa* in previews, both in Venice and in Germany, were clamouring to know more about the girl with the exotic appearance and unique voice. And once in Venice, though her part in the film was so brief – simply two songs in the *shebeen* scene – Miriam became the sensation of the festival, admired, fêted, photographed and followed by the press wherever she went.

'There were really glamorous film stars there, all of them far more glamorous than me,' Miriam said, 'but I was the one everybody, including the press, was following all the time, wherever I went.' It is easy to see why. Even apart from her unforgettable voice, she was such an exotic and magnetic creature, and would have been unlike anybody most of them would have ever come across in those days. People from southern Africa were a rarity in Europe, and even more so in the film world.

And then there was the fascination with her hair. Everyone wanted to touch it, children in particular. According to Miriam, it took them by surprise: it looked like wire, but to the touch it was soft as wool, and they were entranced.

Come Back Africa was showered with praise at the Venice Film Festival: 'Burning with integrity; it is the most damning indictment of apartheid and the pass system that I have ever seen,' wrote the *New York Post*. 'If you want to see and understand South Africa, there is no better way than this picture of Johannesburg: the bitterness of the whites, the growing anger of the Negroes and the horror of the shacks and tin shelters of Sophiatown.' And Time magazine: '*Come Back Africa* . . . looks deep into the private nightmare and social desperation of a man and his people.' The film won many awards, among them, at the Venice Film Festival, the prestigious 'Italian Critics Award'.

★

Come Back Africa remains entwined in my mind with *King Kong*, because it too drew its energy from the extraordinary high-octane and sadly short-lived optimism of the times. But it was *King Kong* which was at the heart of it. As singer Abigail Kubeka told me, when speaking with affection about the brilliant musicians, singers and dancers in the townships in those days: 'If you weren't in it, you were nobody!'

Again and again my mind has been drawn back to that astonishing opening night, which those who experienced it have never forgotten. It is vividly alive in my mind. But in my case it is not memory but reconstruction – pieced together in my imagination by hearing so many accounts of it.

Because I was not there. Not for any of it.

When I had spoken to my husband Joe about divorce, I had told him in desperation that if he continued to ignore the issue, he would come home from work one day and find me gone. He didn't believe me, in spite of my insistence. And then, when a few months later the opening date for *King Kong* was set, it turned out to be the very date I had so wildly plucked out of the air all those months before: February 2nd.

It sounds implausible, I know. No novelist would dare put a coincidence like that into their story. But this was the date I had warned Joe I was going to leave, with a note pinned to the pillow to tell him I'd gone. And that is exactly what I did.

★

By the time the curtain went up on opening night, I was speeding in my sturdy Simca Aronde over the Limpopo and across the border towards Zambia, on my way overland up Africa, in those days a journey dreamed of by many but made only by the occasional few, and rarely by women.

Eight months later, after wandering about in East Africa, a sojourn in Zanzibar and another in Kenya, and then a slow cargo boat from Mombasa to Genoa and trains through Europe, I reached Folkestone and then London. But all that is another story.

All these years later, I still regret the manner of my going, because of the hurt caused to the one person, my son Dan, whom I loved beyond all words. He was not yet two years old, and I had debated endlessly with myself over whether to take him with me into what would inevitably be a rackety and chancy future. In the end I decided that it was in his best interests to leave him secure, surrounded by people who cared for him, and on whom he could depend. Later, many times, I have regretted that I was not strong enough or wise enough or clear-headed enough to have managed things differently. But I doubt whether at that point I had the inner resources to do anything else. I was fighting to survive, driven by instinct. I knew if I stayed I would die or go mad.

There are times in life when the pressure to act in a certain way is beyond all logical explanation – though later one looks for plausible reasons, which may or may not be the correct ones. But all I knew at the time, deeply knew, was that had I stayed, even if I managed to survive, I would ultimately have succumbed to family and social pressures, and be living like an automaton, an unhappy creature of the prevailing society, no use to Dan, myself, or anyone else.

That desperate dash out of the country saved my life.

It also meant that for many months I had no idea whether *King Kong* had been a success or a failure.

5

I arrived in London with a heavy heart, high hopes of a new start, and virtually no money. The immediacy and limbo of travelling had allowed the dramas and unresolved difficulties and consequences of my actions to drop temporarily off the stage of my conscious mind, though they lurked close by, in a dimly lit spot in the wings. Very soon I found myself a bedsit in Notting Hill, drab and somewhat dangerous in those days, sharing a flat with five members of an undistinguished pop group. I can't remember what went before, how I met them, or even any of their names or faces, just as I'm sure that if any of them happen to be alive still, none of them will remember mine.

During that first winter, by now in another bedsit, still in seedy Notting Hill, there were times I sat and wept, simply because I was shivering with cold and couldn't yet afford a warm coat. There was a slot machine into which you put money to turn on the gas heater, but it felt like an age before any heat built up in the room. I took short-lived odd jobs, waitressing and cleaning, at all of which I was terrible.

Most of what I was doing, though, remains a blur. The only thing I remember clearly is the dominating and un-remitting fog of sadness I felt for Dan, the son I had left behind. I couldn't speak of him to anybody, partly because I was so ashamed, but chiefly because of the overwhelming pain in my heart – and the tears, the seemingly endless tears, when I thought of him. I would have drowned in those tears had I tried to speak. If there was a child in a film, I would have to leave the cinema: the sight tormented me – not so much for what I had done, and by doing it lost this beloved child, though that grief was there too, but overwhelmingly and unbearably, because of *his* vulnerability, and the pain I had inflicted on *him*. His pain was mine, and yet for him, so much more overwhelming than mine. He was so small: too small to handle such a burden or understand what had happened, and yet he would have to carry it. My mind and body would spasm in anguish. How could I have put him through it? How *could* I? These strong feelings and regrets remained with me down all the ensuing years. *King Kong* at this time was virtually forgotten, lying somewhere in the back of my mind, a vague question mark. Occasionally it would surface momentarily, and I would wonder whether it had worked, and how it had all gone.

At some point, though, a pinprick of light penetrated my mind, my survival instinct telling me to pull myself out of this mode of ducking, diving and hiding, and get in touch with my rather conventional elder brother Peter, whom I'd been avoiding, expecting considerable criticism from him because of what I had done. He had emigrated some years earlier, and was a GP in a practice on the Holloway Road in north London. To my surprise, he responded instantly and generously: he and his wife Amy took me in for several months while I sorted myself out. I was, and remain, endlessly grateful, but looking back I am shocked to find no memory of ever telling them so.

Amy, whom I hadn't met before, was only nine years older than me, but so strong and sure and dependable within herself that she soon became my rock, somewhere between an utterly reliable bossy older sister and the mother I'd never had. Of cockney origin, she was clean in mind and spirit; tough, honest, funny, cheerful and hard-working. She was also an opera singer, the dramatic soprano Amy Shuard. At the time I moved in with her and Peter, she had recently left the Sadler's Wells Opera House for Covent Garden, and was preparing to sing Lady Macbeth there. Her voice was so big, she told me, that although from the very start she had sung leading roles at the Wells, she had never been able to 'sing out' because the theatre was too small for her voice. It was a relief, she said, to be at the Royal Opera House, because it was 'nice and big'.

The few months I stayed with Peter and Amy helped me find my feet in London. At first I did nothing but watch TV, particularly news magazines, current affairs programmes and documentaries – it was a superb education into what life was like in Britain, how people thought and behaved, how they saw and treated each other, what the social buttons and triggers were. I absorbed it all like a sponge. It was also a novelty: there was still no television in South Africa. TV arrived there only seventeen years later – two years after Afghanistan, and eleven years after Ghana. The South African regime resisted TV as long as it could, knowing that all sorts of disruptive ideas could flow into 'unsuitable (that is to say, black) minds', and knowing too that the State could never fully control every minute of what was on TV, or who watched it –

though when it finally arrived, in 1976, there were ludicrous attempts to do so.

Some months after arriving in London I went on an anti-apartheid march. On our way, a herd of antagonists, members of the British National Party and their ilk, turned up and started heckling and shouting racist abuse – words like 'kaffir lovers', I suppose, things like that. The people I was marching with promptly shouted equally heated insults back. In seconds, the encounter escalated, and probably all that stopped it becoming violent was the momentum of the march pushing us forward. But the experience provided me with food for thought. We, the marchers, saw ourselves as the decent people, the ones on the side of the angels – but were we really any different from these others? If we could be prompted to react so easily, so automatically, behaving exactly as they did when our buttons were pushed, then were the differences between us simply those of opinion and bias, and in reality no deeper than that?

During that march I ran into a friend who had recently arrived from Johannesburg, and asked her, tentatively, if she knew anything about a musical I'd been involved with before I left South Africa. It was called *King Kong*. It had probably sunk without trace, I said, preparing myself for the worst. After all, it was nearly a year, now, since it had opened. But *had* she by chance heard anything about it? She stared at me in astonishment.

'You mean you don't know?'
'No, what?'
'It was a huge success! *Man!* It's coming to London.'

183

King Kong had been bought, as I've said, by British theatrical impresario Jack Hylton. A former bandleader, Hylton was a man of many talents and great successes. In the 1920s he won fame, respect and towering popularity for his big band, which played and recorded what was then the new jazz style known as 'swing'. He was in touch with all the famous jazz artists of the time – indeed, he brought Duke Ellington to England in 1933. By the 1950s he had turned impresario, and for a decade or so his productions of musical theatre dominated the West End stage. On the face of it, he was the best and most auspicious producer we could possibly have had for *King Kong* – even if, from time to time, I still wondered whether we'd missed a trick by not accepting Jerome Robbins' offer from Broadway.

But in fact Jack Hylton was not entirely enthusiastic about our show, according to our friend Robert Loder, who had already been helpful in getting *King Kong* onto the Johannesburg stage, and had later flown to London to negotiate the contract with Hylton. It transpired that Hylton had made his offer to stage *King Kong* sight unseen, at the urging of his friend Lord Derby. The two men were major shareholders in Harlech Television, and Lord Derby had been entranced by *King Kong* when he had seen it in Johannesburg. Left to himself, it seems that Hylton might not even have been particularly interested. As far as Robert could tell when they met, he was producing the show partly out of genuine sympathy for 'the cause' – he was human, and he cared – and partly, perhaps mostly, because Lord Derby had pressed him to do it.

Robert had been briefed by Leon Gluckman, the *King*

Kong stage director, about the two things he needed to hold out for in the negotiations: first, that *King Kong* should play at the Adelphi Theatre, in the Strand, which specialised in musicals and was the perfect size; and second, that Miriam Makeba should be the leading lady. Nothing else mattered, just as long as Robert could get Hylton's consent on those two matters. Leon was very clear about the need for Miriam: 'Don't let them replace her with anyone else,' he said. 'It *must* be her.'

But by now Miriam was in America. After her success at the Venice Film Festival, her life had changed phenomenally fast. Taken up by Harry Belafonte, launched by an appearance on the *Steve Allen Show*, she was immediately applauded by the jazz greats and also by the giants of film and show business, all of them clamouring to meet her and hear her sing. Within weeks of her arrival she had taken the American entertainment world by storm. She was booked for concerts and cabarets from coast to coast, and performed for the likes of Duke Ellington and Miles Davis at the Village Vanguard, the legendary Greenwich Village jazz club. It was a meteoric ascent to stardom.

Eddie Cantor once said in a telling epigram: 'It takes twenty years to become an overnight success.' But Miriam proved the exception. *Time* magazine summed up her progress: 'She is probably too shy to realise it, but her return to Africa would leave a noticeable gap in the US entertainment world, which she entered *a mere six weeks ago*' (my italics). What a stroke of luck for our production that our leading lady should now be so celebrated!

However, it turned out that, in Hylton's eyes, he was doing us a favour by putting on our show at all. 'I pretty much met a brick wall,' Robert told me. 'I was 25, inexperienced, and also had a very weak hand to play. So I failed miserably at achieving either of my main objectives – Hylton dismissed the very idea of the Adelphi as our theatre, and he wasn't interested in Miriam. In fact it soon became clear to me that there was no possibility of negotiating much of anything with him.'

Hylton had already decided he would put the show in that great barn of a theatre, the Princes,[1] in Shaftesbury Avenue. It had 3,000 seats, double the number of the Adelphi, which Leon had wanted, and was unpopular with the majority of producers because it was so difficult to fill. In fact in showbiz circles it was said to be jinxed, because so many productions failed there. And as for Miriam: 'I don't see why I should pay for this woman to come from New York,' Hylton said, and that was that. 'Talk to my solicitor,' he said. His solicitor was a young man, Arnold Goodman, later to make an illustrious name for himself as one of the top legal go-betweens in the arts and beyond. The three of them went out to lunch, and came back to finalise the deal. Goodman told Robert: 'Jack Hylton is paying to bring all these people over. I don't know why he wants to do it, but he does. Here's the contract.' Take it or leave it was unspoken, but very clear.

'It was irrelevant whether the show made money or not,' Robert told me years later. 'I realised that we were supplicants, and that Hylton would have walked away if I kept insisting on our demands. In fact at one point in the "negotiations", as I was still trying to talk to him and Arnold Goodman about what we thought absolutely essential, I looked across at Hylton and saw that he was fast asleep.'

But in the end Jack Hylton *did* bring seventy people out of South Africa, and in doing so was instrumental in changing their lives.

Back in South Africa, the cast had been waiting to find out whether all or even any of them would go to London with the production. Hylton decided only very shortly before the meeting with Robert Loder that in fact he would bring across the whole South African cast, because it would be impossible to capture the essential quality of the show with British performers. For the same reason, he decided that Leon Gluckman should direct it. As Leon himself said when he heard the decision, 'A professional London presentation would probably be slicker than ours, but there would have been no set pieces which would look anything like, or have the flavour of, scenes like the Township Bus Queue, or Township Sunday, or the Kwela Dance or Gumboot Dance.'[2]

When at last they heard that they actually *were* going, the cast was stunned. Who would have ever believed they would get to London. To *London!* None of them had imagined such a thing would be possible in their lifetime . . . not unless there were somehow some inconceivable magic at work behind the scenes. And yet the impossible had happened – the gates to the outside world were opening for them. It was yet another unfolding of what Joe Mogotsi was to call the *King Kong* 'miracle'.

Up till that point in South Africa's history, it was exceptionally rare for any black person to be granted a passport, or even for them to consider applying for one. The more usual exit route for anyone even slightly 'political' was a carefully planned cloak-and-dagger escape over South Africa's borders.

But now, here was this application for seventy passports, requested from a government undecided about letting *any* black people out of the country, let alone so many at once. That could be opening the door for too many potential loose cannons. Who knew what 'lies' they would spread about their lives under apartheid? It took a while before the government came to see that refusing passports to our cast would *also* attract attention — attention of the wrong sort — plus a fair bit of ridicule too. I learned many years later that Helen Suzman, the South African MP implacably opposed to apartheid, played an important part in getting the government to realise that it would be more harmful to stop the *King Kong* cast from leaving than to simply let them go. Indeed, only recently I discovered archived documents showing how Helen used her influence to ensure the passports were granted.

It was a cumbersome task for Ian Bernhardt and the Union of Southern African Artists, collecting all the necessary documents, character references, birth and marriage certificates, and so on. Most of the cast were not organised to keep such records to hand: life wasn't like that for them. It would also take time for the backgrounds of all the cast members to be exhaustively examined by the police and the Special Branch. But in the end only Dan Poho, who played Popcorn, a member of King Kong's boxing entourage, was refused on 'political' grounds. It took fourteen months, hard to believe these days, before the rest of the passports were granted and ready — and over those months, an awareness of the show had been slowly building in London. People in the know had got hold of copies of the recording. Kenny Graham, for instance, jazz saxophonist and one of Britain's foremost jazz composers and arrangers, told the press: 'I have heard of *King Kong*, but never expected the music to be as good as this. It should make a great impact in London if the right people are allowed to hear it.'

Knowing that *King Kong* was coming finally spurred me on to *do* something more each day than sitting watching television. Looking back, I can hardly believe how lucky I was. I wrote to Sidney Bernstein, founder of Granada TV, asking for a job. I told him I admired Granada's current affairs programmes, from which I was learning a lot about Britain, and mentioned my journalistic experience. The very next day a phone call came from Jeremy Isaacs, a Granada producer at the time, who offered me a temporary job on a documentary programme scheduled for broadcast two weeks later. Several people working on it were ill, and I could be a stopgap. The work went well, helped by a whole series of lucky coincidences, and when a permanent job became available shortly afterwards, I was offered it. However, that would have meant moving to Granada's headquarters in Manchester, and I couldn't face that. I'd only just managed to get myself to London. And *King Kong* was coming.

By some sort of beginner's luck, plus my willingness to work long hours and find it all such fun, opportunities to write for newspapers, radio and TV kept falling into my lap. The freelance work kept coming, until I had an offer to join the newly formed *Sunday Telegraph*, then in its early planning stages. We produced several dummy editions before it hit the streets. I was part of the team on what was to be the Mandrake column (very different from what it is like today), and soon after became stand-in film and theatre critic as well.

Some time before the *King Kong* cast was due, Todd Matshikiza and his family arrived in the UK. After their hurried applications for passports, when they realised they just *had* to get out of South Africa, the process had taken nine months. In *Chocolates for My Wife*, Todd described the deluge of paperwork needed: birth certificates, marriage certificates, photographs, savings account certificate, testimonials of character, native reference books (the new name for the pass book), bankers' guarantees, 'and £100 each in case you get stuck over there and you got to be brought back'.

Once all that was sorted, they were told, again in Todd's words: '"Now go to the Special Branch. See if they'll give you a police clearance. Are you a member of the Communist Party? African National Congress? Ever been in trouble with the police? Anything to do with Huddleston? Any liquor offences? Rent up to date? Which church do you belong to? By the way, you the one making fun of the South African police in your Hong Kong play, an' you want us to give you a passport?"'

Thus, he said, the machine rattled on. For months. Finally a '*King Kong* grapevine', comprising South African friends living in London, had word that the Matshikiza family was coming, and a number of us started looking for a place for them to live. To my amazement, suitable apartments suddenly became unavailable when I said I was looking on behalf of a black family. 'He is a very distinguished musician and composer,' I would add hopefully. My idealised vision of London, as an open-minded city of and for the free, temporarily soured a little.

In the event, I think the Matshikizas started off staying with their good friend, the writer Anthony Sampson, former editor of *Drum* magazine, for which Todd had been a writer/reporter. Later they moved to a basement flat in Primrose Hill – by chance just a few doors down from where I was by then renting a large, sparsely furnished bedsit. I have a vivid memory of happy parties in their basement flat, full of music, humour, goodwill and old friends.

With *King Kong* due to open in three weeks, I asked for a £100 bank loan to tide me over.

'I came to this country with nothing, so have no savings,' I explained to the bank manager.

'What security do you have for a loan?' he asked.

'Nothing yet. But a musical I co-wrote is opening in the West End in three weeks' time, so I should have some money after that.'

'Hmph. Shows can open and close overnight, you know.'

I was shocked. 'But it's bound to last at least a week. There's to be a royal gala opening.'

In the event, he grudgingly let me have twenty pounds. I treasured my first purchases and remember them to this day: a 15-amp electric plug for my kettle, an electric light bulb, a blanket, and a beautiful beaded and sequinned Victorian Indian silk portrait of a peacock in a glossy black frame, costing two shillings and sixpence – 12.5p in today's decimal currency. I have it still, hanging above my desk.

Soon after Todd and Esmé arrived, I suggested an outing to celebrate – tea at Fortnum & Mason. Deliberately posh, but just within my means. I admit I felt a bit uncomfortable about it. Even though I knew there was no apartheid in Britain, the prohibition against going out socially, in public places, with non-white people was strongly conditioned into us. I remember standing at a pedestrian crossing on Piccadilly, with Todd and Esmé and their young children Marian and John. As we were about to cross the wide road a policeman walked purposefully towards us. All of us instinctively froze, fearing the worst. But he smilingly offered a hand to each child, and escorted them and us across the road. It felt like largesse from the djinns, as if they were underlining the new reality: nothing to fear now. But it was still hard to believe.

As we walked through Fortnum's gilded doors, Todd asked with a trace of anxiety, 'Are you sure this is OK, Pat?' 'Yes of course,' I said, with more reassuring confidence than I felt. We went down to the basement café, seated ourselves at a table . . . and yes, they let us order and they brought us what we asked for, and it was all perfectly normal, and though we were a little bit on edge at first, soon I was beaming, proud that Britain had lived up to its reputation, and that it was true after all – there was no legal discrimination against where people with black skins could go.

In his book, published about eighteen months later I think, Todd assigned the charming incident with the policeman to other company in another part of London. That surprised me when I read it, because my recent memory of that event was very strong. But it was a lesson, to be repeated many times, in how one person's perspectives and recollections can be entirely at variance with someone else's version.

My nervousness at Fortnums was yet another signal of how deeply conditioning can bite. I'd had my first experience of this on my way up Africa. I had needed to buy a pair of shoes in Dar es Salaam, and was served by a black shop assistant. Never in my life had a black man touched my feet in a professional, detached, but – by its very nature – intimate way. I noted with pleasure that I had reached a country where such things were 'normal', yet at the same time, as the assistant fitted the shoe on me, taking hold of my ankle as he did so, I began to shake uncontrollably, as if possessed by a *rigor*. I was utterly shocked at this response, so completely beyond my control, in spite of the fact that I firmly believed with both my intellect and emotions that I was free of any trace of racial prejudice. The experience helped me begin to realise, appalled, how deeply I had been brainwashed. I began to see that the process had started in my infancy, and been reinforced daily thereafter, by my parents' attitudes and those of everyone around me. Rather as some people today would feel repelled if asked to eat their dinner out of their dog's food bowl, however clean, so we had been indoctrinated to feel instant, apparently 'instinctive' but actually primitive and insane, disgust at the prospect of drinking from the same cups or eating from the same plates as our black servants. Their crockery was kept separate. As were their toilets. And as for black strangers touching us . . .

Until that day in the shoe shop, I was unaware that the powerful process of conditioning had nothing to do with my opinions or intentions or intellect. It had driven itself into my very body.

★

I wish I could have shared the uproarious journey on the specially chartered plane which flew the *King Kong* actors and musicians to London. I heard about it from Joe Mogotsi. Not one of the cast had ever been on an aeroplane before, and when, after they were airborne, the staff came round routinely to ask if they would like soft drinks or *alcohol*, it was as unexpected as it was wonderful. After all the restrictions they had faced about booze back home, here were *white* air stewards politely offering them the alcohol of their choice.

As Joe later wrote later, it seemed they had finally broken through the colour bar. During the first stop, in the Congo, there was a change of aircrew, and they found themselves on an all-black-run plane. 'That got us really excited! We'd never seen a black pilot before, and when we took off again we were served by black attendants. We could hardly believe it – they too offered us any drink we wanted!'³ They had drunk the plane dry by the time they reached Paris, he said, and the catering crew had to send for fresh supplies.

The landing at Heathrow is etched in my memory. I had been wondering how the cast would react, thinking to myself, *How great it will be for them to step into such a different world!* I pictured their amazement, and me beaming at them as if I had invented the freedoms of London single-handed. I anticipated the scene with pleasure – the emotion, the tears, the joy, the escaping into a land of liberty! But my petty and patronising excitement had not reckoned with the *King Kong* group's way of handling the experience. They were *so* cool. They came down the gangway and strolled across the tarmac into the arrivals building (which didn't take long in those days) looking jaunty and unbothered but clocking everything. I remembered doing the same when I had arrived. *White* men labouring in road gangs. Gosh! No policeman carrying guns. Wow! For the first time in their lives, white porters were helping them with their luggage. And then, as Joe wrote,[4] 'at our Bayswater hotel, the staff were also all white. This was all so new to us, but we settled in looking as if we were accustomed to such treatment.'

. Though not completely accustomed. Before they went out on the streets for the first time, they made sure to ask the hotel manager whether the police would want to see their passes. They must have been told more than once that no one carried a pass in England, but after a lifetime of doing so, they needed to make sure once again.

A few days after the cast arrived, we were all called to an Equity meeting. Equity, the trade union for actors, stage managers and models, ran a closed shop, which meant that no 'alien' performer or musician could be employed if a local person could do the same job. In fact it was one of the last of the closed-shop unions in the UK, made illegal in 1988, after criticism a few years earlier from the European Court of Human Rights. But back in 1961, in order to work in London at all, our musicians and performers needed to become temporary Equity members. We all duly assembled in a small theatre, and an Equity official, a rather dull 'grey gentleman', I thought, began his speech – one he must have given scores of times before. He matter-of-factly welcomed the performers and musicians and explained why it was necessary for them to become Equity members for the run of the show they were in.

I doubt whether 'Mr Equity' had ever had such a reception before. His monotonous, rather bureaucratic way of talking was interrupted by frequent cheers, whistles, stampings and applause from the cast. He was visibly energised by their response – his voice rose, his demeanour became more friendly, he made eye contact, he even *smiled*. It was a lesson how even the most seemingly unlikely people can blossom with encouragement.

Before they left South Africa, I was told – my informant, as so often, being Joe Mogotsi – that some of the cast were invited to meet white families in their homes, to be able to study their manners and social behaviour. This was no novelty for the Manhattan Brothers, of course, but it was for many of the others. 'We were given a lecture on what we could expect in London,' said Joe.[5] 'We were told to respect English institutions, be disciplined and behave properly. But we still had a lot to learn. We soon realised that even our way of speaking was a bit much for the hotel staff. Back home we were used to shouting across a room to get someone's attention, but now we had to remember to control ourselves and speak quietly. Often we used to forget, of course. Especially in the Tube.' Indeed, the *Evening Standard* published an article about the way the *King Kong* cast shouted at each other in the carriages, completely changing the atmosphere there.

And they certainly forgot all instructions about how to behave on the day of the Equity meeting, making a routine event so joyful that I remember it to this day.

I imagine that the oppressive restrictions in the South Africa of those times, so indelibly written into every minute of every day, will barely be comprehended by the majority of people now. Indeed, once we had got away from it ourselves, we not only found it hard to believe the kind of world we had just come from – but also the fact that we had somehow been able to tolerate it. A memory worth a thousand illustrates this: Shortly after the *King Kong* cast had arrived in London, I was a guest at a dinner party, along with the South African poet and writer Lewis Nkosi, whom I'd known for some years in South Africa, but not well. Because he was black, meeting socially was not easy, and I hadn't been able to see as much of him as I would have liked. Lewis was one of the two writers (the other was Bloke Modisane) who had worked with Lionel Rogosin on the script of his film *Come Back Africa*, which had propelled Miriam Makeba to fame. He was slender, soft-spoken, wry, and with an air of danger about him. On this particular evening in London, those round the dinner table were asking with genuine interest what it was like in South Africa. They were not particularly 'political' people – just ordinarily well-informed individuals, probably left-leaning, and curious about our former lives. We answered all their questions as truthfully as we could, but our answers, in the sanity of Britain, sounded quite mad. I would tell a bit. Lewis would tell a bit. It was all coming out . . . how we were kept from each other along rigid lines of colour, how even having a drink together was breaking the law, how sleeping with each other would have put us in prison . . .

The questions kept coming, and although we answered as openly and frankly as we could, at the same time we found ourselves looking at each other somewhat anxiously. Was it true, *could* it really be true, when we answered this, or said that? Had we really managed to live in such a regime, taking all the difficulties as daily norms? How on earth had we done so? Was *I* exaggerating when I answered a particular question? I'd glance at Lewis. Was *he*? He'd look across for confirmation from me. We didn't want, either of us, to embellish or overdraw it, to play for sympathy to this genial, sociable and welcoming audience. We had to reassure each other all the time by small nods of the head and complicit glances that yes, this had been our world. It really *was* like that.

The experience in the Dar-e-Salaam shoe shop, the Fortnums visit, the incident at the anti-apartheid march, and now this amazement at how we had kept the lid on what we allowed ourselves to notice about our lives, in order to live under circumstances which now looked close to impossible. I began to see more and more how the laws and social conventions had caged me. How I had deceived myself that I was free of this contamination. At some point, I realised, I would have to deal with it carefully and consciously.

Other memories:

- A story going the rounds among us: at a lunch in the Houses of Parliament, a member of the House of Lords who has been immensely helpful to the *King Kong* visitors wants to get a picture of what Todd is going to eat from the menu, here in the Lords' restaurant, and as well as that, in London in general. 'What sort of food do you like?' she asks with interest. 'Do you like yam?' Todd handles it beautifully. 'Yes, I do,' he says with a gentle smile. 'Strawberry yam.'

- Some kind of grand tea party, full of South Africans, connected, I think, with a committee organising the opening charity night for *King Kong*. I am caught between two fashionably dressed women, older than I am, and talking across me. One of them leans forward, putting her hand on my knee to speak more confidentially to her friend, as if I wasn't there, and my knee no more than a handy prop. 'I just found out the real reason Pat Williams left Joburg in such a hurry,' she says. 'Have you heard yet?' The other woman is all ears. 'No, what happened?' 'Well, when she got to England . . . she had a black baby!' 'NO!' gasps the other. Such a thing is unthinkable in these social circles. I sit in the middle of them, an anonymous young woman, keeping silent, hugging the incident close, knowing that later it will make a great anecdote.

- Talking to Peggy Phango, who has replaced Miriam, the former leading lady, as Joyce the *shebeen* queen. I have an enormously soft spot for her. She has an uncomplicated zest for life, a wide, cheeky grin, and a fine strong voice. After she left school, she had become a nurse. 'Jesus God, Pat, I used to make the patients scared of me,' she said. 'I would say to them, just shut up and do what I tell you, or you'll *die.*' She is nothing like Miriam, more solid and robust, with a thicker body and a more pronounced swagger and sway. She has a noisy joy about her, and a raunchy kindness. While still nursing, she had started singing in the local jazz clubs, where she had been spotted and given a role in African jazz and variety touring shows. From there, she was cast in *King Kong*.

• An appointment at the Princes Theatre a couple of days before the opening gala charity night to meet one of the Queen's ladies-in-waiting. She is teaching us how to do the deep curtsy required when we meet Princess Margaret and her husband Antony Armstrong-Jones. We repeat the curtsy several times under her careful eye until she judges we have it right. She also briefs us on the rules of conversation: always address the Princess as Ma'am, allow her to take the lead in conversations, never change the subject yourself – that is her prerogative. Arthur Goldreich (our flamboyant set designer), Todd, Esmé and I will have champagne and sandwiches with the royals in the interval, in a private room. Harry and Leon and various cast members will meet them backstage at the end of the show.

The opening night itself was a scrum. I was thrown off balance by the buzz and clamour and shouts of 'Hello!' coming at me from all sides. The audience seemed to contain every South African in London, and nearly every local person I had met since my arrival. So many hands and voices were trying to catch my attention, while the press of bodies almost swept me off my feet. Too much was going on. I was unable to keep my focus. Even while my eyes registered the many people I knew, and saw them greeting

200

me, my brain couldn't pull me out of the noisy, glittering, dizzying blur to muster any sort of greeting in return.

However, once safely in my aisle seat in the stalls, I got myself together. Todd and Esmé were sitting directly behind me, and turning round to them as the band began to play the overture, 'Sad Times, Bad Times', I whispered to Todd, with a huge grin, 'Darling, they're playing our songs!' His dark, shining eyes twinkled, and his returning smile was as wide as a bay.

During the interval, after our well-rehearsed bows and curtsies to the royal couple, Arthur broke all the conversational rules. We had gifts of elaborate South African tribal beadwork for them: a necklace, bangles and an intricately patterned apron. Arthur told Princess Margaret that all the designs had a meaning, and when she asked him to tell her what some of them were, he was, as usual, entertaining, funny, interesting and unstoppable. I wasn't sure whether he really knew what every design, colour and symbol meant, or whether he was making it up as he went along, but soon there was an enthusiastic interchange taking place between him, the Princess and her husband, in which the rest of us played supporting roles. We chatted and munched our smoked salmon sandwiches and drank wonderful champagne and admired Princess Margaret's quite extraordinarily clear complexion and diminutive prettiness, while, in spite of our instructions from the lady-in-waiting, the subject was changed quite naturally, usually by Arthur, and flew wherever it wanted, with the rest of us flying on his coattails . . . and then, very quickly it seemed, it was over, and Act 2 began.

Back in the theatre, we experienced again the increasing joy and pleasure of the audience. They loved the big, dancing moments, the animal sexiness of the *patha-patha* [touch touch] *shebeen* dance, the vigour and precision and rhythmic handslaps on rubber of the gumboot dance, and the spirited, bursting-at-the-seams, whistling energy and action of the set piece 'Township Sunday'. There were fifteen curtain calls at the end, an onstage atmosphere of exhausted relief, and enthusiasm and delight in the audience.

And when, finally, after all the congratulations and hugging and signing of each other's programmes, we emerged from the theatre, we found some of the audience dancing in the street outside, imitating the moves of the *Kwela*, or the *patha-patha*, bursting with exuberance, unwilling to go home. That happened every night after the show, right through its run. I was told it was the first time anyone could remember any London audience dancing in the streets.

I'd often go down to the theatre just to watch it happening, slipping into an empty box in the theatre just in time to catch the *shebeen* scene, which never failed to enthral. It started with the curtain down, the stage dark, no sound at all . . . then, hypnotically, the rhythmic swish of feet would begin to penetrate the silence. And as the stage slowly became lit, moving bodies, first in slow motion and then speeding up to explosive animal vigour and human joy, became visible, and as the sound of the music began and grew, a full stage of dancers moved in the serpentine and irresistible *patha-patha* dance, their hands roaming freely over the bodies of their partners. It was very erotic, which I had imagined was the point of it, but someone – Hugh Masekela, I think, or possibly Todd – laughed when I said that and told me that it was also an excellent way of picking pockets.

With remarkably lucky timing, *King Kong* was part of the prelude to the 'Swinging Sixties'. It seemed to me an interesting irony that Ezckiel Dhlamini, who could never fulfil his dream of coming to London, was enabling our cast, players and musicians to live out that which had been utterly beyond his reach. And then I think: it's more than irony. This fulfilment is a demonstration of how life can work: things conceived but never realised by one generation may become the living experience of the next.

But I was sad that Clive and Irene Menell were not there. They were in America, where Clive was studying and also had business commitments. I found it sad, too, that from that point on they disappeared from the story. But then, beginnings of things are often shrouded in mystery. Probably only Irene, Robert Loder and I are left to remember how *King Kong* had started. Had Clive not promised Todd he would somehow get a *King Kong* musical on, and had he and Irene not enabled its progress at every turn, it is unlikely that it would have happened at all.

★

Most people who had seen the Johannesburg production were a little disappointed by the London one. After the comparative intimacy of the South African venues, the Princes Theatre, with its 3,000 seats, seemed vast and draughty. And to cater for British tastes, there had also been a noticeable watering down of the music, which lost the show some of its magic. Jack Hylton had put one of his arrangers on the job of taming the music, saying, 'It's not quite English, so there are some things that we will have to put in.' According to trombonist Jonas Gwanga, 'they changed some of the orchestrations . . . and they always wanted to have the ends of songs going higher and much louder than we had them'[6] – making it feel more like English musical comedy, in fact. But even so, as Jonas said, 'we still had the flavour'. And with no basis for comparison, neither the British audiences nor the newspaper critics realised that anything was missing.

The review I liked most of all was American, in *Time* magazine on Friday, 3 March 1961, because it 'got it' more than the British critics did, and was especially pleasing to me, of course, because it quoted my lyrics:

Theater Abroad: Cry, the Beloved Country
    King Kong – brave as a lion
    King Kong – a hundred feet tall
    King Kong – champ without trying–
    That's me. I'm him. King Kong.

With notes as big as thunderheads starting and falling low at the end of the lyric, South Africa's *King Kong* was introduced last week to the London musical stage. Drawn from life in the shantytowns around Johannesburg, it gave its West End audiences a chance to see the result of a big event in theatrical history: a superb jazz opera written, directed and produced by South African whites, scored, sung and acted by South African blacks.

With raw flair, swivel-hipped sex, lurid color and fundamental rhythms, *King Kong* has clapped a rough hand on English shoulders to lead its new audience through the *shebeens* (speakeasies) and back alleys around black Johannesburg. Great gum-booted miners dance with precision, township spivs glitter with menace as they re-enact a primeval war dance; *shebeen* Delilahs strut their stuff in the sinuous dance of the *patha patha* (touch, touch). Racy, swinging rhythms interweave tribal chants, European liturgical music and 1925 Dixieland stomps. Such certified-hit solos as 'The Earth Turns Over' alternate with pennywhistle blues and a road gang's traditional chant. Wrote Critic Bernard Levin in the *Daily Express*: 'Certainly the show lacks the fine cutting edge that the Americans grind onto their musicals. But the more sophistication, the less vitality. And *King Kong* triumphs in the end by its bursting, smoking, glowing life.'

Against Odds

Built on a legend, the opera has itself become one. Its central theme follows the life and death of a Zulu giant named Ezekiel Dhlamini, a prizefighter of the 1950s who became the heavyweight champion of black South Africa and was known throughout the union as 'King Kong.' A hero until his death four years ago, he has since become something of an African god. He would clobber his challengers in the ring and later pulp them for good measure in the street outside. Braggart as well as warrior, he let his crown slide, and ended up as a dance-hall bouncer who jealously murdered his mistress. Begging for capital punishment, he was given twelve years at hard labor and drowned himself by a prison dam.

To many, he symbolized the wasted power of his people in his country in his time, and his life was a readymade libretto. The music, too, was at hand – in the jazz concerts of the shantytown *shebeens*. A group met soon after the fighter's suicide and planned what may have seemed an impossible production: book by white Lawyer-Novelist Harry Bloom, lyrics by white Journalist Patricia Williams, score by black Jazz Composer Todd Matshikiza, direction by white Actor-Director Leon Gluckman, a veteran of London's Old Vic. When rehearsals began, they had to be conducted against odds: the curfew, threatening Johannesburg hooligan gangs, the rules of apartheid.

Cracked Barricade

Opening Feb. 2, 1959 in the Great Hall at Johannesburg's University of the Witwatersrand (the only place in the city where an opera-sized production could be staged before a mixed audience), *King Kong* was an instant hit, and played before 120,000 persons – two-thirds of them white – in Johannesburg, Durban, Port Elizabeth, and Cape Town. Then, as now in London, heavyweight Jazz Singer Nathan M'dledle (pronounced Muh-dead-ly) played 'the King.' His girl was played by Miriam Makeba, whose success in the role catapulted her to solo spots in U.S. nightclubs; she has been replaced in the opera by 29-year-old Peggy Phango. From the beginning, the semipro chorus has been filled with carpenters, shop clerks, schoolteachers, messengers, housemaids, typists, even an X-ray technician.

Surprisingly, the government granted passports for *King Kong*'s trip to London (it may come to New York as well) and, slightly cracking the apartheid barricade, the mayor of Johannesburg gave a farewell party for the cast. In London, moving out tentatively from their modest hotel near Notting Hill, cast members were welcomed by everyone from underground conductors to Princess Margaret, and few in the show's enthusiastic audiences could resist the African rhythms:

King Kong bigger than Cape Town
King Kong harder than gold
King Kong knock any ape down –
That's me, I'm him. King Kong.

In spite of the many standing ovations on opening night, the London critics were not as unanimously ecstatic as they had been in South Africa, and with good reason, I thought, given the 'adjustments' to the production and the absence of Miriam's extraordinary voice and presence. Even so, the majority were glowing (if at times somewhat patronising about 'the naivety, vitality and eroticism' of the black African cast). The rest were favourable, but one or two reviewers, while liking it, felt that the political edge they were hoping for was lacking. Having lived in a free society themselves, they didn't understand that *King Kong*'s very existence was a political statement in itself. But without exception, the critics fell in love with the music. Milton

Shulman, of the *Evening Standard*, wrote: 'Undoubtedly Todd Matshikiza's music is the best thing in King Kong.' Bernard Levin wrote, I think in the *Daily Express*: 'the music of Todd Matshikiza is as violent as the story; blaring brass, thudding drums, with the tunes weaving around the hypnotic volume of noise. Though Mr Matshikiza can be gentle too, and if we are not all singing "It's A Wedding" very soon, it won't be his fault.' And W.A. Darlington, of the *Daily Telegraph*: 'Above all, we shall remember it for some superb musical effects, composed and lyricised and sung by members of that race whose sense of rhythm and harmony has so profoundly influenced our own ideas.'

The party after the first night was hosted by Pearl and Edric Connor in a spacious house in Hampstead. Edric was an attractive and engaging Caribbean singer, folklorist and actor, with huge warmth and also – I always sensed – enormous depth. He knew South Africa because he had been there when filming – and like black American film stars Sidney Poitier and Canada Lee before him, he had been kept away from the townships, accommodated in a luxurious 'white' hotel, and given no access to other non-white people. Pearl, who was founder, with Edric, and manager of the only Afro-Asian-Caribbean theatrical agency in London, already knew all the musicians and members of the cast, because before they arrived Jack Hylton had asked her to find accommodation for them. I remember very little about that party except that it was a gloriously high-spirited and warm-hearted celebration – very crowded, abundantly supplied with food and drink, and with a great deal of dancing to *Kwela* and *patha-patha* – and to the music of *King Kong*. The only 'lit' memory that survives is of a rather stiff but enthusiastic upper-class Englishman, a lawyer I think, confessing to the beautiful Hazel Futa, who played one of Joyce's girls in the *shebeen*, that he was standing on the sidelines because he didn't think he'd be able to get the hang of this sort of dancing. 'It's easy,' said Hazel, who at one point had been Miss Black South Africa. 'Just do what you do in bed.' The man looked at her blankly. 'You know,' she said, miming graphically, '*between the sheets*.' Another blank moment, and then light dawned. 'Oh yes! Yes I see!' He took her by the hand and gyrated enthusiastically with her and other partners for the rest of the night.

This is perhaps the appropriate place to mention something I learned at a different party. I loved our 'mixed' parties in South Africa – the music, the goodwill and accord, the drinking and dancing with people we liked and often loved – and the fact that we were breaking the law, though in a real way unimportant, intensified and heightened the pleasure. But this episode actually took place in London, at a party at Joe Mogotsi's apartment. It was a small incident, but it brought with it a wealth of understanding.

A young black woman was dancing a couple of feet away from her son. He was not much more than a toddler, and with her encouraging smiles and gestures she was inviting him to dance too, to copy what she was doing. In a sense, she was hauling an innate potential out of the child. Her eyes held his, he watched her carefully, fathoming what he saw, and then bit by bit I could actually *see* him finding a matching rhythm and movement inside his own body. It was fascinating to observe. He moved tentatively at first, checking his mother's responses to see if he was doing it right, never taking his eyes off her face. But quite soon, as he continued more and more confidently to find the pattern of his mother's movements within himself, he discovered the joy of it, and his face changed from concentration and uncertainty into a picture of sheer rapture.

It really begins that young, I realised, as I watched the process. And it had very little to do with the patronising phrase I'd heard so often from the lips of people like my parents and their friends that 'these blacks, they just have music in them' – as if song and dance and an ability to 'let go' were part of the primitive 'wiring', unsophisticated, indeed almost regrettable, and certainly not quite desirable for us higher white mortals. But humans all have music and song within them! It's just that my own Anglo-Saxon culture has for the most part lost the idea of activating the music template early enough – by allowing children to match what is inherent in them to what they see others doing, as they move to the rhythms of music. I, with my inability to sing, was a victim of something similar. It seems to me that a community surrounding children with music and movement and song so that they come 'instinctively' to dance and sing works in exactly the same way as surrounding children with words, so that they may learn 'instinctively' to talk.

*

It would have been so much slower, and a lot more difficult, to make my way in London, arriving as I had with £25 in my pocket and knowing no one but my brother and Amy. But *King Kong* short-circuited all of that, propelling me headlong into a stimulating and hectic social and working life. There were all sorts of job opportunities in radio, on TV and in newspapers and, with hindsight, perhaps far too many parties, frivolities and excitements.

Shards and splinters of memory from those days:

- Before the show has opened, I am asked by people I barely know, on behalf of a lord and lady I have never met, if I would like to go with them to a nightclub I have not heard of. Sammy Davis Jr, blazing fireball of all the talents to entertain, is the cabaret. When he joins us afterwards for a drink, I am so dazzled and bemused, I say nothing at all for the rest of the evening.

- My friend the singer and writer Shusha Guppy tells me that her friend Alexander, who lives in Wiltshire, is throwing a Saturday night party, and has asked her to invite me and Francis, my boyfriend, for the weekend. It is high summer, and Shusha's husband Nick drives us for what seems like hours through countryside as green and lush as a tropical rainforest. At last we come to huge gates set in a high wall – 'This is it,' says Shusha – but once through the gates, we drive on through what looks like a park for what seems like too long a time. 'Where's the house?' I wonder anxiously. 'Are we in the right place? What were those gates about?' Finally the house comes into view, and appears, to my colonial eyes, to be a palace. It is Longleat, seat of the Marquis of Bath. As far as I can tell, all the celebs of the month, in the arts at least, have been invited – the one who wrote this week's most applauded book, the painter whose exhibition has just opened to excellent reviews, the actress who stunned the critics and the man who wrote the play she is starring in. I remember the hand-blocked wallpaper in our palatial bedroom and through its windows the long green views of the garden and estate outside, as well as the sumptuous breakfast to which we all helped ourselves from a variety of heated silver salvers lined up on the sideboard. And I remember, too, thinking how grateful I was to Ezekiel Dhlamini, whose difficult and tragic life was my ticket to all this luxury.

- A night out with Arnold and Dusty Wesker, who have become good friends. After a meal at their house, we ride around London, driving first to the Royal Court, where Arnold's play *Roots* is on, whooping and hooting and calling out like banshees, and then to the Princes, where *King Kong* is on, and caterwauling with equal gusto there.

- For a while I frequent a Soho drinking club called Muriel's, the haunt, mostly, of artists of all sorts. The atmosphere is very louche. One evening I hear the resident pianist playing something from *King Kong*. 'Gosh,' I say in surprise, 'I *wrote* that! Well, the words to it anyway.' At first the pianist thinks I'm having him on. Then we both take a closer look. I recognise jazz-man and band-leader Chris McGregor, of the Blue Notes, and he sees it's me. How unexpected and delightful!

- At more than one party, I notice that my friends Bloke Modisane and Arthur Maimane, fine black journalists who have recently managed to get out of South Africa, have an 'interesting' technique on the dance floor. They pull whichever (white) girl they're dancing with too close, too fast, cheek to cheek, groin to groin. The girls, as was customary in those more circumspect days, instinctively try to

212

make the gap between their two bodies wider. As they pull back to where they feel more comfortable, Arthur or Bloke would ask: 'What's the matter? Don't you like black men?' 'Oh no, it's not, it's not . . . well yes of course I like black men,' they fluster. So they pull the girl right back, groin to groin again, and this time, to make their 'liberal' point, the girls snuggle even closer. Bloke and Arthur are both brave, humorous and clever men, good writers and delightful and interesting company, and part of our 'gang' – but in these circumstances, I realise, they are incorrigible 'Jack the Lads'.

• At a party given by Julian and Juliette Huxley, my boyfriend Francis's father and mother, I notice that all the men there, and many of the women, seem to be famous for something, or else they are the head of something – a scientific organ-isation, a university college, or a bank or financial institu-tion. 'I suppose they know each other because they're all at the top of what they do,' I say to Francis, trying to fath-om how so many luminaries managed to arrive in the same room on the same night. 'Not at all,' Francis says, contrib-uting a nugget to my British social education. 'They were all at school together. They're childhood friends.'

• Francis also enriches my experience of British landscape and history by taking me on a series of journeys – using a map of ancient Britain. I am astonished by all the forts, castles, stone circles and ancient forests of this country's history, so different from the hundreds of miles of uninhabited land-scapes back in South Africa. I also see in my mind's eye, as if it were a moment ago, the time on one of these jour-neys that I come across a bluebell wood for the first time. These flowers, massed in an airy haze of violet-blue, make me genuinely high. I am utterly intoxicated by them. Those bluebells are as miraculous as everything else in my life at the time.

And thus it continued for the next five or six years. I had no concept of 'building' a career. All I did was career about from one thing to another as opportunities turned up, as at that point in my life they always did. Life was so *interesting*. I was open, avid and eager every new day. It seemed as if the djinns were helping me, *willing* me to flourish. With the energy of *King Kong* still propelling me, I was like a brightly burning meteor. In those extremely social years of the 1960s, I also managed to fit in a dizzying list of jobs, including writing and presenting radio programmes (the second woman – after Dilys Powell – to chair BBC radio discussions); scripting various TV documentaries and presenting others; writing a weekly column for the *Observer* and features for the newly formed *Sunday Times* colour magazine; scripting a documentary on the suffragettes, voiced by Sian Phillips; scripting a documentary, *The Search for Ulysses*, made to launch the CBS colour TV service in America, and spoken by actor James Mason. The suffragettes documentary was nominated for a Screen Writers Guild award.

A few months after *King Kong* had closed, I visited the offices of Aldus Books. These publishers wanted me to write a book to be called *The Supernatural* – a kind of encyclopaedia of human belief. Maurice Richardson, the author Aldus had first commissioned, had dropped the project, confused by the impenetrable nature of the material he was having to deal with. I, on the other hand, had made no secret of my interest in the subject (it was one Francis and I had researched together), and Aldus was now asking if I would be prepared to take the book on instead. The deadline, by now, was only five months away. 'Not possible in the time,' I had told them. So they suggested I might write it with Douglas Hill, who had been Maurice's editor. I had come to the Aldus offices to meet him, to see if we thought we could work together. We could and did, and became lifelong friends. Douglas always remembered, he said, how I had turned up to the meeting with a 'purple' kitten on my shoulder. I had been given it about half an hour before by my friend Doris Lessing, and there hadn't been time enough to take it home before the Aldus appointment.

The first person I saw as I walked in through the door of Aldus House was Gwigwi, my musician friend from *King Kong*. He was wearing a cotton dust coat, his shoulders were drooping, and he was working as a messenger – that is to say, he was doing exactly the kind of job he might have done if he'd stayed in Johannesburg. It was a bittersweet sight, prompting in me both an instant and impulsive sadness – because outwardly at least, so little had changed for him – and simultaneously, a joy at seeing this dear, gifted, thoughtful man again, and remembering what he was *really* made of. Before typing this sentence I decided to look him up on Google, and there are tears in my eyes as I write down what I found: there is now a street in central Johannesburg named after Gwigwi. It is just a stone's throw from Eloff Street, at the bottom of which, at Numbers 5–7, is Dorkay House, still functioning and now famed as a cultural heritage site, around which many legends have accumulated – among them, that this was the place where Nelson and Winnie Mandela first met.

Gwigwi had not shared the same soaring success as some of the others. It seemed to me he found it hard to keep his head above water in London. But he was a 'musician's musician', respected and immensely admired, and having a street named after him pays homage to his essential greatness. Hence my tears. And I have also never forgotten what Gwigwi confided in me in the *King Kong* rehearsal room, about his possession beyond price: his initiation group: 'We are part of each other for ever, we can rely on each other for ever.'

In one way, Gwigwi had almost nothing to do with my day-to-day life – the hours and minutes we spent together would probably barely add up to a month's worth, if that. But he has always been so alive in my mind that I can never think of him without a fond smile on my face, and a deep feeling of warmth in my heart – along with the stern reality, but reality nonetheless, of that initiatory taste.

★

King Kong, with its glorious music and its unchained sense of freedom, fitted well into the atmosphere of the early 1960s. Liberation struggles against racial restrictions and prejudice were part of the Zeitgeist. It was the time of the civil rights movement in America, of sit-ins and marches and freedom songs. It was also the point, some would say, at which American jazz reached its highest peak. In spite of continuing oppression and ever more restrictive laws, there was an atmosphere of hope in, and about, South

Africa: an anticipation of change. Perhaps this hope was the result of the growing political awareness – and accompanying resentment – among black South Africans. In the very month that *King Kong* opened in London, that anticipation was reinforced by the British Prime Minister, Harold Macmillan, in his famous 'wind of change' speech, in which he said that Britain could not support South Africa's racial policies.

Indeed, *King Kong*, now seen as a watershed of South African theatrical history, was very much part of the mirage that seemed to herald the approaching change. There was an unforgettable exuberance, energy and lightness about the show itself, and around any of us, whoever we were, who had anything to do with it. We were a club, you might say, a brotherhood of optimists, to which many people who had nothing directly to do with the show also belonged. People like Bloke Modisane, for example, who was around with us in both Johannesburg and London. Lionel Rogosin had financed and backed Bloke's escape from South Africa and his transition period in London, where he wrote *Blame Me on History* – a book which now seems to me even better than it did on first reading, all those years ago.

Many other people, too, who dreamed of a different kind of South Africa, thought that time was on our side at last; that with just a little push and protest from the African National Congress and with the solidarity of people of goodwill, apartheid would soon somehow crumble. There would be a change of heart among the white citizens, and non-white citizens would finally get the vote and live with equal privileges in a unified society. Some, includ-

217

ing me, thought we were only short steps away from this holy grail.

But a little over a year after *King Kong* first opened in Johannesburg, our hopes were shattered in the space of a few hours by events in Sharpeville, a small township just an hour's drive away. On 21 March 1960, between 5,000 and 7,000 people had gathered outside Sharpeville's municipal offices to protest against the pass laws, which implacably restricted black people's movement in white areas. Any black person found in a public place without their passbook could be arrested and detained for up to thirty days – a restriction which had recently been extended to include black women as well as men.

The march was intended to be the first of a five-day non-violent campaign by black South Africans to persuade the government to abolish these laws. People were urged to leave their passbooks at home and present themselves at police stations for arrest. This, it was thought, would cause prisons to become overcrowded, labour to dry up, and the economy to grind to a halt. But three hours after it began, the 'peaceful' gathering at Sharpeville turned into a bloodbath. Up to 300 police officers began shooting at random into the crowd of 5,000. More than fifty people were killed, and scores more suffered gunshot wounds. Eyewitnesses said men, women and children fled 'like rabbits' as they were shot in the back, running from the gunfire. In the ensuing days the casualties rose to sixty-nine dead and 180 injured.

In London, I was listening obsessively to every news broadcast. A BBC report said: 'It is not yet clear why the police, in armoured vehicles, opened fire at approximately 13.15 local time today, although it is understood some protesters had been stone-throwing.' When Police Commander D.H. Pienaar was interviewed, he said: 'It started when hordes of natives surrounded the police station. If they do these things, they must learn their lessons the hard way.'

Three days later the government banned all public meetings in twenty-four magisterial districts, and a fortnight after that banned both the ANC and the Pan African Congress. When later that year more than 224 of the victims of the shooting lodged civil claims, the government passed a special Indemnity Act clearing all officials of any responsibility for what was by now known as the Sharpeville massacre. Not only were no police officers ever convicted, but Prime Minister Verwoerd actually thanked them for the 'courageous and efficient' manner in which they had handled the situation. Though the police at times found it difficult to control themselves, he said, they had done so in an exemplary manner. Verwoerd's comments were typical of the government's cynicism. He told the South African Parliament that in no way could the riots be a reaction to the government's apartheid policy. Such disturbances were simply 'a periodic phenomenon', he said – and had nothing at all to do with poverty or low wages.

Just one week before Sharpeville, Lionel Rogosin's film *Come Back Africa*, which had launched Miriam Makeba's international career at the Venice Film Festival, premiered at the Bleecker Street Cinema in New York. The reviews were unanimous in their enthusiasm. 'Makes me ashamed to be white,' wrote the critic in the *Daily Herald*. 'The very spontaneity of the scenes gives his story illumination, shock, and intense poignancy,' wrote Hollis Alpert in the *Saturday Review*. The film had already been selected by *Time* magazine as one of the 'Ten Best Pictures' of 1960.

After Sharpeville, it became clear that the demolition of apartheid would not be quick or easy, nor would it just naturally wither away. Instead, it became nail-hard state policy, administered with an iron hand, reinforced when necessary by swiftly passed new laws. Now there were fewer cracks and spaces in the social fabric within which, as had happened up to that point, lovely near-accidents could manifest between people of different colours – unlikely blossoming encounters and friendships, unlooked-for exchanges of ideas and dreams, or just fleeting expressions of ordinary human warmth. Now the air was harder to breathe and minds found it harder to fly, as if pinned to the ground by the extra weight of all the daily hazards. Within two years Nelson Mandela would be arrested, along with many others, and thereafter he would disappear from public sight for almost three decades. Because it was against the law to mention his name, or even say anything about him in public, he was rendered invisible – never spoken of, and all but forgotten by the majority of white South Africans. It took the activities of Oliver Tambo, Nelson Mandela's political 'other half', to build awareness of him in the world outside and keep it alive. Tambo came to London several months before *King Kong* arrived. He was penniless and unknown, with the police on his tail. His wife, Adelaide, and their young children were smuggled out later. While Mandela was in prison, Tambo travelled the world, winning friends for the ANC, keeping the silenced South African struggle alive, giving it a voice. That Mandela's courage and honour and very existence came to be remembered at this point is largely down to Oliver Tambo.

*

By the end of 1961, audiences for *King Kong* were tailing off, just as, for some reason, audiences were waning for other popular West End musicals too. Members of our cast naturally began to be concerned about what would happen to them after the show's run. Any decisions could at first be deferred because of an extended tour to the north of England, and then Scotland. 'Wheee,' I remember Gwigwi saying, 'those audiences, man – they *really* friendly, they warm, they make a noise, we know how they're taking it, more like us at home. In London, they're very polite and quiet.' But despite this shared satisfaction, the cast was in fact falling apart. Individual performers and musicians began trying to negotiate their own fees. In Liverpool, leading man Nathan even threatened to walk out over his pay. At that point Leon Gluckman asked Joe Mogotsi to mediate in the dispute, and Equity, at Nathan's request, sent a solicitor to represent him. I'm convinced it was such an agitated and unsettling time because, after a year of 'normality' – that is to say, a year without apartheid – members of the cast were having to confront the implications of returning to the insane asylum back home. For months they had probably kept such thoughts at bay because there was a possibility that the show might go on to America, but the hoped-for deal had not materialised.

Then one day after they had returned from their tour, the *King Kong* cast members were called together by Hylton's management and told that a plane had been chartered to take them home. They had just forty-eight hours to make up their minds whether to stay or go. If they decided to stay, there would be no offer of help forthcoming, and if they subsequently changed their minds, the management would not pay their fares home later.

It looked like a tactic for scooping everyone back to where they came from as fast and as quietly as possible. I wondered if the South African government was behind it. But to have to make such a life-changing decision and organise themselves to leave or stay in just two days! It was heartless. A quick campaign was organised to let the press know how our cast were being hustled. A few newspapers, thank goodness, kicked up sufficient fuss for the decision day to be extended by, if memory serves, another three weeks. On the whole, the majority of those who had no spouse or family to return to, or whose marriages were shaky, chose to stay in Britain. That amounted to nearly half the cast, among them all four Manhattan Brothers, Peggy Phango, Hazel Futa, Gwigwi, and my dear friend Sophie Mcgina, who in the London production played Petal, girlfriend of King Kong's trainer Jack.

Almost half the musicians stayed too, though a handful soon went to America, where the door to the jazz world had already opened wide for Miriam. Hugh was first to leave, after *King Kong* closed, to take up a scholarship arranged for him by Father Huddleston and sponsored by Harry Belafonte and Sidney Poitier. Astonishingly (as Hugh writes in his autobiography), on the very evening of his arrival in New York, he was welcomed and embraced by the giants of world jazz. He had been taken to the Jazz Gallery on East Eighth Street, where Dizzy Gillespie, with whom he'd been in correspondence for some time, spotted him in the audience. Right after Dizzy finished his set he greeted Hugh like a long-lost brother. He introduced him to Thelonious Monk, who strolled in shortly afterwards, then later took him across to the club where Charlie Mingus and Max Roach were playing, so Hugh could meet and hear them too, then back again to the Jazz Gallery to hear Monk's band. 'My favourite albums were coming alive right in front of my eyes,' Hugh wrote in his autobiography. 'I could have been dreaming.' Later that night Gillespie suggested going on to meet John Coltrane, and made sure Hugh met McCoy Tyner and Elvin Jones from Coltrane's band as well.

What a welcome! Shortly afterwards, Caiphus Semenya and Letta Mbulu, the teenage sweethearts of the *King Kong* cast, and Jonas Gwanga also arrived in New York, and found themselves, through Miriam and Hugh, part of that same welcoming 'family' of jazz artists. They too were reaping the good fortune which landed like a mantle over so many of us during those early years away from South Africa – the still unfolding 'miracle' of *King Kong*. Doors opened easily, and their subsequent careers were dazzling. Their huge talent and dedication were equal to the challenge.

The price of exile is high, however. I've heard from all of them about the pain of longing for home and missing their families. They couldn't return for decades to see their loved ones, nor even attend the funerals of their parents. From time to time it nearly broke their hearts.

My charmed life couldn't last for ever, of course, particularly because I wasn't doing anything to build on the dizzying opportunities that had been handed out to me. For some reason I held back, ambivalent – enjoying it, but worried. Partly it was because both socially and, to an extent, in my working life, I was flying high because of what I *seemed* to be, not because of who I really was. I began to understand the price of admission into circles of excellence and advantage: if you're not born into them, you get there through money, achievement, good looks or marriage. I was young and attractive, I'm told, full of energy, but not an outstanding beauty. I was neither rich nor 'born'. I had no belief that I had sufficient talent to achieve on my own anything comparable to *King Kong*. And I remained alone until my early sixties, when I first lived with, and later married, David Pendlebury, a dear friend of many years. My achievements as journalist, broadcaster, columnist and writer kept me 'up there' for a bit. Perhaps it could have lasted a bit longer if, while the djinns were lavishly opening doors and bestowing success on me, I hadn't been stubbornly running as hard as I could in the other direction. I couldn't yet put my finger on the reason why.

The Supernatural, the book I co-wrote with Douglas Hill, became a bestseller, and remained in print in one form or another in many countries and languages around the world for more than twenty years. Because of its timing, it initiated and was for a while, a source book for many writers on what later came to be called the 'New Age' movement. That book should have made me, if not rich, at least comfortable, for life. However, when the publishers offered me either a royalty or a £1,500 flat fee, I chose the fee. It was exactly the same type of offer that the Manhattan Brothers, and other musicians, had received from the South African recording company Gallo, and which they had accepted for the same reason – I needed the money. And in spite of the success of *The Supernatural*, I never wrote another book, except for a pseudonymous novel which won a joint Book of the Month award from the American journal *Psychology Today*, shared, very pleasingly for me, with Jacob Bronowski's *Ascent of Man*. Also, in spite of the Screen Writers Guild award nomination and the prestigious CBS documentary, I never wrote another film.

I was in my very early thirties at the height of my successes. A photograph of me at the top of my *Observer* column featured in a huge poster campaign run by that newspaper and plastered on the walls of Tube stations. But suddenly I started to panic, and that panic crystallised into a clearly remembered thought: 'Is *this* what I want my life to add up to? Superficially successful Fleet Street journalist? There *has* to be more to life than that!'

And then I remembered a clear intention that I had stated to myself when planning to leave South Africa, but which for some years the intense busyness of the everyday had virtually buried: 'Apart from ensuring that Dan remained in a stable environment, my only justification for leaving him would be to become more truly myself, a proper person waiting for him in the future, instead of the neurotic and discontented woman he would have known had I stayed.'

There was another crazy sort of sense behind my

behaviour too. Throughout my life I have reacted against any sort of 'belonging', whether national, social, political or professional. It would have been delightful to have continued my professional success (and, of course, I still had to work at some level to make my living), but the prospect of reaching dizzying heights as a 'star' brought with it the fear of investing too much in that status and getting stuck there. My instinct has always been to remain an outsider, (a spy?), with the kind of mobility and perspective that would never have been possible if I had fallen for the temptation to 'come in from the cold'. While my behaviour looked, and indeed *was*, irrational and self-destructive, it was driven by a longing for something more human and truly meaningful.

6

On a visit I made to Johannesburg late in 1978, Ian Bernhardt, who had produced *King Kong* two decades earlier, asked me to lunch. How fortuitous it was, he said, that I had arrived when I had. A group of businessmen had offered to back a new production of *King Kong*. The reputation, and love for, the show rested mainly on its music, its brilliant musicians and performers, the manner of Leon Gluckman's staging – the gumboot dancers, the *patha-patha* players, all the brilliant set pieces – and what might be called the known basic story. But the script itself, while holding the show together, was generally accepted as having problems. Ian asked me whether I was up for doing a rewrite.

'Well, I'll only be here a few weeks,' I said, also pointing out that after nearly twenty years in London, I was out of touch with the township speech patterns and idioms that had once been familiar to me, though they had never been my own. So he suggested I work with someone else, and he had in mind a brilliant young mixed-race woman called Fatts – short for Fatima – Dike (pronounced Deekay), who was the resident playwright at the Space Theatre in Cape Town. He'd find out if she was interested or even free. But first, he said, I should meet the man who wanted to sponsor the revival. Which meant another lunch, this time with Ian and the chief backer of the team prepared to bankroll the production. For the life of me I can't remember his name, and in the circumstances that is probably a good thing. I'll call him Monty.

Ian had been wanting to stage a revival of *King Kong* for years. The show's reputation remained undimmed. People who had seen it at the time kept telling Ian that they wanted to see it again. And others too young to have been there were also curious to see it, to find out what this legendary show was all about. And then, fortuitously, Monty had turned up. When he and two colleagues got in touch with Ian and told him they were interested in backing a production, it seemed like a wonderful opportunity.

These were difficult years economically in South Africa. Increasingly restrictive apartheid laws held society ever more tightly in their grip. Indeed, in 1961, two years after *King Kong* opened, South Africa was forced to leave the Commonwealth by the other member countries, all of whom opposed apartheid. The atmosphere inside the country was one of increasing isolation, almost as if the place was under siege. A boycott of South African goods and sport was also beginning to have an effect – psychological as much as anything else. And one consequence of the Sharpeville massacre the previous year (probably felt only by the comfortably-off white population) had been a panicked outflow from the country of such significant amounts of money at such an alarming rate that strict exchange controls had been put in place. Individuals could take a very limited sum of money out of the country, the equivalent of around £100 I think it was – not nearly enough for a trip abroad, and even more limiting for the growing number of people who were planning to emigrate. In this bleak economic atmosphere, enterprising individuals concocted a variety of different ways to smuggle out their cash. An acquaintance of mine, for instance, bought a lot of expensive paintings and furniture, apparently for himself, which he then shipped out and sold when he emigrated to California. And the scheme concocted by Monty and his partners was to back a production of *King Kong*.

They had it all worked out: after a short and magnificently successful season in South Africa, in effect a very-out-of-town try-out, the show would go straight on to New York and earn them back their original investment plus handsome profits. The money would flow in from multiple sources – the stage show itself, recording sales and very possibly a world tour. During our lunch, I noticed that Monty's attention was mainly fixed on all the various means of exploitation: T-shirts and other clothing, together with perhaps *mbiras* and whatever other exotic and 'ethnic' musical instruments the band could be persuaded to play. And, of course, King Kong dolls. There was virtually no talk about anything to do with the show itself. That clearly didn't interest Monty, except as a medium for the franchising.

This was the commercial atmosphere and frame of mind from which the second production of *King Kong* arose – as mean-spirited and greedy as the first had been innocent and hopeful.

Fatts Dike, however, was a delight. The first time we met, she emphasised the fact that there were two 't's in the diminutive of her name: 'I'm not a carbohydrate,' she said. And though she was certainly plump and bouncy, she *wasn't* fat. She had what in Nigeria is called a *jolly-body*. She was nearly twenty years younger than me, but was from the start the senior partner in the work we were doing. At 28, she was already an actress, stage manager, storyteller and playwright, and much richer in all-round life experience than I was. She had started out intending to be a nurse, but after rattling around for a bit, life led her elsewhere.

'When I left school,' she said in an interview with a mutual friend, 'I worked in a Steakhouse for a few months, and then I left and went to work in another Steakhouse for another few months, and then I was employed by my brother-in-law and a few shops in the location, worked as a blockman in butcher-shops, then worked in a bookshop, and then in a supermarket for a couple of years.'

But in 1974 a child in Guguletu township near Cape Town, a girl just seven years old, was raped to death, and her body was found inside a dustbin behind the shops. From that moment on Fatts knew what she had to do. 'I wanted to burst out and push the walls of those shops away. I had something I wanted to say to my people. In 1975, I went to work in the Space Theatre as stage manager for a year, and then started writing in 1976.' As a result of that rape and its consequences, Fatts's 'say' took the form of a moving drama, *The Sacrifice of Kreli*. Although South African theatres were segregated at the time, the Space, a fringe theatre complex, somehow managed to sidestep this by looking the other way. The celebrated playwright Athol Fugard had also developed his craft there, working

230

with black actors. Fatts became the Space's resident play-wright, and also became known for speaking out on behalf of the rights of black people in South Africa, and women in particular.

I felt lucky and happy to be working with her. She was a robust and colourful character, wacky and hugely funny, with a mind that flew high and sometimes wild. She had been born in Langa, a township close to Cape Town. It was the oldest of such suburbs (as the township has now become) and was designed to allow the authorities max-imum scrutiny and control of the residents. The word Langa itself means 'sun' in Xhosa, a lovely name for any place, but in fact the township was actually named after Langalibalele, a tribal chief, renowned rainmaker and folk hero, who in 1873 was imprisoned on Robben Island for rebelling against the government. Langa was always a place of notable resistance to apartheid.

In my teenage years I used to teach night classes in liter-acy there to men often twice my age and older. The class-es were organised by well-wishers, and were an education for me as valuable, if not more so, as learning to read was for my students. I had never met people like this before – all men, mostly labourers, patient, resilient and soldier-ing on, determined to take this opportunity to learn. I felt like such a lightweight in my role of volunteer teacher, when I could sense the essential substance and strength of character of these men. And their humility. So there was gratitude on both sides.

Fatts was tough, sparky, creative, perceptive, brave and driven. Given the odds against a mixed-race girl from the townships succeeding at all, she needed inordinate helpings of all those qualities, and more, just to survive. Her stories of township life were as entertaining as her insights were penetrating. I remember her talking about how, as a child, she tried to understand why the white people on trains had carriages to themselves, in which they sat quietly and comfortably, with plenty of space around them, and even had their meals served to them. Her people, on the other hand, were crowded into third-class carriages, crammed in higgledy-piggledy, all on top of each other, no spare space, rowdy, noisy, sometimes dangerous, always full of life, sharing food, singing, arguing. 'I thought about it a lot, and I decided, Pat, that the only explanation that made sense was that white people were very fragile. They wouldn't have been able to survive the way we lived, and so they had to be carefully looked after.' It seemed to me she was accurately describing people who, quite unawares, had been 'spoiled'.

She also told me a memorable story about a man in Langa who was not only a respected leader of the community whom everyone looked up to, but was also as good-looking as he was reliable. Every day he would go off to work dressed in a suit and carrying his briefcase. No one quite knew what he did, but they knew that whatever it was would be important and worthwhile. 'Jesus God, Pat,' Fatts told me, 'I was in my teens, walking down Adderley Street one day, and there, standing outside the main door of this luxury hotel, I saw this man . . . in a *doorman's* uniform. His job was to open a door for people and close it after them! And perhaps they would sometimes tip him! I crossed over to the other side of the road before he could see me, and never mentioned it to anyone.' I have a hunch there were probably many people from Langa offering him the same consideration.

The incident reminded me of a rather similar experience in the pleasant suburban hotel where I was staying at the time. The black porter at the reception desk, a man probably in his early forties, was – much like the man Fatts described – an individual of striking good looks and noble bearing. He was also friendly and helpful – that is to say, very good at his job. I was standing with an old friend in the hotel entrance hall waiting for a taxi, and was struck once again both by his looks and also a lovely quality that emanated from him. I said to my friend, 'That man there is so terrific looking, isn't he?'

She looked puzzled. 'Where?' she asked, staring straight at him.

'There.'

'Huh?'

'*There* – behind the desk.' Still bafflement on her part. 'The *porter*,' I said.

'Oh!' Light dawned. She looked with new eyes. 'Oh, you mean the *boy*!'

Fatts and I were light-hearted as we worked on our version of the script, keeping it based on the original show as much as we could manage. I was still too ashamed of my original 'idiotic, amateurish effort', as I remembered Harry calling it, even to suggest that she, a professional, should take a look at my first version. But with her experienced and creative mind, keen eye and practised ear for character and dialogue, the script became sharper, more authentic and more truthful. We laughed as we worked, acting out scenes together, and were reasonably pleased with what we'd achieved. It looked as if we should have a good enough rough copy by the time I had to leave. There would be more to do later. In the meantime, I appreciated collaborating with – and learning from – someone who had real experience of the theatre and who was so interesting both in herself and also because she was from a community different from my own. And beyond all that, I just liked, indeed loved, Fatts. Our work was a genuine, unselfconscious sharing, and a memorable experience.

But it didn't last very long.

*

Once Ian knew he would be able to produce a funded revival of *King Kong*, he immediately wanted Krishna Shah to direct it. Krishna had been born in India but had spent much of his life in America, and also a few years in South Africa. A graduate of Bombay, Yale and UCLA, he was the first Asian-American writer/stage and film director/producer to win critical acclaim both on Broadway and in Hollywood. He had an already flourishing career and an impressive list of productions, including co-authoring the play *Sponono* with Alan Paton (author of the seminal novel *Cry the Beloved Country*) and also directing it on Broadway.

But although Ian wanted Krishna, Krishna knew immediately, without even having to see it, that he didn't want the script Fatts and I were working on. He already had someone else in mind for that job – Joe Walker, an award-winning black American playwright, screenwriter, theatre director, actor and professor. In other words, he was far more high-powered than we were, and with all the right credentials to get *King Kong* to Broadway.

Krishna intended to direct the revival himself, and Joe Walker would revise the script. Monty and his friends were enraptured. Krishna and Joe's track records as good as guaranteed their quick ticket to Broadway, and promised great success. How could anything possibly go wrong?

When Ian told us that our services were no longer required, even before our work was finished, I was surprised to find myself really relieved. It meant I could go home and concentrate on my life in London. So Fatts and I went our separate ways, and would not meet again for decades.

However, the day before Krishna was due to fly from New York to Johannesburg to start on the new production, the Indian government dropped what was for him personally, at that precise moment, a bombshell. It issued a statement which said that because of the apartheid regime in South Africa, from that day onwards no Indian national would be permitted to travel there. And Krishna held an Indian passport. There was no legal way he could even *go* to South Africa, let alone stay and work there. So he suggested to Ian that as well as revising the script, Joe Walker should also direct the show.

And thus the disaster began.

From time to time I heard from Ian that casting and rehearsals were going well, and then later, that he would like to fly me out to Johannesburg for the last few days of rehearsals and the opening night. Thus I found myself, having arrived at the airport a couple of hours before, sitting in the plush auditorium of Johannesburg's His Majesty's

Theatre, about to watch a complete run-through of the first act of the revived *King Kong*.

It was an unexpected, almost surreal shambles. I remember sitting in the almost empty theatre, jet-lagged and stunned with disbelief, as an unrecognisable first act played out in front of me *for nearly six hours*, with no pauses for refreshments for the cast. There was, I thought, an atmosphere of chaos, desperation and madness in the theatre. Joe Walker may once have been a brilliant exponent of his craft, but at this point he had either been swept up in such a manic episode that his sense of reality had ceased to exist, or else he must have been high on drugs.

For the next few days I sat in the theatre's stalls, often with Joe beside me, watching repeated, seemingly endless run-throughs of Act One, trying to understand what was happening. The songs had sunk virtually without trace: those old, much-loved friends, Todd's familiar melodies and the character of the music, were so submerged under an alien treatment that they were almost – and sometimes completely – unrecognisable. My lyrics had similarly been swallowed up, except for the odd line here and there. And the script had suffered the same fate: Joe had not only re-written much of the dialogue but also introduced quite unrelated new scenes. Only a shadow of the original show remained. The rest was the chaotic fantasy of a black New Yorker with no real interest in, or understanding of, South Africa.

So much of what Joe and his wife had done needed to be challenged, and with only days until opening night, it was hard to know where to start. So I began with the show's most crucial asset, Todd's music.

'Why can't I hear any of it?' I asked Joe.

'That man's music was terrible,' he said aggressively. 'My wife Dorothy is a composer and she has saved the show by redoing it.'

'*What??*' I boggled. 'For a start, Joe, that music is Todd Matshikiza's copyright, and is known and loved by everyone in this country.'

'I don't care about that', he says. 'It's no good and it's out of date. That widder-woman Matshikiza should be grateful for what my wife's done with his music. It would never go down the way it was. Not on Broadway.' And that was his mantra – 'not on Broadway' his justification for everything anyone objected to. He was the experienced Broadway writer. We were the hicks.

I learned later that a line in his contract said that the music could not be changed, so whenever I asked what had happened (how *could* that gorgeous music have been thrown away?), I was told that Joe's brilliant wife had simply re-orchestrated it, that it was all there if you listened, and any fool who knew anything about music would know that much. 'Re-orchestration' became the excuse for the Walkers to do what they wanted and yet stay within the terms of the contract.

I remember very clearly one of Joe's new scenes, and a few lines of its dialogue, unforgettable because of its shamelessness. It couldn't be allowed to pass. King Kong has, in the scene – for no good story-reason except, presumably, the force of voices in Joe's own mind – returned home to visit his parents in Zululand. His father says to him, 'Why do you not come back home my boy, and live here with us in this beautiful place, where the long arm

237

of the white man does not reach and our stomachs are always full?'

'Joe!' I exclaimed. 'Don't you know what you've done?'

One of the central tenets of apartheid was that black people *should* go back to their tribes and live in their pseudo-national homelands, so in effect Joe was enthusiastically endorsing the State president's policy. But when I explained this to him, he wouldn't – or wasn't able to – take it in. His judgement in this was no doubt further clouded by the fact that, as he told me portentously, he had been to a *sangoma* (witchdoctor) a couple of days earlier, and the spirits, speaking through the *sangoma*, had revealed his 'roots' to him. *He* was a Zulu too! In fact there was to be a ceremony the very next day, at which an ox would be slaughtered for a ritual feast, and he, Joe Walker of New York, former lieutenant in the US Air Force, would be formally initiated, with great rejoicing, into the Zulu tribe. Which meant that he wouldn't be around next day until the evening, but everyone else must keep on working.

Next day, I got a greater measure of what was happening to the cast. In Joe's absence they were less afraid to speak up. They were desperate. They didn't know what to do or how to be. *Please help us*, they said to me, coming up one after another with their anxieties, wanting to know how to say their lines, and all reporting the same thing: 'Sometimes I say the line the way he's told me and he says OK, and the next time I do it like that he says it's quite wrong. I don't know what I'm doing any more.' Some of the cast were actually in tears.

Joe had created a chaotic atmosphere. Nobody knew what was happening. Because he wasn't playing by the

238

rules, he was able to manipulate nearly everybody. Sometimes he bawled the cast out, sometimes he praised them, and they could never work out why he did either at any precise moment. He was also working them from morning till late at night, without stopping for meals. So they were all exhausted, and when they complained that they needed a meal he questioned their dedication and made them feel ashamed. Though I noticed he always sent for food for himself.

In fact his actions were consistent with current psychological understanding of the mechanism of brainwashing – individuals are confused and destabilised by lack of food and sleep, and also by the paradoxical behaviour of the brainwasher, who turns fictions into facts, and without explanation, can be toweringly angry or wonderfully friendly. The victims' own coherent world view is thus systematically broken down, until there is no stable ground left under their mental feet, so to speak. At that critical point the brainwasher's view of the world, however blatantly it contradicts the victim's former good sense, will 'take', because it is the only lifeline of certainty once all other certainties have been demolished.

This had already happened to the cast by the time I arrived. Bewildered and off balance, they hung on to their single article of faith, the brainwasher's message – in this case, that Joe was the brilliant director, black like them, who knew how to deliver success and take them all to America and to freedom. Such a wonderful prospect! All they had to do was work hard, obey him, measure up, do what they were told. By the time I arrived it had reached the point where they might even have jumped off the highest building in Johannesburg for him, had he demanded it. By a technique which I assume he must have understood instinctively, he had turned the members of the cast into his creatures.

As the days went by, it was hard to see how the show could open. I spent my days in the theatre, working some of the time with the cast, and at other times just watching. Often Joe would come and sit next to me and bend my ear with his truly insane ideas. He had always known he was a Zulu. He didn't believe that black and white people were equal: blacks were far superior. He was the saviour of *King Kong*. More than once he said: 'I'll show these people something they won't forget.' In that, at least, he was right.

And what *I* have never been able to forget, apart from the distortions of the words and the music and the general craziness, were the episodes of casual individual cruelty. Two backstage incidents are lodged in my memory. Three days before opening night, Joe announced: 'I want a dwarf. Bring me a dwarf.' He had decided that this dwarf was to be King Kong's shadow, wearing whatever King Kong wore, always at his side, mimicking everything he did. Word must have sped through the townships, because very quickly a small individual was presented, and met with Joe's approval. A message was sent to the wardrobe mistress that she must make dwarf clothes, identical to King Kong's own, scene by scene. Within the hour the wardrobe mistress, spitting fire, raged into the auditorium. She let Joe know in no uncertain terms that she was already struggling with constant unexpected extra work because he changed his mind so often. If he thought that with less than three days to go she had time to make more costumes, even for a man as small as this dwarf, he had another think coming. She would walk out, leaving all pending work undone. Joe could see that her determination and anger were utterly beyond his manipulations. So he abruptly fired the unfortunate dwarf.

More brutal, though, was the treatment of a man who had been in the chorus of the original *King Kong*. I can't remember his name, but I do remember his situation. Things were going badly for him, and he was desperate. Underfed and depressed, he had been hanging around the theatre for days, longing to be one of the cast, and part of the music, the fun and the fellowship he remembered so well from the original show. Perhaps, he asked members of the cast who would chat with him, it would be possible to have a part, any part, even just a walk-on, in the new show? Could they ask Joe? And they in turn, whenever it seemed like a promising moment, tried – unsuccessfully – to talk Joe into hiring him. Finally, on the day the dwarf was fired, Joe relented. The happy man was brought back onstage again, eager to bond with this new *King Kong* community. And as well as that, he would soon have some much-needed money in his pocket!

Then, less than two days later, on the afternoon of the day before the show opened, and for no discernible reason, Joe fired him.

Two days before opening night, Act Two was run through for the first time. It was much shorter than Act One, which was a relief, but equally a shambles, and unredeemed by the music and song. Then, with only about a day and a half to go, the cast members found that their parts were savagely cut, as the *nine-hour show* was pared down to a little over three hours in total.

Why hadn't I just walked away? For once I had a quick answer. It was because of the sincere, hard-working cast. They were bewildered, confused, desperate even – but still hopeful. And the impulse to observe, and help, is usually stronger in me than good sense. I couldn't do much to save the situation, but I could do the little they were asking for. So I spent most of my time helping cast members in any way I could, by reassuring them, going over their lines – and also, like a den mother, making sure they were fed.

Ian Bernhardt's daughter Linda, manager of the group of musicians called Spirits Rejoice, who formed the major part of the band, later asked herself the same question. Why did she not leave, taking her ill-treated musicians with her? And why was Ian, the *producer*, not intervening, not making some effort to get the show on course? Was he not seeing what was happening? I remember early on asking him the same question I had asked Joe: 'Why can't I hear any of Todd's music?' 'I'm not a musician, but Joe says it's all there, just re-orchestrated', was Ian's uneasy reply.

Ian was hamstrung. He was the show's producer in name only. Monty was named in the contract as executive producer, and whenever Ian attempted to intervene, to alter something or straighten out the mess, which was, after all, part of his job, Joe Walker would go to Monty directly with his own version of what was happening, badmouth Ian a bit, and reassure the investors that all was well. Whatever Joe said, Monty believed. The magic word 'Broadway' mesmerised him. Joe was the expert who could get the show there. Joe was the one who could ensure that the backers' investment was safe, that their money would be multiplied. In the light of such dazzling promise, Ian and his concerns didn't stand a chance. He was just a hick like the rest of us.

A few days before the opening night, Todd's widow, Esmé Matshikiza, now remarried and living in Namibia, had slipped into the back of the theatre during a rehearsal, presumably invited by Ian. Esmé was prohibited by the government from returning to South Africa, but Irene Menell had asked Zach de Beer, an influential liberal MP, to arrange entry permission for her for a brief period. I think I was not in the theatre at the time that Esmé, Irene and a journalist friend sat at the back and watched the unfolding travesty of *King Kong*, appalled by what they saw and by the virtual massacre of Todd's music. As Irene wrote to me later: 'the extraordinary distortion of the story, the music and the blatant ignorance of the real context, which was an urban and not a rural one at all, left us completely stunned. We adjourned to a coffee bar across the road, all three of us agreeing that such a complete travesty should not be allowed to open. On Helen Suzman's advice we went to consult a lawyer that she had recommended. He cannily advised us that the effort of trying to interdict the opening, which would have needed a court order, would be unnecessary – and expensive – overkill, particularly since the show was clearly so terrible that it was unlikely to survive the opening night. We accepted his advice.'

The opening night *was* a disaster. But what I hadn't expected was the degree of hurt and upset among the audience. At the interval, most people were clearly in shock. What had happened to their much-loved show, *their* show, they said in bewilderment. Some were actually in tears, and all of them were asking, 'Where's the music?', 'Where's our *King Kong*?', 'How could this happen?' I'm told Esmé was there with her sister and nephew, presumably to see for themselves quite how bad the completed production was. Irene had come with a friend, but after suffering through the first act, they couldn't bear to see more, and left. Clive Menell, warned by Irene's report, had refused to be there at all.

The theatre was noticeably emptier after the interval. And when the curtain came down at the end of Act Two there was virtually no applause. Joe, however, bounded onto the stage as if it had been the greatest of successes, and to this day his words resound in my memory. Wherever he thought he was, it was certainly not the Johannesburg we knew. 'They said we couldn't do it!' he cried. 'But we showed them!' What fantasy world was he living in? No one had ever said we couldn't do it. In fact we *had* done it, brilliantly, nearly two decades earlier. Then he made what seemed to me a nonsensical speech, and as I watched from the wings he called onstage various members of the backstage team to take a bow. Finally he called for, of all things, 'my drama coach – Pat Williams!' What on earth possessed me, zombie-like, to go on stage? And then, worse, by God, in front of the remaining audience, Joe grabbed me in a bear hug and attempted to kiss me while I struggled out of his grasp.

244

The reviews next day all reflected the event with a mixture of outrage and sadness. A later story in the *Rand Daily Mail* summed it all up:

'King Kong' created a legend, a legend that lasted twenty-one years. Then, sadly, it crumbled. In April 1979 a revival was staged at His Majesty's Theatre, Johannesburg. At least, those of us who fondly remembered the old show thought it would be a revival. But the new 'King Kong' had little to do with the smash hit of two decades earlier. An American writing and production team jettisoned the original 'book', used only a few of the original songs. Most of these were given a disco treatment that caused Mrs Esmé Shipanga, widow of Todd Matshikiza, to give the producers an ultimatum to 'stop this travesty of my husband's work' or face legal action.

Rave notices had greeted the initial 1959 staging, The Star headline proclaiming '"King Kong" Is Greatest Thrill In 20 Years of SA Theatre Going'. Now the headlines read: 'A Defeat for Comeback Kong', 'Cheap and Nasty', 'Kong is a King-Sized Disaster'.

Almost immediately after the first reviews appeared, the visiting production team walked out of the show and returned home. The première had been packed. Two performances later, roughly one tenth of the seats at His Majesty's were occupied. Corney Mabaso, the local assistant director, tried to salvage the show by restoring as much as possible of the original, but the damage was done. Critics attended again, and commented on the improvement, but to no avail.

On the third night of the show, a Monday, only nine people arrived to see it. They were given their money back, the production closed, and Monty and his partners must have lost all the money they had staked on it.

The morning after the disastrous opening night I was sitting with Ian in his office when Joe Walker stormed in, clutching the various reviews. 'I've experienced race hatred before,' he yelled, 'but this is worse than anything I've ever known. How can you people sink to such depths? This is a terrible country. I want my money and I'm getting out.'

I don't know if he was paid, and if so, how much. What I do remember is that, it transpired later, he had left a profusion of unpaid bills, some rather large. I assume that in the end these were met out of the pocket of Monty and partners.

And thus their dreams of Broadway died.

During that insane week, as I watched Joe Walker destroy *King Kong*, I imagined it could only be an inexplicable, perhaps drug-fuelled, downward step in a waning career. But to my surprise, according to Joe's Wikipedia entry, his award-winning career appears to have resumed undiminished until his death in 2003. According to that entry, he 'wrote, directed and choreographed *A Proper Zulu Man* [whatever *that* was] and *King Kong* at His Majesty's Theatre, Johannesburg, South Africa 1979–80.' After 'choreographed', he could have added 'and buried'.

Looking at his behaviour, from where I am now, I find a simpler, more charitable reason for the disaster – Joe's intentions for the show were quite different from ours.

He had made no effort to understand South African culture, nor had he spent any time absorbing the context and flavour of the original show, because in his eyes he was merely taking some amateur production and turning it into a show that would fit into the 'dialogue' of contemporary New York theatre. In a sense he was also a prisoner – of *his* own cultural context. Starting with those assumptions, his efforts would have been counter-productive from the start, as he tried to turn *our* show into *his*. And then everything he did was exacerbated by whatever drug he might have been taking. I had thought it was cocaine, but am told that his paranoia and paradoxical behaviour were more typical of marijuana.

Two days after the show closed, I flew back to London, and more than thirty years passed before Linda Bernhardt and I finally talked about what, at that time, looked like the sinking of *King Kong* for ever. I had been aware that whereas the first production of *King Kong* had been conceived with sincerity, inexperience and raw talent, from the start the revival (now *there's* a misleading word!) had been an utterly ill-conceived means to an end – a conception fuelled by greed and misunderstanding.

But it was a story with elements of greed on our part too. Not Ian nor Linda nor I had listened to the voice within each of us which knew the enterprise was suspect, so wrongly motivated that it was unlikely to work. But because Ian so much wanted *King Kong* to be staged again, because Linda wanted the opportunity for the musicians she managed, and because I had thought during the initial lunch with Monty 'well it's not ideal but let's see what happens', and later, during those ghastly rehearsals, 'well I have to hang in here now, because I'm being asked for help and that at least is *something* I can do . . .' For all those reasons and more, none of us were prepared to take the drastic step that would end the fiasco.

What paralysed us over and above everything else, Linda and I agreed, was that the cast and musicians had in many cases given up their regular jobs to be in the show, and none of us wanted to pull the plug on work they were being paid for. But even so, while an explanation may or may not shed accurate light on a situation, what matters in the end is what one can learn from it. Linda says hers was a strong and painful lesson – never again to hang on and make excuses or remain in a situation when her gut instinct is to walk away. For my own part, I learned that regardless of loyalty or good intentions, if a situation is taking more than it is giving, then it is time to bring it to a close. I learned, too, that if one comes upon a con man, or someone seemingly not in their right mind, nothing can be reasonably negotiated (except possibly by a perceptive and skilled clinician) and the best thing to do is walk away fast, and thereafter keep a very low profile.

I returned to London after that traumatic week exhausted, regretful, and also disappointed in myself. Why couldn't I have at least something of Esmé's insight and strength of character? I had always admired her for her steadiness and dignity, and also for her capacity to read people and situations. And now Joe Walker had left such disappointment behind that perhaps there would never be any prospect of further productions of *King Kong*.

*

Soon after my return to London, aged forty-seven, a few weeks before Christmas 1979, I was diagnosed with colon cancer. There had been a bundle of stresses and disappointments in my personal life during the previous six months, but the *King Kong* calamity and the part I had played in it was a strong factor in the mix that precipitated, if not the illness itself, then the diminished efficiency of my immune system, which might otherwise have held it at bay.

7

The Joe Walker catastrophe was, however, not quite the lid on the coffin it had seemed at the time. The *King Kong* story meandered on over decades, now no longer a sustained narrative but surfacing from time to time in isolated incidents, each one materialising like a little blast of fresh air, prompting the realisation that somewhere off-stage the heart of the show was still beating, and not quite forgotten.

I mentioned earlier the odd request from an American producer who wanted to cast boxer Muhammad Ali as King Kong, and which predictably came to nothing. But most of the time these tiny events were no more than requests for permission to play the music, or to perform or broadcast one of the songs. In one case I remember, a representative of Castle Beers, the South African brewers, thought the *shebeen* song, 'Back of the Moon', would be the ideal background for a planned TV commercial. Todd's widow Esmé and I were against it. Let's keep the music together as a body, we decided, rather than letting it go out piecemeal as wallpaper for advertising projects. For above all, what was clear on every occasion I played the *King Kong* CD to anyone, was how immediate and full of life that music and those songs still were, and how strong the essential story remained.

From time to time, lovely chance meetings with former members of the cast reminded me how much we were all still linked. On one occasion, I bumped into Peggy Phango, who had replaced Miriam as leading lady for the London show. She was as feisty and robust as ever.

'What are you up to, my darling?' I asked.

'I'm in opera at Covent Garden now!' she said.

'Wow!' said I. 'What opera?'

She rolled her eyes mischievously: 'I'm in *The Trojans*. In the *orgy* scene,' she said with relish. I always delight in invisible connections. My opera singer sister-in-law Amy happened to be singing the part of Cassandra. They would be on stage together.

On another occasion, on a glorious autumn day, Miriam Makeba was the star attraction at a huge outdoor concert in Richmond Park. Hundreds of people were there picnicking, myself among them. I hadn't seen Miriam since she left South Africa, about thirty years earlier. At the show's end, I knocked on the door of her caravan, wondering if she would still recognise me. As I put my head in, I saw she was with Peggy Phango. Miriam looked at me for a mini-moment and said in amazement: 'Pat Williams! I was thinking of you *yesterday afternoon!*' The connection, I realised, remained unbroken. As we started talking, we were as close within seconds as if it *had* been yesterday afternoon.

And then another welcome incident: a letter from the South African writer Denis Hirson. I'd not known him before that point, but would later discover that his boyhood experience of the *King Kong* musical had been a pivotal moment in his life. When he wrote to me this first time, he had just completed a novel,[1] and was asking permission to quote in it the first three of the verses from the 'King Kong' song.

It is roughly at this stage that the film and theatre producer Eric Abraham makes his appearance in the story. A man of immense talent, intelligence, charm and courtesy, in looks somewhat resembling a taller, leaner Gene Wilder, he has a 'can-do' attitude, a huge capacity to make things happen, an iron determination to see his projects through, and is altogether a master of the art of the possible. In my experience, he is also stupendously generous. At the time of writing he has won two Oscars for feature films he has produced, and a number of other awards for film and the-atre productions including an Olivier, BAFTA and Golden Globe. He is also South African, and so knew from the start the reach and potential of *King Kong*, which of course he had heard of, even though he had been far too young to see the show himself.

It seems to me that Eric's two Oscar-winning films, *Kol-ya* in 1996 and *Ida* in 2013, reflect in their themes Eric's own rejection of authority and ideology; his determina-tion, in fact, to live his life free from any controlling dog-ma. As a young freelance journalist and activist in Cape Town, he had chosen to report and broadcast on black politics and human rights (or rather, the lack of them) for the international media, including the *Guardian* and the BBC. Inevitably this made him a thorn in the flesh of the apartheid regime, which did its best to render opposition to its policies invisible by 'banning' people and organisa-tions in order to silence them.

Such banning (and less frequently house-arrest orders) issued personally by the Minister of Justice in terms of the Suppression of Communism Act (later the Internal Security Act), were extra-judicial – and as such could not be challenged. What is more, the breach of any one of the many restrictions became a criminal act, usually attracting a prison sentence. The effect of such arbitrary bans was political excommunication, with severe restrictions on the individuals' freedom of speech, association and travel. Publications, organisations and assemblies could be similarly outlawed and suppressed by the Minister under this Act. Indeed, while Nelson Mandela was becoming a well-known and celebrated figure in the outside world, he was at the same time rendered invisible back home because it was against the law to quote him in a public forum in any way. The fact that it was in the Minister's sole personal discretion to act against persons or organisations he deemed a threat to the security of the State, made people fearful of even talking about these proscribed people and organisations. Self-censorship and fear flourished.

Anyone he considered a threat to the security and public order of the state could be confined to a magisterial district – and in the case of house arrest to their home – for between twelve and twenty-four hours a day, and allowed no visitors at any time. These banning and house arrest orders were for an initial term of five years, which in a number of instances were renewed for further five-year terms. Banned persons were not allowed to meet or speak to more than one person at a time, since a social gathering was defined as 'more than two people'. They were also forbidden to attend any gathering or meeting, could be made to resign from any official positions, and were barred from such places as law courts, schools, universities, black townships, newspaper offices, airports and railway stations.

Between 1948 (when the apartheid government came to power) and 1990, more than 1,400 people in South Africa, mainly black, were subject to such bans, among them, as I have said, *King Kong* musicians Todd Matshikiza and Jonas Gwangwa, and then, seventeen years later, in 1976, Eric Abraham, then aged 22 – about the age I was when I was working on *King Kong*.

Eric told me how he had come to receive such a ban. He had been trying, he said, 'in a very small way, to cast some light on an important segment of South African society. He felt that foreign correspondents were reluctant to report on Black South Africa for fear of having their entry permits withdrawn. 'So in the early to mid '70s I got to know black student leaders and activists like Winnie Mandela, and also the SWAPO (South West Africa People's Organisation) internal leadership.[2] Their views were important because I knew that sooner or later there *would* be black majority governments in both South Africa and Namibia, and I wanted to help this process, in a small way, by providing another channel for their ideas and voices to be heard abroad. To that end, I started a news agency for the international media – the Southern African News Agency (SANA). It had a number of (mainly black) reporters and specialised in news about black politics and human rights abuses. Most SANA publications were banned, and its reporters restricted.'

So in a sense Eric had been a conduit – one which the government was determined to shut off.

While he was banned and under house arrest, Eric told me, he received many threatening phone calls, and frequent harassment from pro-apartheid extremists on the periphery of the Security Police – people who were known to have petrol bombed and fired shots at activists' homes. Amnesty International even hired a private bodyguard in an attempt to protect him.

Then in January 1977 he escaped South Africa and fled across the border to Botswana. Luck was with him: he was given an emergency travel document, to take up the offer of political asylum in the United Kingdom. At Heathrow, the press was out in full force to meet him, and as a result of all the publicity, he was offered a number of interesting jobs within a fortnight of his arrival. The one he accepted was from the BBC TV current affairs primetime programme *Panorama*, even though he had never seen either the programme or television itself – which only came to South Africa in 1976. He flourished as a producer there for several years, and then 'just fell into' an independent drama production company, Primetime TV, which a friend, David Elstein – a former editor of ITV's flagship current affairs programme *This Week* – had been offered to run, but which he felt he could only do with a partner. Between them, their prolific output included, among much else, *Fortunes of War* with Kenneth Branagh and Emma Thompson, for the BBC. As an independent producer he went on to produce films which included Roald Dahl's *Danny the Champion of the World*, John le Carré's *A Murder of Quality*, the peak-time crime series on BBC1 based on Reginald Hill's novels *Dalziel & Pascoe*, and a number of foreign language films. All this experience led him quite easily towards becoming the independent producer, both for theatre and film, that he is today.

Fifteen years of exile followed.

He was finally allowed back to South Africa in 1991 – a year after Nelson Mandela walked free.

In my opinion, Eric's spectacular rise in show business and his influence in that world, have come about because, as well as being an enthusiast and a brilliant organiser, he is also an uncommonly intuitive man, and a storyteller at heart. I've often heard him quote Karen Blixen, author of the famous autobiography *Out of Africa*: 'I think all sorrows can be borne if you put them into a story or tell a story about them.'

*

The possibility of reviving *King Kong* must have been in Eric's mind, on and off, for at least twenty years. In fact at one point he had contacted me to write a script for a feature film about the making of King Kong – something along the lines of *Strictly Ballroom*. That came to nothing, but some years later he asked me, out of the blue, if I would give him an option on my rights to the lyrics of *King Kong*.

I was very reluctant at first. But bit by bit he talked me into it. I remember him saying, 'Let me take it off your shoulders, I can make the decisions for you,' and slowly realising, once I had his measure, that this was a good idea – I could stop sitting on the rights, with no sense of what to do for the best, and lease them to a fellow South African for whom I had an instinctive respect and liking, who was a good communicator, and most importantly, who had a genius for making things happen. With his experience, will, vision, connections and innate understanding of *King Kong* and its meaning, both as a 'jazz opera' and as a marker in South African social history, I came to see that the show could still have a future.

Round about this time, a black theatre group, Ysango, had been put together by the British stage director Mark Dornford May, who had moved to South Africa and already had a track record of successful shows, both in Cape Town and the West End. I had seen Mark's adaptation of the early-fifteenth-century Chester Mystery Plays in London in 2001, and thought it sensational. It featured South Africans of all colours, speaking a mix of South African languages, and displaying that innate South African flavour of music, dance, humour and vigour that had so distinguished *King Kong*. 'Divine, defiant and dazzling . . . This is one of the most moving, beautiful, humane and courageous shows you will ever see in the West End,' wrote Charles Spencer in the *Telegraph*. Eric saw it too, and was 'bowled over by it'. And in 2006 Eric and Mark joined forces.

Eric's backing, creative understanding and capacity to make things happen, wedded to Mark's stagecraft and harmony with the people he was now working with in South Africa, made for a fruitful association. There were wonderful productions, including South African transformations of *The Magic Flute* and *A Christmas Carol*. On several occasions Eric brought the company to London's West End, and thereafter toured them in several countries. *The Magic Flute* had Mozart's score transposed for an orchestra of marimbas, drums and township percussion. Mozart would have loved it. The show won numerous awards, including the 2008 Olivier Awards for Best Musical Revival, the WhatsOnStage Choice Award for Best Off West-End

Production and the Globes de Cristal for Best Opera in Paris.

Eric underwrote and actively produced the now re-named Ysango Portobello theatre company for six years. 'I was so proud of the players,' he said. 'Most of them were from very modest backgrounds – only some of them had a decent enough education – but they were without exception brimming with talent. I had brought them to London with the various shows, but started to think about how good it would be to have a permanent space in Cape Town. Then I found a warehouse and church hall in District Six, and thought, "It's the perfect place – we can transform this building into a theatre." Which we did.'

*

District Six stands conveniently within sight of the docks, close to the thriving tourist area of shops and restaurants along the waterfront and harbour. It was also a particularly appropriate site for the kind of theatre Eric visualised because it had once been a 'non-racial' haven, one of those rare areas in apartheid South Africa that were relatively free and racially integrated. It had a lively community of artisans, merchants and other immigrants, many of them Malay people originally brought to South Africa in the seventeenth century by the Dutch East India Company to be slaves, plus a number of black Xhosa residents and a sprinkling of whites and Indians. I first knew the area in 1947, when I was removed from my parents and was living with my cousin's family in Cape Town. By the late 1950s, almost a tenth of the city's population lived in District Six.

And just like Sophiatown was in relation to Johannesburg, District Six was virtually a suburb of Cape Town, and similarly distinguished by its sheer life, warmth and energy. Once known as the 'soul of Cape Town', it too was home to what felt like a disproportionate number of artists and jazz musicians. The place was jumping. It was a pressure-cooker for talent. There was a large Muslim population, but virtually no hint of sectarianism. Children of different faiths would often go off to any mosque or church their friends went to. Pianist/composer Abdullah Ibrahim, in those days known as Dollar Brand, lived nearby and was a frequent visitor, as were many other local jazz musicians. Interviewed in the Guardian in 2001, Abdullah described District Six as 'a fantastic city within a city . . . when you felt the fist of apartheid it was the valve to release some of that pressure'.

It was also an immensely attractive place to me and my friends because it brimmed with the 'more' that results when people of different backgrounds of race and culture mix and nourish each other. From the calm and pleasant steadiness and beauty of the city and suburbs of Cape Town, delightful enough if you happened to be white, transitioning to District Six was like entering a new dimension, a place of far greater fluidity and unexpectedness. This was the first and only place in my life, for instance, where I saw an extraordinary Malay ceremony: in front of a large audience, in a heightened atmosphere of heart-catching drumming, several men were sticking sharpened skewers through their cheeks and hanging by their necks on finely honed swords, all without drawing blood. In its way, it was almost a metaphor for life in South Africa itself.

But of course, in apartheid South Africa this was too good to last. In 1966, the government declared District Six a 'whites-only' area. Between 1968 and 1982 the old houses were bulldozed and over 60,000 inhabitants were forcibly removed and crowded into an inadequate complex of small box-like 'township houses' on the bleak and sandy Cape Flats, some 25 kilometres away. And as there weren't enough of these to accommodate everyone, a shantytown quickly grew up right next to them. The government claimed it was clearing the area because it was a crime-ridden slum, but few believed this. The same words had been used before, in the Sophiatown 'clearance'. To most residents there, as well as to people like myself, it seemed more likely that the government wanted the land because it was attractively near the city centre, Table Mountain and the harbour. Yet even so, when Eric signed the lease on the derelict building for his theatre, just over forty years after the removals, it was still largely surrounded by waste land, and pretty much still is today.

*

The theatre Eric created, and named in honour of that fine South African playwright Athol Fugard, opened on 12 February 2010. It had a flavour about it reminiscent both of London's Wilton's Music Hall and the Donmar Warehouse. Mark Dornford May became its first director.

A year or so after the theatre's opening, Eric managed to secure options to *King Kong* from Esmé Matshikiza, Todd's widow, for the music, from me, for the original script and lyrics, and from Harry Bloom's widow Sonia (who had met and married him some time after he came to live in London) for the final book of the musical. It had taken Eric over twelve years to achieve this.

The opening night of the Fugard Theatre began with a performance of *The Magic Flute*, and ended with a party. Eric had generously flown me and my husband David to Cape Town to be part of the happy and glittering evening. The Deputy President of South Africa, Kgalema Motlanthe, was there, together with several cabinet ministers, the Brazilian ambassador, the vice-chancellors of two universities – and also, wonderfully, the remaining handful of elderly people who had been citizens of District Six before the removals. Athol Fugard himself arrived from America, and actors Janet Suzman and Alan Rickman flew in from London. Noticeable in the crowd, among all the finery, excitement and expectation, was a scattering of huge men, twice the size of any of the rest of us, looking suitably dour in dark clothes, dark glasses and dark facial expressions, obviously bodyguards watching out for the distinguished government guests. For some reason, *King Kong* was also in the air. People who had seen the show half a century before were coming up to me to talk about it, and without exception each sang a stanza or two of one of the songs at me, word perfect. Each asked, too, when they would see the show again. They all felt that at some point, preferably soon, it just *had* to happen.

From 2006 Eric supported the Ysango Portobello group, always on the lookout for material for them. '*West Side Story* was at the back of my mind,' he told me.[3] 'And of course, from the same era, the icon, *King Kong*, was waiting for its moment. It was so enormously special in affirming the narrative of the black story, and black music, at a time when South Africa was very gloomy and was going to become even more so. Yet somehow, in the midst of the impending gloom and doom was this shining star, *King Kong*. I thought: here in this theatre company are some extraordinary talents, and here is *King Kong*, this unique work which *is* South Africa. If anyone could pull it off, this group would.'

With the possibility of *King Kong* in the air at this point, I began to wonder whether I should take a deep breath and show Mark my original script. My intention wasn't to 'sell' it to him, because I wasn't sure how much there was to recommend it. Even so, I reasoned, perhaps a line, or an idea, would provide him with a thought, or an extra resource, if the show came to be staged.

But then, could I bring myself to allow him to see what I had written when it had been so rubbished before? I dithered and debated. Could I bear to expose myself again? But the thought kept coming back to me that the script might just be of marginal use – and if so, it would be worth tolerating the discomfort. So I asked Mark if he would like to see my draft script, and then sent it to him with an apologetic letter, excusing its worthlessness.

Here is part of my letter, dated 12 March 2009:

Dear Mark,
Attached, as promised, is my original KK draft. As you'll see, it's a piece of juvenilia really, with all the many shortcomings that implies. I was 22, had left school at 15, had no further education, had never worked in the theatre or seen much more than Hollywood films, and it shows. But even so, in my

opinion it really is the basis on which everything in the finished production was built.

At the time, I thought this enclosed draft, which I knew was thin and inconsistent, was just a start, a pencil sketch – and was hoping that it could grow into something substantial by means of working closely with the stage director. I wanted to be guided by his needs for the production, and learn and learn and learn from him. But that was not to be . . .

Anyway, that's in the past. I'm sending you this now just in case there's a line of dialogue, or song, or situation, or anything else (like the idea, for instance, of KK's body never being found) that might be useful to you.

Mark's response to my apprehensive letter was utterly unexpected:

March 17, 2009, 9:46:26 AM
Subject: RE: draft script.
Dear Pat, This first draft is brilliant! Many of the things that concerned me in the 'later' version in terms of staging, structure and development are dealt with here. You might not have had any experience, but like Shelagh Delaney's landmark play 'Taste of Honey' which she wrote at a similar age for the Royal Court in the 1960s, your script has a passion and depth which throws any nonsense about experience out of the window. It is a remarkable piece of theatre in first draft. It also seems to me much more 'black' without the patronising tone that sometimes crops up in the later

version. So I would like to make this 'first draft' the main script, and borrow from the other if need be.

Best, Mark

At a stroke, Mark's letter set me free from the idea that I was not a real writer, which had haunted and inhibited me for so many years. I knew I could write 'factual' things, and had done so, but had decided I was hopeless at anything 'creative'. And all this because what I had written with a sincere heart, and thought was a good-enough beginning, had been dismissed by an established, best-selling writer (and thus to me an authority figure) as infantile and incompetent.

However, I also knew and respected Mark's work, and had taken a great deal of pleasure in it. In my eyes he was an 'authority figure' too, and one who outranked Harry in my personal pecking order. Thus I was able to believe what he had said, and finally begin to put my burden down.

Decades later, unaware of Mark's words to me, Eric, in a taped conversation, described my original script in very similar terms. And *that* endorsement completed the breakthrough.

In the end, however, the possibility of a *King Kong* production with Ysango Portobello came to nothing, and shortly afterwards, Eric and Mark parted company.

*

The visit to South Africa for the opening of the Fugard Theatre, however, gave me a chance to get together after many decades with most of the remaining survivors of

King Kong, and catch up with their stories. I also found, to my great delight, that we really were a 'family'. The ties held, as encounters recorded in my notebook made clear:

Visiting Thandi Klaasen, that utterly spellbinding dancer, with an effortless, animal flow of movement which, in *King Kong*, made it nearly impossible to look anywhere else if she were on the stage. Her life turns out to have been tough and often traumatic. The first thing I see, though, is her spirit: she is not damaged in any essential – she is a burning flame, beautiful, fierce, strong and direct; she has the fortitude of a survivor.

Unlike the exiled musicians who were justifiably garlanded with praise and success because of their exceptional talents and achievements in the US, and who as far as I can tell are now living in the comfortable northern suburbs, working on fine projects to 'give back' to today's young musicians the benefit of their experience, Thandi toughed it out in South Africa, and in spite of a significant career as a solo performer, today is very isolated. She lives on her own in a township outside Johannesburg, in a tiny four roomed house, the whole of it not much bigger than the bedroom David and I have in our Johannesburg guesthouse. The township is flat, virtually treeless, baking hot, with dusty streets, and identical small square brick houses squashed together like teeth in a mouth. No white people live there. Colin, the taxi driver who has driven me many miles to see her, is very concerned. 'It's too dangerous for her here on her own,' he says.

Meeting her now, more than 50 years later, her

spirit and energy seem undimmed. Her face bears the scars of terrible burns. Entries about her on the Web speak of having an acid bomb thrown in her face when she was in her teens, but I have no memory of scars on the face I saw at the time of *King Kong*. She describes the event to me in great detail, with such immediacy that I assume she must have been older when the acid attack happened. Her neighbour, she says, jealous of her success and celebrity, asked Thandi to bring some of her showbiz friends to a party at her, the neighbour's, house. Presumably she wanted the clout of having such people under her roof. Thandi, characteristically forthright, refused. 'You don't have anything in common,' she said. 'You can't just "shop" for them to make yourself feel important. These are my friends, we've known each other for years, we've worked together. What will you talk about? We have plenty to talk about. You don't.'

The woman exacted a terrible revenge. She invited Thandi round to her house, and for some invented reason asked her to go to the kitchen. As Thandi went in, she saw two thugs with hoods waiting there, and suddenly heard the woman shout an imperious 'HAK!' (do it!), at which the one threw petrol in her face and over her head and the other set her alight. Thandi was ablaze, rolling round the floor, trying to put the fire out. She tells me she doesn't know how she got to hospital. All she knows is that she was there for a year, in unbearable pain, fighting for her life. She couldn't speak. Her lips were blistered and swollen, her face burned beyond recognition.

The fact that she survived at all is a miracle, a testament to her fiercely determined spirit. She shows me the truly gruesome burns on her head. The ones on her face are obvious. Yet when she puts on a wig and masses of concealing make-up and dares the world to find her anything but beautiful, she is stupendous. Amazingly, heroically, she is still performing, often with her daughter Lorraine, a singing star herself these days. Thandi's tiny living room is stuffed with photos and posters and framed citations and awards, including the Order of the Baobab in Gold 'for her contribution to the art of Music', and a picture of her on a sofa, holding hands with Nelson Mandela.

This morning when we meet, however, she is in a shower cap, cotton 'overall' and slippers, looking her age and seeming very sad. She's just out of hospital again, having had a complex operation on her hip and leg, and has no one to look after her. The neighbour's son stole her car, and people keep away from her, probably because she speaks her mind – in a Yorkshire sort of way – and doesn't suffer fools gladly.

It is an emotional, bitter-sweet meeting. Thandi embraces me when I arrive, and is very tearful. She says she had seen me on TV a couple of hours earlier that day, and had cried then too. But I know her. She's tough and resilient both by nature and through hardship. When she can walk properly again after this recent op, she'll get right back up on a stage if she can. She's not finished yet. She is a lion. But right now, a very wounded one.

Even so, there's not much dent on her spirit. She

tells me she's scared of death, but I imagine that when it finally comes she will pick herself up, leave her shabby surroundings, and march into heaven as feisty as ever.

★★★

Next I see Abigail Kubeka, who as a young girl had the chance to be in *King Kong* after Miriam Makeba promised her parents she'd look after her. She also has remained in Johannesburg, though she's done many gigs abroad. We saw each other last when she was 20. Though she must be into her seventies now, she is still beautiful, and carries herself with the relaxed easiness of a young girl – in fact she still seems like a young girl, her face and her demeanour radiating uncritical warmth and kindness and freely given trust.

We meet at the guest-house where David and I are staying, and embrace like long-lost sisters. What a difference from Thandi's situation! Abby is a TV soap star now. She arrives looking magnificent, in a black, white and grey artistically patched coat, a long skirt, impossibly high-heeled grey shoes in which she walks with nonchalant grace, and on her head, an elegant circlet of quilted velvet, studded with large ornamental pearls. She looks years younger than she can possibly be – strong, shapely and lovely. One by one, the excited staff at the guest house, all of whom know her from her 'soap', line up to shake her hand, and are excessively solicitous as they serve our tea. Many of them even give little curtsies. The same excitement is generated at the local restaurant where the three of us go for lunch. A group of girls walking past the restaurant see her through the window, do a double-take, and then walk backwards and forward several times to catch glimpses of her.

Abby has emerged from all the years truly admirable, rich in experience, deepened by it, and very grateful. Apart from the present 'soap' there are corporate appearances, government gigs, spots in concerts. She drives a huge white Mercedes, celebrity style (and in my brief experience, drives it somewhat alarmingly) but explains that she also has it because it is big enough to fit her whole family into. I truly love Abby, just as I love Thandi, and know she feels the same. I wonder if in fact it's untested love, wrapped in a film of emotion, as often happens in the theatre. But then I realise that under that emotion is the bedrock, the unshakable depth of it, born of our unique shared experience, which forged us into a community.

Irene tells me that Abby is the one who keeps in touch with all the other survivors, and looks out for them when they are in difficulties.

★★★

A phone conversation with Helen Gama, who played the girlfriend of King Kong's trainer. I have been unable to meet her because she was away for all but the last day of my visit. Again, as with everyone else, it's as if we saw each other yesterday. She tells me she's very well, except for arthritis; that she walks with crutches, and can cope with that. But she hasn't seen anyone from *King Kong* for years, though she bumped into Abigail a few years ago at the funeral of a family member, and saw Thandi and Abigail at the Menells' house many decades ago. The light of her life, she tells me, is her granddaughter, a university graduate with a degree in finance, working at one of the major South African banks. What prospects that girl must have – unthinkable in the days of *King Kong*!

'How many grandchildren, Helen?'

'Just this one.'

'I have two, the younger one still at school, sparky and pretty and clever, and the older one more serene and inward. She's a university graduate too, and they are both beautiful girls whom I adore.'

'Oh! That is just how it is with my granddaughter! She is so beautiful inside. God has blessed us, Pat, with health, and with these beautiful girls. It is so good, and so lucky, when children these days are so unpredictable.'

'And tell me Helen. After *King Kong* did you carry on in show business?'

'No, I didn't. I went to nursing.'

We laugh over that. In the part she played, the girlfriend of King Kong's trainer was a nurse. Life took her on a different path. That explains why she hasn't seen the others.

'So you made your *King Kong* character come true!'

'Yes, I have had a career as a twice state registered nurse, working first in a hospital and then with my brother-in-law in Diepkloof, Dr. Montera.'

'And has life been good to you on the whole?'

'Yes God has blessed me in many many ways. And you?'

'Yes it has been like that for me too. I'm so grateful.'

A long drawn out aaaaah of agreement.

'And tell me something else, Helen. They used to call you the best dressed woman in *King Kong*. Are you still so well dressed?'

Another long laugh. 'I don't stop! It makes me happy. Life is very short, and I will not stop doing that.'

We say we will write to each other, and exchange photos of ourselves, and of our granddaughters. But the slow-going pace of old age has taken its toll, and neither of us have done so.

★★★

Tea with Abdullah Ibrahim, the pianist and composer in *King Kong* days known as Dollar Brand. Next to him sits the American journalist who is writing his biography, travelling with him and, by the look of it, recording every word we speak. I tell Abdullah that I remember him at Dorkay House, always seeing him at our early gatherings there, and ask him what part he played in *King Kong*. 'In spite of what everyone says, I had nothing to do with it,' he says dismissively. Though he does say yes he was around Dorkay House at the time, and that he asked Ian Bernhardt to get him a passport while arranging the passports for the *King Kong* cast – something Ian refused to do, says Abdullah, but in fact I imagine something Ian couldn't do. We are sitting in the Rosebank Hyatt Hotel, where Abdullah is staying. At one point he suddenly looks at me and utters the introductory lines from the Back of the Moon lyric:

271

'Like paper riding in the breeze . . .' he intones,
'Like penny whistle melodies,
Like birds that fly
Across a sky they know . . .'

and looks challengingly at me. What is it, I wonder. Is
he sending up those lines? Or showing me he remembers them? But no. 'You are creative. That is why we
can speak to each other,' he says. He tells me he has
plans to open a huge meditation centre in the Tran-
skei area. I ask why. 'Because of the healing power
of music,' says Abdullah, explaining that he believes
musicians are miscast as entertainers when their role is
more akin to that of healers.

And indeed, his music has a profundity and
ineffable effect all its own, pouring itself into the
channels, byways and outer reaches of the mind, as
well as lifting the attention, seemingly, towards other
worlds than this. There is no mistaking his genius
both as piano player and composer. He is venerated
in South Africa, his concerts always sell out, and he
is known as one of the greatest international jazz
musicians of the day.

***

I think of Abdullah's words later when I visit Jonas
Gwanga, trombone player, composer and singer, who
returned to South Africa some years earlier. He has
had a car accident, the third in his life, and for the moment is confined to a comfortable looking chair in his
large and beautiful living room. Both before and after
King Kong days, increasingly restrictive laws made life
impossible for him, and with the help of others al-

ready there, he too left South Africa. The turn his life took thereafter would have been inconceivable even a year earlier – he studied at the Manhattan School of Music, and then produced, performed and composed music both for film and theatre. Jonas, the self-taught boy, who even had to learn how to hold a trombone by studying a photograph of Glenn Miller! The group of Huddleston/*King Kong* boys stuck together – among many successes in a rich career, Jonas toured the US with Hugh Masekela and Caiphus Semenya, and co-composed the sound track for the film *Cry Freedom*. He also composed, created and toured the world with a 'cultural ensemble' for the ANC called 'Amandla! A Revolution in Four-part Harmony', hailed by all involved, and also by its results, as brilliant PR and propaganda for the anti-apartheid cause.

He tells me, echoing Abdullah Ibrahim: 'The thing about working in music, and growing through music is that it develops you spiritually also.' I see this later in Letta Mbulu and Caiphus Semenya when we meet. They are glowing. There is a beautiful lightness about them which speaks of inner fulfillment. They are also lit, of course, by the love between them, which began in their teens in the Dungeon – the rehearsal space of *King Kong*. Their achievements, too, have become part of world music: Letta's glorious voice can be heard in films and TV series that include *Roots* and *The Color Purple*, as well as on numerous discs. Caiphus's music for *The Color Purple* won an Oscar. I have always thought that certain musicians who have personally evolved through their music, become, together with their music, like angels. Or in Abdullah's words, like healers. Letta and Caiphus, self-exiled when young, seem to me to have that flavour. They tell me they are now helping talented youngsters in Johannesburg, many of them socially disadvantaged, to grow and develop as musicians.

There was also a hugely enthusiastic and affectionate reunion with Fatts – now always Fatima – Dike. She too had grown in strength and knowledge, and was managing director at Siyasanga Cape Town Theatre Company. Still bouncing and bursting with energy, but far more 'serious' now, and deeply absorbed in her work, which has an educating purpose as well. She spoke, too, of spiritual experiences that took her completely by surprise and utterly transformed her understanding of life. This is what she really wanted to talk about and share the wonder of. We managed a quick lunch at the theatre – she had to be back at work – and planned a proper, longer get-together soon after.

But before that could happen, my South African visit came to an abrupt end, my reunions incomplete. A headlong tumble down a crowded staircase onto the sharp edge of a concrete platform resulted in an emergency hospital stay, long surgery, and – as soon as I was well enough to fly – a return to the UK.

*

Back in London, I thought yet again that *King Kong* could be no more than a high point in my memory. But reminders kept knocking at the door. As time went on, I heard more stories about people in our *King Kong* community. What I hadn't realised was how many of them had made significant contributions to the social history of our country, either through their political actions or their music. As Joe Mogotsi put it:[4] 'To some people only political exiles were considered to have helped the emergence of our new nation. Yet it was also the committed artists, musicians and singers, who touched the hearts of nations and brought South Africa the support and encouragement needed to overcome the hard years of apartheid.'

Miriam's life was lived in a blaze of fame. Celebrated as Mama Africa by friends and fans, and the first artist to popularise South African Xhosa and Zulu songs around the world, she had been, right from the start, a forthright spokeswoman against the apartheid regime and the suffering of her people. From the late 1960s she was, for five years, wife of the revolutionary and former Black Panther, Stokely Carmichael. Later she became a close friend of Sékou Touré, head of state of Guinea, the country in which she was invited to make her home when not touring. I'm told her house still stands there, untouched. In 1990 she was finally able to return to South Africa – a longed-for but rather lonely homecoming, apparently, and died in 2008, aged seventy-six. I remember a friend of hers telling me, with tears in his eyes, how before travelling to her final concert Miriam had confided to him that she really didn't want to go, she was tired out, too tired to travel, too tired to sing. She was due in southern Italy, booked to appear at a protest concert against organised crime and criminals. Her friend urged her to cancel, but she would not. Perhaps she was hearing the *Amadlozi* within her signalling her to go, telling her that this would be her last concert, that she had discharged her life's task. Only as she was leaving the stage, to the sound of the audience's roars of applause, did she suffer the heart attack which killed her. The words she was often heard to say had been prophetic: 'I will sing until the last day of my life.'

I learned from many of our *King Kong* musicians and performers how Miriam had generously helped them in various ways; indeed, it seemed that throughout her life she helped just about everyone she could. I wish I could leave it just at that, but like the rest of us, she was also human and fallible. Joe Mogotsi told me how he had spent years trying to get from her royalties which should rightfully have gone to the Manhattan Brothers. His obituary in the *Guardian*[5] confirmed what he had told me years before: that they never made a decent profit from their estimated 2–3 million records sold; that even in 1956, when their song 'Lovely Lies', with vocals by Makeba, Mogotsi and Nathan Mdledle, became the first South African record in the US Billboard Top 100, they were paid only a small fee and no subsequent royalties. Years later, when Miriam was a star in America, she accepted royalties for her rendering of a number of songs originating from the Manhattan Brothers and mostly written by Joe. He told me he had tackled her about it on several occasions, and in the end, Miriam acknowledged the Brothers as composers and lyricists of some of the work, including her trademark Click Song, a traditional number adapted by Mogotsi.

Hugh Masekela's story, too, is well known and well documented. His has been an extraordinary life in music, much of it known to the public since he was a schoolboy, when almost incredibly, through the agency of Father Huddleston, Louis Armstrong sent him one of his favourite trumpets, a portentous gift which has become part of South Africa's cultural legend. An international star for decades now, Hugh has successfully battled the demons of alcohol and drugs which jazz musicians and exiles often face. After arriving in the United States in the early 1960s, he was briefly married to his old friend and lover Miriam Makeba. And even after the marriage ended, over all the years that followed, I imagine that the deeper connection between them was never broken. And like Miriam, he too could not return home for many years.

Today Hugh still tours the world. Shortly before writing these words, after a gap of at least thirty-five years, we met in London at Ronnie Scott's jazz club one afternoon. He had arrived to prepare for a gig that night, and I was standing a few yards back from the club's low-lit entrance corridor. To my surprise and delight, he looked up from the group who were greeting him, spotted me, instantly left them standing and came towards me, wrapping me in the warmest of bear hugs and kisses. 'I bet you thought I wouldn't recognise you,' he murmured into my ear – and of course he was right. He is now, eight years younger than me, smaller than I remember him, and clearly exhausted from travelling. He had just flown in from Los Angeles and had a punishing schedule ahead of him, in yet another world tour.

But as we talked, and also later, while he was being interviewed by Sarah Swords for a an excellent BBC programme on *King Kong*,[6] I watched the young man's mischievous grin flashing frequently across his face – split-seconds of time travel, taking me back to the teenager I still remember.

He was sombre when I asked what his return to South Africa had been like. After a silence, during which he seemed to be assembling the relevant thoughts, he said, 'You know, in the US we didn't have the family and friends and support we had in South Africa. But South Africa now is not like it was before. Apartheid has damaged and spoiled so much, so many . . .' Hanging unsaid, I surmised, was the sense that, as with Miriam, there was no general open-armed, full-hearted joy at his return either. 'And nothing has changed,' he said, after another pause. 'The same people are still there running things, the same things are still happening. Mandela was pushed forward as the acceptable face of the new nation, but behind it . . .' His voice trails away. Then: 'I would defect from there, but there isn't anywhere to defect to.' Together we mused on the state of a world where there are no longer any countries which you could call oases of comparative sanity and calm.

I told him I was writing this memoir, and asked if at some point he would look at the passages about himself and correct any inaccuracies. 'Is there anything in it that would put us in prison?' he asked in his slow, gorgeously gravelly voice. And that perspective, presumably born out of his early life in South Africa's townships, dealt with *that*!

It also added to my understanding of why memoirs and autobiographies are seldom completely accurate. They are usually written by people, like myself, with far more years behind them than lie ahead. And when you try to check the facts, you often find that the people concerned have conflicting stories, or have departed this life, or you have lost touch with them, or can't find them, or they are too far away or too busy or too preoccupied – or, as in Hugh's case, too wise – to trouble themselves.

*

In the years after *King Kong* ended, virtually every member of the *King Kong* community contributed in some way towards the emergence of a 'new' South Africa. That was particularly true of two people in our creative team, Clive Menell and Arthur Goldreich. Both notably influenced the course of South Africa's history – each in ways that reflected their own personalities. Clive's contribution was one of substantial, steady, unobtrusive, service. Arthur's was as dramatic as the man himself.

The drama with Arthur began, from the Menells' point of view, with a simple missed appointment. He had been due to meet a group of students before they departed from South Africa for America, as part of an annual student exchange which Irene and Clive had been involved in organising for some years. Clive had instituted an orientation period before any group left, an element of which was a meeting with Arthur, who gave each student an informal lecture on art – something which he and they greatly enjoyed. But on the afternoon of 11 July 1963, a day burned into many memories, Arthur failed to show up for the scheduled appointment. And when a student phoned Clive to ask where Arthur was, Clive – though he never flew into rages – was thoroughly annoyed and irritated by Arthur's absence.

But at roughly the time the student was waiting to meet him, Arthur was already in the hands of the security police, arrested along with nineteen others, including his wife. The charge was sabotage – a charge which carried the death penalty.

Arthur and his family had been living on Liliesleaf Farm, in an affluent outlying Johannesburg suburb. Servants, gardeners and farm labourers, came and went – normal enough, except that they were not what they seemed, but in fact allies, colleagues and fellow members of the 'militant underground'. Arthur had bought the farm with his friend Harold Wolpe to serve as a safe house and secret headquarters for the armed wing of the ANC. The year *King Kong* opened in London and Arthur presented Princess Margaret with the Zulu beadwork, Nelson Mandela, under the assumed name of David Motsamayi, had moved into the farm, more or less permanently, as chauffeur, gardener or cook – the stories differed, presumably depending on the occasion. So integrated were the day-to-day lives of the Goldreich family with the underground activities that at one point, as the high command met round the table to discuss tactics, Arthur's five-year-old son was found contentedly sitting underneath it.

Clive and Irene, like the rest of us, had been utterly in the dark about Arthur's activities. We were astounded at the arrests, news of which quickly reached me in London. We knew that Arthur was politically engaged, but had no clue how deeply. It wouldn't have crossed our minds that he was part of the underground leadership of the ANC's liberation army. Right through the time we were working so closely together, building our jazz musical and meeting so regularly, and then later on, through the high times when *King Kong* came to London (which included an intense love affair between Arthur and one of the top supermodels of the day), Arthur gave no hint that he had any worrying preoccupations, let alone that he was leading a double life. But looking back to all the meetings of the 'creative team', and particularly the night when Arthur 'became' a bicycle, transforming himself into so many real and inanimate characters, I realise that his capacity to switch personalities so easily, and to act them out so brilliantly, would certainly have served him well in secret work.

And then I suddenly remember, during the *King Kong* period, a long car drive with Arthur, during which he pulled into a lay-by and seriously and methodically questioned me about my attitude to 'the situation'. On reflection now, it is clear that he was probing to see if I was willing or suitable to be enlisted, as a helpful contact in his wing of the 'struggle'. The more we talked, the more obvious it was that we saw the human aspect of the situation in precisely the same way, but as the conversation became more searching it began to feel uncomfortable – right in one way, but wrong for me.

Arthur had grown up in an Afrikaans area during World War II, a time when most Afrikaner nationalists expected the Germans to win, hoping for a post-war Nazi state in South Africa – which would, of course, 'deal with' the

Jews. Indeed, the German language teacher at Arthur's school gave out Hitler Youth magazines for the class to read. Possibly in reaction to this, Arthur developed the mindset of a freedom fighter while still a schoolboy. Early in 1948 he went to Israel to fight in its war of independence. But later that same year the implacably racist Nationalist Party won the South African general election for the first time ever. This would change everything. I remember my mother took to her bed for a couple of weeks, in fear and trembling at what might ensue. And Arthur, realising there was a righteous battle ahead, came home.

When they met soon after, his wife-to-be, Hazel, a young teacher whom I remember being as calm and steady as he was passionate and electric, was already an active member of the Young Communist League, and Arthur joined it too. Then in 1950, when such membership was made illegal, the Communist Party voluntarily dissolved itself, while at the same time some of its members went 'underground'.

After all the years of patience and restraint in the teeth of ever harsher laws, the ANC decided it would have to resort to armed struggle against the continually escalating government oppression and hatred. And here Arthur's brief military experience in Israel proved useful. Nelson Mandela noted that the two of them often discussed tactics, because Arthur knew about guerrilla warfare and helped fill in gaps in his understanding. Also, he said – and this comes as no surprise – Arthur's flamboyant character 'gave the farm a buoyant atmosphere'.[7]

At the time of the arrests, Nelson Mandela was already on Robben Island, serving a five-year sentence for inciting workers to strike and for leaving the country without a passport. He was brought out of prison in 1964 to stand trial with the others. That trial lasted nine months. During his speech from the dock, Mandela referred to Arthur's involvement while he was staying at Liliesleaf farm: 'We had numerous political discussions covering a wide range of subjects. We discussed ideological and practical questions . . . Because of what I had got to know of Goldreich, I recommended on my return to South Africa that he should be recruited to Umkhonto weSizwe, the armed wing of the ANC.' Which meant that, as a member of the military arm, Arthur helped to locate sabotage sites and draft a disciplinary code for future guerrillas.

Arthur and Hazel were held at Marshall Square, Johannesburg's central police station, under the law which allowed the police to hold for ninety days anyone suspected of committing a politically motivated 'crime', with no warrant or access to a lawyer. When the story of the arrests came out, I was awed by Arthur's strength of purpose and the depth of his commitment. His natural gaiety was a perfect cover for his dedication.

He and his co-prisoners were immensely lucky in their prison guard, Johan Greeff, a teenage policeman who had no idea of the importance of his charges. He would obligingly collect food and cigarettes for them – on one occasion, even a pair of shoes and a new suit. Arthur actually persuaded the station commander to allow him out of the building, accompanied by Greeff, to visit his barber! In Hazel's words, and as all his friends well knew, 'Arthur could charm the birds out of the trees.'

Greeff loved fast cars, and dreamed about owning a Studebaker Lark – something only the rich and powerful could afford (the President of Israel had one). Knowing this, Arthur and his friend and fellow-detainee Harold Wolpe offered him enough money to buy one if he would help them escape. So on a quiet Saturday night, Greef opened the prison's inner and outer doors, temporarily switched off the lights, and faked an injury – while Arthur and Harold, together with two members of the Indian National Congress, ran swiftly through the open doors, where friends were waiting to spirit them out of sight. There followed a furious nationwide manhunt, several days spent in hiding, and then, disguised as priests, a flight in a single-winged Cessna from an airstrip in Swaziland to Bechuanaland, since 1966 known as Botswana. Although four had escaped, it was Arthur who got the lion's share of the government's attention and fury. Hazel, concerned about the safety of their children, chose not to escape, and in fact was released three months later.

When the news of the getaway broke, I was staggered. Soon after, Arthur arrived in London, still very close-mouthed about much of what had happened. But typically, he adapted the elements of the truth he felt able to reveal into a good story, telling me a breathtaking tale of coincidences: there was a sudden power failure, the lights went out, he had seen the warder's keys on the table, in the dark he just grabbed them, ran as fast as he could, unlocking doors as he went, and found himself standing outside, where coincidentally the streetlights had also failed. So, astonishingly, there he was, suddenly a free man, along with the others who had followed him out. He made it very convincing. I believed every word of it.

Greeff, the warder, was arrested within the hour, sentenced to six years in prison and paroled after two. More than forty years later a courier arrived at his motor repair shop in the remote northern Cape and handed him an amount believed to be in the region of 110,000 rand, payment at last of a portion of the money the escapees had owed him. Nelson Mandela had encouraged the earlier promise of payment to be honoured.

Arthur returned to Israel and, true to his nature, continued to fight against oppression and discrimination in the country whose independence he had briefly fought for decades earlier. He compared the treatment of Palestinians to apartheid in South Africa, and spoke out publicly, I'm told, against 'the abhorrent racism in Israeli society, and the brutality and inhumanity imposed on the people of occupied Palestine'.

Over the years I have come to realise not only how connected we are, but also how sometimes we mistake the real source of our actions, emotions or opinions, and assign to them a very different cause. Attribution, it has been said, can be very different from origin. I have often wondered if this explains Clive's uncharacteristic edginess and irritation on the day Arthur was arrested. It seems to me very possible that a different part of his awareness had actually picked up the danger surrounding Arthur. And then, not knowing the real reason for it, he assigned his anxiety and frustration to Arthur's (also uncharacteristic) failure to keep an appointment.

Today, Liliesleaf Farm is a museum and conference centre. You can take a virtual tour online, or visit it for an entrance fee of sixty rand.

*

Clive Menell's contribution to our country was quieter and steadier. His life of privilege and duty was lived within the friendship and deep mutual love between himself and Irene (she as exceptional, in my eyes, as he). He died in 1996, at the age of sixty-five, and his friend Nelson Mandela captured the essence of his contribution when he spoke at Clive's memorial service. The words still remain on the official ANC website. Speaking of Clive as 'a leader of great distinction and a person of rare quality', he continued, in part:

> The rich contribution he made to our society and the imprint he has left on its history goes far beyond what is known by each one of us who had the privilege to work with him or to count him amongst our friends. It is only now, when we come together from the many walks of life that he touched, that the sum of his gifts can be felt.
>
> Born into privilege of a kind that few people can ever know, he gave of his energies and talents not only in his inherited station, but also to the cause of changing our society and the upliftment of the poor. The combination of vision with the capacity to give it practical effect, made him a leader in many spheres.
>
> Transformation in South Africa and global economic change have brought historic challenges to our business community — it will sorely miss the leadership of Clive Menell, who has helped guide it through this period of economic, political and social transition.

I am one of the many people who deeply loved and respected Clive, for everything that he essentially *was*, in himself, as well as for all that he *did*.

Irene herself was as much part of Clive's journey as he was – so much so that she was awarded one of South Africa's highest honours, the Order of the Baobab, in silver. Part of the citation read:

> For over 50 years, she committed herself to the service of humanity by promoting democracy, equal education, human rights and non-racialism. In this regard, Menell made a significant contribution to different spectrums of South African society, including politics, education, community development, poverty-alleviation, philanthropy and the arts. Her passion for education, especially among black learners, remains one of her greatest legacies. She stood up to be counted during the height of apartheid and fearlessly pioneered literacy initiatives for the benefit of disadvantaged black children. At the time when it was uncommon for members of the privileged white class to relate with others across the race barrier, she and her husband initiated countless relationships with people across all races and classes. Through these efforts, she contributed towards creating a united South Africa where diverse people live together in harmony. She continues to focus on developmental issues that affect the country.

And, happily, she still does.

Over the years, Clive Menell and Nelson Mandela had collaborated on many social initiatives. Very recently, when I asked Irene about their friendship, she spoke affectionately of them being 'very sweet together: Clive absolutely worshipped Madiba,[8] with an innocence and love you could see on his face whenever they were together.'

The close friendship had been cemented after Mandela had parted from his wife Winnie. He had needed somewhere to stay that offered sufficient privacy before his own house was ready. So his chief of staff, Barbara Masekela, asked Clive and Irene, who were in Cape Town at the time, whether Nelson Mandela could perhaps stay in their house for a few weeks. It was the same house, with the studio on top, where *King Kong* had been created. And yes, of course he could stay there.

At one point, Clive had an important and unexpected meeting in Johannesburg, and phoned to ask if Mandela would mind him staying at the house overnight. Well, of course he wouldn't mind. Over dinner together and afterwards, the two men talked with growing warmth and a mutual recognition of their deeply shared harmony and outlook. Irene told me about it fairly recently. 'They bonded very deeply that night,' she said. 'And guess what they were talking about for so long, that brought them so close? They bonded over *King Kong*!'

8

Looking back, there is so much sadness in the stories I've told. Too many of the *King Kong* people died too soon, often tragically, and far from home. Black people's lives on the whole ended noticeably earlier than most of those who were white.

It is a melancholy catalogue. I heard that Ronnie, also known as Scarab, of the Woody Woodpeckers, a group of marvellous musicians, was found dead in his London bedsit, after having lain there for several days. The gravely beautiful musician Mackay Davashe died in his forties of tuberculosis. If my memory is correct, Patience Gcwabe, who briefly played the lead in the London production of *King Kong*, fell out of a window. I remember my shock and sadness when told this the day after it happened. It was thought she was pushed, but by whom and why was a mystery – one I have never heard any more about. After some time in menial jobs in the UK, Gwigwi, who had been drinking hard, pulled himself together, went to the United States to study music at university there, but then died after a year, aged fifty-three. Diabetes and high blood pressure took him away. The incidence of diabetes in black South Africans was disproportionately high, according to Joe Teeger, the *King Kong* cast's doctor, who looked after the cast members at the time and continued to do so for most of them thereafter. Rufus Khoza, the last of the Manhattan

Brothers, mouldered in London in the few years before his death, refusing to go home to a family who wanted to look after him, and who considered it would be an honour to do so. I heard that he refused because he felt guilty at having abandoned them at the time of the show by staying on in Britain. Rufus's guilt was something I well understood, having had to learn for myself, when my son Dan started visiting me in London in his early teens, and we were trying to build our relationship, that guilt can be a boulder in the path. Focusing on past wrongdoing can poison present possibilities. Sufficient unto the day . . .

To continue the melancholy litany of those who have gone: Kippie Moeketsi, the foremost South African jazz musician of his generation, to his peers the greatest musician of them all, died alcoholic and penniless in 1983 aged fifty-eight. I remember so well his beautiful sound, his moodiness and friendliness, his seamed face and slanting eyes, his shrewd, tough, warm look. He was, in the words of Abdullah Ibrahim, 'the father of us all, an alto player, the first person who made us aware of the riches inside South Africa, [and] who convinced me to devote my entire life to music.' His name lives on through Kippie's Jazz Club in Newtown, Johannesburg. On the patio outside it, a wonderful life-size statue of him sits on one of the benches under the trees.

Ian Bernhardt lived long enough to take part in the memorable 1994 general election, the first in which South African citizens of all races were – at last! – able to participate. He was in a hospice, so election officials came to his room to witness and collect his longed-for vote. Two days later he died.

Arthur Goldreich survived him by six years. After 'the great escape' he had lived in Israel, remarried there, and headed the Industrial and Environmental Design Department of the Bezel Academy in Jerusalem – helping transform it into an internationally recognised centre for design. He ended his days in a care home, aged eighty-one, with failing mental ability but with his charm undiminished. Having been adored by women all his life, even in the home he was constantly surrounded by admiring female residents basking in his company – and I hear that they did so right to the end.

Our leading man, Nathan Mdledle, also diabetic and dogged by alcohol, lived into his seventies. He had a huge, traditional East End funeral, his transparent coffin borne in a carriage drawn by black horses wearing white feathered plumes. Hundreds of people were there, myself among them. Nelson Mandela sent his condolences in an affectionate message, writing also that Nathan had been an inspiration to so many young musicians, and would be remembered fondly for his significant contribution to South African music. It was only by chance, some years after Nathan's death, that to my surprise I heard from my brother Peter – whose social world barely intersected with my own – that he had been Nathan's doctor throughout all the years in London. Another invisible connection.

Like Gwigwi and many of the other *King Kong* cast and musicians, Nathan had yearned for more than the inadequate township schooling he had received. Three years before he died, though still drinking, he registered at the University of Sussex, propelled by a long-standing wish to do a thesis on Louis Althusser, one of the most influential Marxist philosophers of the twentieth century. In the words of Abdullah Ibrahim, this quest for knowledge 'was insatiable in the ghetto'. Abdullah himself had read everything in the public library 'three times', he has said. 'We were reading Langston Hughes and Richard Wright, Shakespeare, the Bhagavad Gita, Confucius. We realised that though we were in bondage, our minds were not.'[1]

Sophie Mgcina, who in the London production of *King Kong* played the character Petal, innocent, dewy eyed and very sweet, had the same hunger for learning. She had an exceptional, multi-faceted intelligence, and great depths, but you had to know her to discover this – it was never worn on her sleeve. She matured into a formidable woman who with huge efforts qualified herself to study music at Goldsmiths. When she graduated, she told me, she would be the first black South African ever to get a doctorate in music. She was fascinated by many topics, including language and translation – another deep interest we shared. Indeed, she translated English songs into Zulu, Xhosa and Sotho, served as a voice and dialogue coach on such films as *Cry Freedom*, did voice-overs on many productions and wrote a book on the pronunciation of South African accents. She also wrote the music for the first South African film to achieve international recognition – Jamie Uys's *Dingaka*.

Her most towering achievement was probably her performance in *The Long Journey of Poppie Nongena*, a production in which (in early performances) she not only played two leading roles, but also composed and directed the music. The play became an instant hit when it premiered at the Market Theatre in Johannesburg in 1980, was re-staged in New York that same year and then again at the Edinburgh Festival in 1983, followed by a world tour in 1984. She won an Obie Award for best achievement in New York, and was nominated for the Laurence Olivier Award for best supporting actress.

Sophie became a Quaker, was a close friend of the pianist and composer Donald Swann (of Flanders & Swann and 'At the Drop of a Hat' fame), for a dreadful period was an alcoholic, then a recovered alcoholic, and then returned to South Africa to build choirs in the townships – as a way, she told me, to draw children off the streets and away from delinquency. As well as all its other facets, our friendship in London was also a very 'girlie' one – we used to swap clothes with each other. She enjoyed the high-style way I dressed, in 'designer clothes' in those days, and it excited me to wear her dramatic and very theatrical robes. They always suited me, as my clothes did her, but neither of us would have thought of buying such things for ourselves.

Towards the end of her life, Sophie was honoured by the State, as Irene and the Manhattan Brothers had also been. In Sophie's case, the citation spoke of 'the sustained excellence of her extensive and versatile body of work' which had made her 'a doyenne of South Africa's performing arts and an inspiration and example for those to whom she has passed on her knowledge and sense of dedication'. It spoke of a career which started when she was nineteen, probably just a couple of years before she played in *King Kong* – and the 'more than four decades of acting, composing, theatrical coaching and translating which have gained her national and international fame and respect'.

I lost touch with Sophie in later years, but heard she was heavily into the bottle again, then had got over it again, but that she was always out there helping the young, urging them towards the education which would take them further. Indeed, she once told me that part of her determined drive towards educating herself was in order to educate others. As the citation said: 'Her role as an educationist tends to be obscured by her activities in the public eye. She became a teacher at the Federated Union of Black Artists Academy in 1980, was appointed its creative director and head of the Department of Music and Voice in 1986, and in 1994 was given the task of establishing the National School for the Performing Arts at Dorkay House.'

Sophie died in December 2005 of heart failure, aged sixty-seven, and it surprises me how often I think or speak of her, or gaze at her picture.

Todd died in 1968. Four years earlier he and Esmé had moved from the UK to Zambia. Even now, all these years on, I am deeply sad that I never saw him again. In London we had lived just a few houses away from each other. I have fond memories of many parties in their basement flat, and an unforgettable mental picture of rolling down a sparkling white Primrose Hill one Sunday morning with the Matshikiza children, enjoying their first experience of snow. When I look at photographs of Todd now, just the sight of his face makes me smile with love and affection. But I think he had begun to find London frustrating. Even with the influential friends he had made, plus his own musical genius, it was hard to break into the English music scene. Sometimes he played jazz gigs in nightclubs. He also wrote lively articles in his trademark 'Matshikeze' for various UK publications, and a regular column for *Drum* back home, entitled 'Todd in London'. But as *King Kong* faded from public view, most of the contacts and encouragement faded with it, I think, and he discovered a truth about London – that when someone says to you 'we must have lunch sometime', this may be sincere when uttered, but rarely acted upon. I remember him talking to me bitterly about the indifference and hypocrisy he encountered, and the alien coldness of more than the British weather.

So I think he must have been relieved to go back to Africa. Yet at the same time, I imagine it must have broken his heart to be so near his own country – and yet, so far. He was still a 'banned' person, and could not go home again. For a while he worked for the Zambian Broadcasting Company, and was a very popular personality on the airwaves. According to several sources, however, he was frustrated by the lack of a creative musical environment, and in 1967, the year before he died, he became instead the music archivist for the Zambian Information Service. I was also told that he was drinking heavily.

*

When Todd died, his friends in London, the majority of whom were connected in some way with *King Kong*, gathered together at the Africa Centre in Covent Garden to celebrate him and bid him farewell. I have only the haziest memory of the emotional party that night, except for the fact that the warmth and love for Todd in the room was palpable and unforgettable; that we listened to, and danced to, his music, much of it from *King Kong*, and that, with sheer good luck, his closest friend from childhood happened to be in London, and spoke movingly about their lives together in those early days. Then a close friend of his adult years, writer and journalist Anthony Sampson, former editor of *Drum*, did the same. It was one of those 'lit' nights which felt utterly outside time. Todd's being, his spirit, was vividly with us – and love and admiration and gratitude for having known him was shared in every mind. 'This,' I said to myself at the end of the evening, 'this *really* is the last night of *King Kong*. After all these years, it's finally over.'

I have often been puzzled that Todd's music from *King Kong* was barely known outside South Africa. It *should* have been. At least *some* of his beautiful songs should surely have become part of 'world music'. It took Letta and Caiphus to explain it to me. Todd was a 'banned' person, so his work was officially ignored. It would be an extremely difficult task, given such an obstacle, to make it worthwhile for anyone to promote his work outside South Africa. I learned later that inside South Africa, however, two songs from *King Kong*, 'Back of the Moon' and 'Strange Things Happen', are standards, and have been sung by entertainers over all the years.

*

I hate even writing down that my dear friend Joe Mogotsi died in 2011, aged eighty-seven. I was closer to him, and for longer, than to any other member of the *King Kong* cast, and still miss him like mad. The composer and performer of unforgettable songs, a musical legend in South Africa, the 'glue' of the Manhattan Brothers,[2] he recorded his last CD in his eighties, still in fine voice. Several years after *King Kong* closed, the Manhattan Brothers had broken up, perhaps inevitably, given the sheer strain of adjusting to London, and perhaps disheartened by the difficulties of finding a place in the British music scene. Before the break-up they worked in cabaret for a while, and Joe appeared in a number of musicals, including *Showboat* and a German production of *Porgy and Bess*. He was always deeply into music and song, always a Manhattan at heart, even when, to earn a living, he worked for seventeen years as head of security for a firm of Scottish engineers. I was surprised when he told me he would often wear a kilt at work, but then thought, *Of course he would!* He was always a stylish dresser.

In 1990, just two months after Nelson Mandela's release from prison, the original four Manhattan Brothers got together one more time to perform at a huge concert at Wembley Stadium in front of their old friend. When they came onstage, Mandela told the crowd: 'I have known these men for 40 years. The Manhattan Brothers were the greatest singers and entertainers in South Africa. The Brothers are like my sons, and supported the ANC.' And when they met briefly later, Mandela specifically asked about *King Kong* and a possible revival. 'People *must* see that show again,' he told Joe emphatically.

I think you could call Joe a truly good person. In the teeth of all the difficulties in his life he was a shining example of warmth, constancy, goodwill and kindness, of always doing his best. I could find in him no trace of meanness, begrudging, or seeking after advantage at others' expense. He gave everyone the benefit of the doubt. With his wide smile and gravelly, Satchmo-like voice, he lifted my heart whenever we met.

*

I have told all these stories, listing, like a smitten fan, the achievements and contributions of just some of the people drawn together by *King Kong*, because it seems to me, now that nearly all the stories are in, that they signal the unusual qualities of the individuals – all part of an extraordinary generation, born at a time when the spirit of challenge and possibility was still in the air in South Africa, and it drew out the best in them, in all of us. It's as if the circumstances and ingredients at the time of *King Kong* had precisely the right measure – greater difficulty might have broken that part in people that made them so energetic and valiant and brave and funny and creative and optimistic and touched the depths within them.

But to my surprise, in spite of (perhaps because of?) their lustrous careers and international success, when those exiled musicians and singers from our cast were finally able to return home, they were largely ignored. On recent visits to South Africa I noticed a dismissive indifference or coolness when I mentioned their names. Even Mama Africa, Miriam Makeba herself, was never booked to sing again in South Africa.

I asked her old friend Abigail if this was really so. 'It is true,' she said. 'Miriam was a very sad person at the end of her days. She was not treated the way she was in the States.

She didn't work at home here at all – the only time she sang was when she was booked overseas. Here, nothing was happening. All she wanted was to be on that stage, telling people the truth the best way she knew, which was through her music. She famously addressed the UN, telling them about the horrible plight of our people under apartheid, but that was to me almost incidental, because that wasn't really her way. All her life, her way was through music.'

★

The very day I put the last full stop on this memoir, on 15 January 2017, I heard that the valiant Thandi Klaasen had died. The South African press celebrated her with lengthy accounts of her life and times – far more column inches, praise and attention than she had earned in later years, when she could have done with it.

Now we are a handful of survivors. I have not seen Boy Ngwengwa again since the show ended, but three years ago I was told he had been working steadily in Johannesburg as a journeyman musician. Jonas, Letta and Caiphus, and Hugh, whose work is so well known to world music, are now all based in South Africa again. Abigail, Helen Gama and Irene have never left. And where once creators, cast and musicians totalled seventy-eight, now – if Boy Ngwengwa still lives – it's just the nine of us.

★

All I possess as if far-off I see,
and now what vanished is reality for me.[3]

We all know from experience, I think, that whenever we go inside ourselves, time ceases to exist. Clocks mark time only in the outside world, recording, calibrating, coordinating; marking and measuring passages, moments, intervals and stations. When I re-read the beginning sections of this memoir I am very aware of this: I see how my approach and tone of voice seem so much younger in the earlier stages of the story than later on. It is almost as if I were writing and sending it from *then* – with the freshness and idealism of South Africa's late 1950s and of my own youth: writing it as raw, in fact, as I was when I was living it, for at that stage life had barely begun to cook me. I am amused, when re-reading now, to see how the young woman returned from the 1950s and early 1960s to give her account of her co-written "jazz musical" through this other me – the calmer, detached, observing woman in her mid-eighties. From my present location in the twenty-first century I can watch the immediacy of the emotions and expectations of my younger self – romantic, inexperienced, impulsive, uneducated, enthusiastic, forlorn, idealistic, hurt and optimistic – as she lived through the *King Kong* experience and battled with her personal unhappiness. Indeed, most of the early parts of this book were originally written in the present tense, and had to be changed later. In Denis Hirson's words 'the past is always there, ready to surface like a deep-sea pearl-diver'.

I have read recently that some physicists now believe that

time travel is possible, perhaps even imminent. Difficult to credit – but in any case I think the real potential for time travelling lies in resources already inside us. Through the internal space of no-time, we might one day travel wherever we choose. Indeed, as I begin to draw together the threads of the *King Kong* experience (a whole series of Ariadne's threads!), I am surprised to discover how much material was lying waiting, unforgotten, and how readily it spooled out of my mind. Memories – some meaning-ful, others trivial, edged – and sometimes poured – into the present, seemingly at random. I remember a book, *The Mind of a Mnemonist*, by the Russian neurophysiologist Aleksander Luria, who closely studied a man he called S, who could never forget anything at all. He would go for mental walks in order to drop his memories of the day in the city's dustbins, or he would visualise a bonfire, and throw his memories into it. But if even a page of a book escaped those flames, he could still read the words not quite obliterated on the charred page. The 'S' stood for Solomon Shereshevsky, an individual to whom I am relat-ed. I often wonder whether I have a small portion of his affliction, but so small that it is actually more like a gift. In my case, however, what I remember is seldom the *when* of incidents and events, but more usually the *what* of them.

As well as there being no clock time within ourselves, I have also come to think that there are not necessarily many real barriers between our own experience and that of others. Human beings are wired to connect. Mirror neurons will normally fire in the brain and body of ob-servers of an action at the same time as those neurons fire in the person making that action – which means that we are constantly engaged in a 'neural ballet'[4] that links our brain to the brains of those around us. Working as I do these days as a psychotherapist, I often demonstrate to my clients how in situations where they normally flounder, they can simply 'borrow' a capacity, or mental posture, of a friend or someone known to them until, through use and experience, surprisingly quickly that skill or faculty becomes their own property.[5] I think it is the same with memory. Indeed this is the means by which in this memoir I've been able to absorb memories not directly my own. For instance, I remember as clearly as if I had been there myself an incident told me by the incredibly brave Myrtle Berman, who (among other things) I think gave Hugh Masekela a place to stay each night during *King Kong*'s run, even when her husband Monty had been taken away by the police, and she herself was in danger of arrest. 'I have a memory of *King Kong* which will never leave me,' she said, describing a night at Dorkay House, where she had been organising the union's paperwork. 'I was coming up the stairs,' she said, 'and heard this almost unearthly sound reverberating through the virtually empty building. It was Nathan singing his heart out, practising the Death Song from King Kong. I stood transfixed in the silence of that empty building. I couldn't move. It was one of those moments of great beauty, unforgettable, and utterly out of time.' That memory, by now, has also become mine. The incident is as vivid as if I had been standing next to her.

Indeed, after hearing the stories of others involved in *King Kong* – as well as through their books – I have lived their experiences again and again in my own imagination, until they have been absorbed into my personal narrative and inwardly *become* mine. And because *King Kong* was in a sense conceived and born through individuals so basically in harmony with each other, our memories are easily shared – though interpreted, of course, from different points of view.

But ah, those individual interpretations . . . there's the rub. We know that memory distorts, erases, assumes and confabulates, while at the same time seeming so persuasive and incontrovertible. All my accurate memories co-exist in the company of others less reliable. In any shared experience, it seems, we tend to end up with both general agreements and a palimpsest of contrary understandings. Almost everyone, automatically – and usually out-of-awareness – edits a final 'film' of what they have seen or experienced, leaving what doesn't fit or suit them on the cutting-room floor. In my personal *King Kong* story, I have my own take – indeed, it *is* what I have taken – out of whatever else I may have chosen, more or less unwittingly, to ignore or misunderstand. For instance, until having a conversation with Robert Loder many years later, I had no recollection (though surely I must have known?) that there were other strong difficulties and disputes between people involved with the show, as well as those that Todd and I had encountered with Spike Glasser and Harry Bloom. To this day I don't know who or what they were, and Robert was honourable enough not to tell me.

*

All of this brings me to this business of 'the record'. I remember accounts coming back to me of events which I can absolutely guarantee are untrue: people saying that I had a black baby when I came to London; claims in a monograph by an American author I have never met that I wrote four versions of the *King Kong* script; being named in one academic book on South African music as the author of *King Kong*[6] and in another on the subject, equally academic, not named at all; while in yet another account Mona Glasser has become the author of the show . . .

Equally untrue is the claim in a review of Letta Mbulu's album *The Village Never Ends* (1983) that Caiphus and Letta 'met in China in the 1950s whilst touring as cast members of *King Kong*, South Africa's first internationally successful musical'. But *King Kong* wasn't even thought of until late 1958, and never went to China. Indeed Letta and Caiphus themselves have confirmed to me that their lifelong love story began in their teens, in the 'Dungeon', the rehearsal room of *King Kong*.

Then there is another aspect of 'the record' – the fact that in the history of any event, certain people (even the very people who initiated and helped to shape the event in question) completely disappear from the story, just as Clive and Irene disappear from the *King Kong* saga (though I hope this memoir puts the record straight), while others, as in the case of Harry Bloom, move forward to take centre stage. In every account I've seen, with the single exception I've mentioned above, Harry is said to be the sole author of *King Kong*, in spite of Clive's durable structuring, the creative team's construction of all the set-pieces, and my own contribution to the final script. Abdullah Ibrahim, on the other hand, has somehow been written *into* the *King Kong* story, and yet he denies flatly that he had anything to do with it.

Indeed, the *King Kong* experience has enabled me to understand how a 'record' comes into being. It is built on little more than an important ingredient in brainwashing – *sufficient repetition* of a particular opinion or point of view, or even a single name. Thereafter the material, now very familiar, takes on a life of its own, recorded and stored in libraries and reprints, reproduced again and again by those who consult these sources, repeated and passed on by those who hear or read these accounts, and travelling thereafter from person to person, often through nothing more than gossip. I remember, when still a journalist, realising that every published newspaper article, no matter how inaccurate, is filed in the cuttings library, and its details are consulted, repeated and circulated each time a related story is written.

This memoir, of course, is subject to all these same hazards, distortions, difficulties, biases and false memories. Even though much of the time I have checked through published books or on the internet – and also, of course with the handful of survivors I have managed to seek out – I know it is riddled with inaccuracies, as well as with perspectives and emphases not shared by others. But then I remember that when people have been present at an event reported soon after in the press, they always find even that report inaccurate. In fact, I can now understand and forgive the inaccuracies in other memoirs, knowing that for the most part what I am remembering here is the emotional residue of my story, on which are caught some of the facts, like solid little creatures in an almost invisible spider's web. Mutual memories are a shared world of endless reflecting mirrors. In the end, I can only say 'this is how it was for me'. Which is the point, after all, of memoir writing.

But although I know that much of what I have written can also be called into question, I always feel my heart sink when I find that later journalists or academics have joined up bits of information about *King Kong* into a confident but misinformed whole. Selected facts, collected but stripped of emotional weight and the invisible human subtleties within a lived experience, can never tell the whole story. The result will always have a serious warp. Just because a storyline is plausible, joining up the discoverable dots is not enough to bring the truth of it to life. Even sacred narratives written after the event get distorted this way, and in any real sense rendered useless as history.

Thus I have learned from the *King Kong* experience that we can seldom trust the record – there is always a story behind the story. If something of as little consequence as a stage musical, which happened within living memory, can become so fogged and distorted – no, I didn't write four scripts, no, I didn't have a black baby, no, Harry was not solely responsible for the *King Kong* script, no, the show never was in China – how much can we believe of the accounts of what happened many centuries ago, even the day after the death of Moses, or Jesus, or Muhammad, for instance, over which, because of their conflicting versions, so many people are still prepared to hurt or kill each other all these centuries later?

★

Earlier in this memoir, when recounting a conversation with Gwigwi about initiation, I said that I'd come to realise that an initiation was a beginning, the opening of a door to a level of experience and understanding that would be fully experienced and integrated over time. Thus it was only much later that I could bring into focus what I dimly perceived while it was happening – that the rich *King Kong* experience contained within itself a wealth of potential life-lessons – lessons which needed to be repeated over and over again in the years that followed, but which had all been initiated at the school of *King Kong*.

Those lessons are registered and embedded in the narrative of this memoir – among them, that neither extreme poverty nor extreme privilege need be prisons; that the stranglehold of conditioning *can* be broken, either by shock or by something else becoming more important than the conditioned perspective; that it is fear that drives and diminishes us; that generosity and sharing augment our possibilities; that 'the record' distorts history, and so on.

But one lesson required much more time to absorb than the rest: that old wounds *will* heal – if you don't pick at the scars. The failings of others, or pain suffered at their hands, over time become like smoke, memories without weight. I find that all my grudges against Harry, all the hurt that I nursed and stoked, have vanished. He did what good he could, which in the end was probably considerable, both as a human rights lawyer in South Africa and subsequently as Professor of Law at Canterbury University. He too was carrying the wants and needs and shortcomings that moulded *him*, and presumably at the time of *King Kong* could have acted no differently.

*

I look back at the truly extraordinary people by whom I was surrounded at the time of *King Kong*. They stand out like beacons in my memory, and I bring them onstage again for one last encore. Clive and Irene Menell, whose great contribution to South African society was made without ever drawing attention to it. Clive, who set *King Kong* in motion, pledging to Todd that even without Harry a musical *would* happen, and then writing the durable outline on which the whole show rested. Irene, staunch and strong, whose humour, humanity, intelligence, insight and sheer *steadiness* encouraged us and facilitated our work. Indeed, without the Menells, there would probably have been no *King Kong* musical at all. And then Todd, unforgettable friend, phenomenal musical genius, extraordinary writer, the sweetest of men. And in the background, Nelson Mandela, icon of our age, to whom *King Kong*, a show he loved, must have represented the promise of all the joy, creativity and talent which could be released into the national community once we as a nation could cooperate rather than oppose or keep apart from each other.

And even before any of this, Father Trevor Huddleston, who, in developing and enabling his schoolboy musicians, was like a stage magician, preparing in front of his audience's eyes the elements of the tricks which would only manifest later on in the performance. Young Hugh Masekela, the teenager, playing in the band and diligently copying out the *King Kong* score, destined to become an internationally acclaimed jazz trumpeter, flugelhornist, cornetist, composer and singer, winner of many decorations and awards, and possessor of four honorary university doctorates. Miriam Makeba, winner of the Dag Hammarskjöld Peace Prize in 1986, generous friend, fighter for freedom for her people, whose unfettered voice uplifted millions around the world. Sophie Mgcina, the ingénue singer in

King Kong, who became writer, actress, director and composer – a formidable woman of concentrated purpose and beauty. Lovely Abigail Kubeka, singer and performer of great distinction then as now, with a remarkable understanding, emotional generosity, and care for others. Arthur Goldreich, whose actions are written into our country's history. Caiphus Semenya, Letta Mbulu and Jonas Gwangwa, extraordinary luminaries in the international jazz world. Esmé Matshikiza, wife of Todd, professional social worker, woman of presence, dignity, strength and wry humour, unbroken by the many hardships she must have suffered under the apartheid regime.

And then the four Manhattan Brothers, to whom, also, the South African government awarded the Order of Ikhamanga in silver. The citation for that award stated that their reputation, 'defined by the South African music fraternity', was as 'the first-ever superstars . . . Not only did they have a huge impact on the music of the day, but . . . their trendy fashionable outlook was a way of asserting their humanity in the face of the dehumanising social conditions of apartheid . . . They were also the first to redefine the style, fashion and trends of the day – in a way that was never done before in South Africa. Their mammoth contribution to music, art and culture can be regarded as ways of engineering a sense of pride in African culture and heritage.'

And on it goes. Harry Bloom, who, nudged by Wolf Mankowitz, and together with Todd, generated what was the original seed of *King Kong*, which – through Clive's agency – set the green shoots growing. Leon Gluckman, inspiring stage director, another prodigious talent, utterly dedicated to drawing exceptional performances from the large, and largely inexperienced, *King Kong* cast, and creating an unforgettable event on the stage.

What incredible luck to have been connected with all of them! A connection that has endured, it became clear, when I re-met survivors more than half a century later. Who would have predicted, at this point nearly sixty years on, such a lasting impact from a single stage show? *That* was part of the miracle Joe Mogotsi so clearly saw.

★

And then, too, all these years later, the overwhelming luck and happiness that my son Dan, who, while still at school, had begun to spend holidays with me in London, emigrated there immediately after graduating as a doctor in Johannesburg. We are good, warm friends now, and every day I thank my lucky stars for him, for both the individual he is in himself, and for our relationship. He is a fine man, utterly without 'side' or showiness – thoughtful, responsible, honest, cheerful, funny, clever, and with a loving, forgiving nature. His quality is such that even if he were not my son I would be very glad of his friendship. I feel close to him, and to his two daughters, and adore them all.

I can be grateful, too, to the very parents I felt so damaged by as a child, and rebelled against so comprehensively. They, like the rest of us, were fashioned and diminished by their own conditioning, and by the wounds, bruises and deprivations of *their* life experiences. But if I look past all that to the essence of their natures, as I can now that the dross of this world has fallen away from them, I see their deeper reality, and respect and honour them.

And I have deep gratitude, too, for David, my husband,

exactly the man who, from the time I began to think about what falling in love would be like, I had imagined might be waiting in my adult future. When we met in the mid-1960s, he told me that in his final term at Cambridge he had gone with his father to see *King Kong* in London's West End. He remembers, even now, the joy and optimism that the music, indeed the whole show, evoked in him – 'so welcome in those years, when there was such terrible news coming out of South Africa'.

Many years later, after almost a decade together, we finally married on the Isle of Arran. Joe Mogotsi, by this time not in the best of health, was determined to make the journey to be with us. He and David had become warm friends. It was a smallish wedding, but I loved the fact that the guests came originally from more than a dozen different countries, and were now living in Britain – while David, who is solidly British, had lived and worked in almost as many places himself. After the ceremony, as we gathered to drink champagne, Joe held up his hand for silence. And when all was quiet, he sang in Xhosa, in a voice as strong and firm and sincere and deep as if he were still a young man: '*Basikelele Nkosi Bawe, Sikelela Bawo Abuntu, Bake, Basikelela Bobabini* . . . [Bless them Lord, Bless them O Holy Father, Bless both these Thy people . . .].'

It was the Wedding Hymn from *King Kong*.

*

The miracle of *King Kong*, it seems to me, was a compound of the time, the place, and a group of people representing the best of South African culture and talent. Because of these factors, an entity emerged in the teeth of difficulty. It transcended all the divisions and rifts there may have been between us, and the justifiable technical criticism of one or two critics. Over all the years only two people have told me of their distaste for *King Kong* – because, they insisted, the boxer Ezekiel Dhlamini was 'the wrong sort of hero', that it was 'the wrong sort of story', that all the 'happy blacks' doing their singing and dancing displayed 'the wrong sort of attitude'. But it seems to me that they must have been speaking from a pre-existing – and theoretical – agenda, and so missed the glory of what was really there.

And critics there will always be. We were not Brecht, or Stoppard, or Rogers and Hammerstein, not anywhere close, and certainly not even trying to be. We were the people available at that time, a naive, enthusiastic, mostly inexperienced group doing their best. Even though you could fault it, or point out the ways in which it fell short of being 'a well-made musical', in the end, because of the timing, the talent, the human chemistry and all the many other contributing forces and elements, *King Kong* turned into a legend, which today exists in the minds even of South Africans who weren't born at the time the show began.

So what, in the end, is left when the excitement is calmed by time, and what may be false memories have sunk to the bottom of the pool? Setting my natural soppiness aside, I can say, simply, that it was an experience beyond price; that I still feel privileged beyond words to have been drawn into the company of everyone connected with *King Kong*, and to have played a part in the story of this first South African musical, which was so much more than just a 'jazz opera'. It is woven into the fabric of our lives, born within the brotherhood of music, dance, the telling of stories, and the rich human harmonies of work sustained against the odds. And it became for many people a memory and reminder, a pinprick of light in the dark days which lay ahead.

The extraordinary afternoon when Doris Fisher from Detroit played her father's song 'Chicago' in the Menells' studio, and the musicians shouted for joy, laid out, as if to be read, how even fixed perceptions can instantly be transcended by a sudden shift of focus, and how what seems infinitely remote may be nearer than one can know. It showed me, too, how all our lives tangle and thread and plait together, whether we know it or not, as do the fragile but unbreakable threads connecting the songwriter Doris Fisher, Nelson Mandela, Todd, the Menells, Miriam, me and every single member of the *King Kong* cast – and through your reading this, connecting you as well.

All this and more was put in front of us – raw materials, spread out on life's banqueting table, to be cooked and digested over time. We had tasted one of the most generous of shared life's gifts, the awakening of a joyful recognition – '*This is how life should really be.*' At a stroke, without any malice, the Phenomenon of *King Kong* demolished every ugly assumption of apartheid and the politics of power. What remains even now is simply love – the love and gratitude which touched and flavoured everything and everyone connected with the enterprise, including its audiences, and does so still today.

313

Epilogue

This morning, as I write, a find a poster on the Facebook pages of the Fugard Theatre. It accompanies a call for auditions for a new production of *King Kong*. I marvel at the dozens of delighted messages that appeared that same day underneath the poster – about a show last seen nearly sixty years ago. Here are some samples:

At last, I can't believe that it will be staged soon.
Wonderful news it is.

Still one of my all-time favourite soundtracks. mentally
jiving to Back of The Moon! Truly cannot wait to be at
this epic show. Best to all your efforts. and Thank You.

Saw the original at Wits as a teenager. Had the LP. Still
remember every word (and sing it in the shower). My all
time favourite.

This is the most fantastic news. I saw the production in
Port Elizabeth at least 4, maybe 5 times when it was on
tour back in 1960/61 . . . I still have two copies of the LP
with the original cast (with words) – with nothing to play
them on! Can't wait to see it again.

Fantastic! One of my favourite LP soundtracks to listen
to when I was growing up. Oh those marvellous
muscles!

What wonderful news. I grew up with the London cast
recording, being considered too young to attend the
show in London with my SA-born mother. Ever since
I've loved the music and hoped that somebody would
re-stage it. Please let me have more details and I shall
try to make a flying visit (assuming that your production
doesn't travel the world like the original!). Best wishes
from London.

★

Eric Abraham has never given up. After a number of promising attempts over the years, which (typical in show business) for one reason or another didn't hold together, he has now assembled a supremely gifted and experienced team – the best possible, in my opinion, to carry *King Kong* proudly back onto the stage. He has solved the script difficulties at a stroke by inviting one of Britain's finest writers, William (Bill) Nicholson, to revise and reshape the script, to make it speak to our own times. Bill is author of the lovely play *Shadowlands*, scriptwriter for the film of Nelson Mandela's story, *Long Walk to Freedom*, and has written much else for theatre and film, as well as a canon of thoughtful and entertaining novels – of which I, along with the rest of his huge audience, am a fan. So the script, I think, is now in safe hands.

'The extraordinary circumstances in which the show arose are long gone,' Bill told me, after reading an account I'd written about the days of the first *King Kong*, 'which is good of course. But I sense that with their passing the special genius of that moment has passed too. Never mind. Something else will emerge, part shadow, part tribute.' And whatever that 'something else' may turn out to be, and however different, I suspect that the lingering taste of our 'miracle' will still be hovering like a mantle over this new incarnation.

*

When our 'jazz opera' closed in London, I thought of it as 'the last night of *King Kong*'. Then nine years later Todd died, and at our memorial get-together in London's Africa Centre, as old friends and *King Kong* cast members and

musicians played his songs, danced to his music and celebrated his life, I told myself that this honouring of Todd
was – this time for certain! – the *real* 'last night of *King
Kong*'. Then after some more years passed and the possibility of revivals kept on bobbing up, I realised that this was
not quite true either – and that perhaps the last night of
King Kong would not come until the handful of survivors,
myself among them, had finally departed this world. But
now I know that even this is not true, because at the time
of writing a new generation of remarkable musicians and
singers and dancers are flocking to the Fugard Theatre auditions, all of them eager to play in a remarkably promising
new production of *King Kong*. So at last Todd's music and
songs will be returned to brilliant life again. The original
King Kong stage-show recordings have never been deleted
from the Gallo catalogue in what is now close on sixty
years. My fervent wish is that this time, orchestrated in a
way which would be more congenial to Todd, they will
achieve the wider audience that was denied them before,
and take their rightful place in world music.

I reflect, too, as I contemplate this future production,
that the whole phenomenon of our 'jazz opera' and all the
miraculous events that have surrounded it rests on the brief
life of one strong, tragic, brave and alienated Zulu man –
the boxer Ezekiel Dhlamini, known as King Kong. I see in
my mind the life-path of this loner, his triumphs and frus-
trations and his defiant bloody-mindedness, and think of
him begging the trial judge for the death sentence, so that
his life, and his story, could be told as a lesson to others.

For reasons more far-reaching than he could ever have
begun to imagine, through our stage show and over the

many years that followed, Ezekiel's wish has been granted many times over. Indeed, I think the ending of my youthful draft of the first *King Kong* script is the truth of it – a truth now expressed visually and very movingly in Bill Nicholson's reworked version. When Ezekiel Dhlamini threw himself into the dam on the prison farm and drowned, on 3 April 1957, he passed from life into legend, and that is where he still exists today.

Acknowledgements

My thanks and gratitude to everyone who has helped me in the course of compiling this memoir. Among them are: Eric Abraham, for suggesting this book, for making it happen, and for all his many kindnesses; Laura Barber, at Portobello Books, for the warmth, humour and delicacy of her help and advice which has made it such a pleasure to work with her; Ka Bradley, Christine Lo and Sarah Wasley, also at Portobello, on all of whom I could rely without question; and copy editor Mandy Woods (a songwriter too), for her friendliness and her formidable attention to detail; Linda Bernhardt, for helping my memory with events concerning her father, as well as in other places in the story; Lady Antonia Fraser, for her willingness to search for memories of entertaining the *King Kong* cast, and her hospitality while doing so; Tarquin Hall, Julia Welstead, Clare Maxwell-Hudson and Nigel Hinton, for all their support and feedback; Denis Hirson, for sharing his childhood experience of seeing *King Kong*, and for the generous gift of his words in this book; Robert Loder, Irene Menell, Abigail Kubeka, Jonas Gwangwa, Letta Mbulu, Caiphas Semenya, Thandi Klaasen, Myrtle Berman, Rob Allingham, Hugh Lewin, and all the others who allowed me to tape-record our conversations and their memories, as well as for their delightful company; Hugh Masekela, for his sustained friendship, and for waving through what I'd written about him; Esmé Matshi-kiza, who helped me see how easily one can be misled by assumptions; Irene Menell, for her constant readiness to read, comment and share her own memories and corrob-orate mine and for a great deal else besides; Dario Milo, of Webber Wentzel, for his sobering legal advice; William (Bill) Nicholson for the encouragement and validation he has so generously given me, with such grace, and with-out even knowing it; David Pendlebury, whose writing I so greatly admire and who saw the first stuttering drafts of my text, for all his advice, thoughtfulness, love and – yes! – 'Behutsamkeit'; Alexandra Sellers for her valuable and penetrating comments, as well as her enthusiasm and encouragement; Jessica Strang and Tim Oliver, for their warm friendship over the years, and their immense inter-est in King Kong and its future; Francie Suzman, now Lady Jowell, for her own marvellous stories of the early King Kong days; Sarah Swords, who so generously shared with me all her interviews for her BBC Radio 3 programme King Kong, the Township Musical; Sasha Richards at Warn-er/Chappell, for her help in making it possible for me to quote my own lyrics; Denise Winn, for her insightful and masterly editing, for sorting out the book's content, struc-ture and flow in places where my story was beginning to stagger, and for restraining me from the worst of my name-dropping and preciousness; Gill Whitworth, who by not wanting to read anything other than 'a proper sto-ry' started me off on the right foot; Dan Williams, for his thoughtful advice relating to Joe, his father; and all those others, whom I may have left unnamed, who have helped me on my way.

320

Notes

Chapter 1

1. Nelson Mandela, *Long Walk to Freedom* (Abacus, London, 1995).
2. Suppression of Communism Act, 1950.
3. Trevor Huddleston, *Naught for Your Comfort* (Fontana, London, 1956).
4. The first Immorality Act, of 1927, prohibited sex between whites and blacks, until amended in 1950 to prohibit sex between whites and all non-whites.
5. All black men, young and old, were called 'boys'.
6. Leon de Kock, 'Reckoning with Athol Fugard', (*New Haven Review*, Issue 14, Summer 2014).

Chapter 2

1. Nelson Mandela, *Conversations with Myself* (Macmillan, London, 2010).
2. '*Mensch*' (German) literally means 'human being', often used to indicate integrity and honour.
3. 6.3 kilogrammes.
4. From *Sophiatown Speaks: A Collection of Interviews*, edited by Pippa Stein and Ruth Jacobson (Junction Avenue Press, Johannesburg, 1986)
5. ibid.

Chapter 3

1. Hugh Masekela and D. Michael Cheers, *Still Grazing: The Musical Journey of Hugh Masekela* (Crown, New York, 2003)

2. In those days, it was only men.

3. South African word for cinema, still in use today.

4. There are varying accounts of how it got to the USA, and sold in the millions. I am telling it as Joe told me – the same version that is in his autobiography, *Mantindane: 'He who Survives': My Life with the Manhattan Brothers* by Joe Mogotsi with Pearl Connor (Booktrader, Copenhagen, 2002).

5. One of South Africa's four provinces, and an Afrikaner stronghold.

6. The story is also told in *Mantindane: 'He who Survives': My Life with the Manhattan Brothers* by Joe Mogotsi with Pearl Connor (Booktrader, Copenhagen, 2002).

7. Hugh Masekela and D. Michael Cheers, *Still Grazing: The Musical Journey of Hugh Masekela* (Crown, New York, 2003).

8. Quotes taken from *Mantindane: 'He who Survives': My Life with the Manhattan Brothers* by Joe Mogotsi with Pearl Connor (Booktrader, Copenhagen, 2002).

9. 'Jou' means 'you' in Afrikaans.

10. Literally 'farmers', used interchangeably with 'Afrikaner' in a context like this.

11. Known today as Abdullah Ibrahim.

12. A story confirmed in *Makeba: My Story* by Miriam Makeba and James Hall (Plume, New York, 1989).

13. As described in *Makeba: My Story* by Miriam Makeba and James Hall (Plume, New York, 1989).

14. Hugh Masekela and D. Michael Cheers, *Still Grazing: The Musical Journey of Hugh Masekela* (Crown, New York, 2003).

15. This was a traditional song adapted by Joe Mogotsi.

16. My own memory of this event has been confirmed and amplified by consulting Mona Glasser's *King Kong: A Venture in the Theatre* (Norman Howell, Cape Town, 1960).

17. We were in a little room at Ronnie Scott's, where he was interviewed by Sarah Swords, for her BBC Radio 3 programme *King Kong: The Township Jazz Musical*.

18. Literally, 'Kaffir brothers', used as an insult.

19. Todd Matshikiza, *Chocolates for My Wife* (Hodder and Stoughton, London, 1961).

20. ibid.

Chapter 4

1. From *Mantindane: 'He who Survives': My Life with the Manhattan Brothers* by Joe Mogotsi with Pearl Connor (Booktrader, Copenhagen, 2002).

2. Published by Jacana Media, Johannesburg, 2005.

3. South African word for 'headscarf'.

4. 'In the Queue' was written by Todd, with moving lyrics in Xhosa.

5. Remembered from our conversation, and amplified by referring to *Mantindane: 'He who Survives': My Life with the Manhattan Brothers* by Joe Mogotsi with Pearl Connor (Booktrader, Copenhagen, 2002).

Chapter 5

1. It was sold the year after *King Kong* closed, and renamed the Shaftesbury Theatre.

2. Mona Glasser, *King Kong: A Venture in the Theatre* (Norman Howell, Cape Town 1960).

3. *Mantindane: 'He who Survives': My Life with the Manhattan*

Brothers, by Joe Mogotsi with Pearl Connor (Booktrader, Copenhagen, 2002).

4. ibid.

5. ibid.

6. Gwen Ansell, *Soweto Blues – Jazz, Popular Music and Politics in South Africa* (Continuum, New York, 2004).

Chapter 7

1. *The Dancing and the Death on Lemon Street*, (Jacana Media, South Africa, 2011).

2. South West Africa People's Organization (SWAPO), now a political party in Namibia, was formerly the national liberation movement in what was then known as South-West Africa, a former German colony which had been administered by South Africa, under a League of Nations mandate, after the Treaty of Versailles, at the end of the First World War.

3. It became the Fugard Theatre's first out-of-house production, was extraordinarily successful, and at the time of writing was awaiting transfer to the Mandela Theatre in Johannesburg in 2017.

4. *Mantindane: 'He who Survives': My Life with the Manhattan Brothers*, by Joe Mogotsi with Pearl Connor (Booktrader, Copenhagen, 2002).

5. 30 June 2011. Written by Adam Glasser, good friend of Joe and son of Spike, the musical director and orchestrator of *King Kong*.

6. For the Radio 3 programme *King Kong: The Township Jazz Musical*, broadcast in February 2017.

7. Nelson Mandela, *Long Walk to Freedom* (Abacus, London, 1995).

8. His clan name, used by many of his friends.

Chapter 8

1. From 'The Sound of Freedom', *Guardian* profile by Maya Jaggi, Saturday 8 December 2001.

2. Some of this information is gleaned from the obituary by Adam Glasser in the *Independent*, 11 August 2011.

3. *Was ich besitze, seh ich wie im Weiten, / Und was verschwand, wird mir zu Wirklichkeiten.* (From the dedicatory poem that opens Goethe's *Faust*, translated by David Pendlebury).

4. A lovely phrase coined by Daniel Goleman, author of *Social Intelligence: The New Science of Social Relationships* (Hutchinson, London, 2006).

5. See *Which You Are You*, CD by Pat Williams (Human Givens Publishing, UK, 2009).

6. *Township Tonight! South Africa's Black City Music and Theatre*, by David Copeland (Raven Press, Johannesburg, 1985).

Permissions